Fondazione Bruno Kessler

Annali dell'Istituto storico italo-germanico in Trento
Jahrbuch des italienisch-deutschen historischen Instituts in Trient

Contributi/Beiträge 33

I lettori che desiderano informarsi
sui libri e sull'insieme delle attività
della Società editrice il Mulino
possono consultare il sito Internet:
www.mulino.it

The Protestant Reformation in a Context of Global History

Religious Reforms and World Civilizations

edited by

Heinz Schilling / Silvana Seidel Menchi

Società editrice il Mulino
Bologna

Duncker & Humblot
Berlin

FBK - Istituto storico italo-germanico

The PROTESTANT

reformation in a context of global history : religious reforms and world civilization / edited by Heinz, Schilling, Silvana, Seidel Menchi - Bologna : Il mulino ; Berlin : Duncker & Humblot, 2017. - 225 p. ; 24 cm. - (Annali dell'Istituto storico italo-germanico in Trento. Contributi ; 33 = Jahrbuch des italienisch-deutschen historischen Instituts in Trient. Beiträge ; 33)

Scritti di vari. - Nell'occh. : Fondazione Bruno Kessler

ISBN 978-88-15-27407-6 - ISBN 978-3-428-15322-0

1. Riforma I. Schilling, Heinz II. Seidel Menchi, Silvana

270.6 (DDC 22.ed.) Cataloging in Publication record: FBK - Biblioteca

Composition: FBK - Editoria

Translations by Korshi Dosoo, Alyssa Evans, Ralph Nisbet, and Mark Roberts
Texts revised by Mark Roberts

This book is published with the financial support of the Provincia autonoma di Trento / Autonomous Province of Trento

ISBN 978-88-15-27407-6
ISBN 978-3-428-15322-0

Contents

Preface

by *Heinz Schilling* and *Silvana Seidel Menchi*

1. *Introductory remarks*

The present volume offers the papers of an international conference held in Trento from October 28 to 29, 2016, at the Istituto Storico Italo-Germanico (ISIG). It faced the task of using the occasion of commemorating the 500th anniversary of the Reformation, so as to reconsider the events within Latin Christianity in a comparative perspective and to consider them globally. The universal religious sociology of Max Weber was used and evaluated in the light of the new theoretical and methodological conditions of interdisciplinary and international research.

This also sets a memorial-political emphasis for the 500th year of Remembrance. If the earlier centennial celebrations were concerned with the recognition of the Protestant identity in the national German framework, or at most the European and North American one, in 2017 it turned to inner-Christian inter-confessional and the inter-religious comparison in a global-historical perspective. It is only the inter-religious and trans-civilizing comparison, as show the lectures of the Conference of Trento, published here, that are capable of reliably determining the particular and memorable aspects of the Lutheran Reformation, as well as the reach and limits of its imputed "world-effects". And last but not least, a diachronic comparative perspective from the past to the present opens up, which may serve to understand better the complex, often irritating, religious fundamentalist and political conditions of our time.

In contrast to a hundred years ago, a great scholarly-sociological approach from a universal-historical perspective can hardly be worked out by a single scholar. Today, a diversified international and interdisciplinary research landscape of specialists is obligatory. In addition, Eurocentric questions are increasingly replaced or supplemented by global-historical

Translation by Mark Roberts

perspectives. Thus, renowned experts on distinct world-religions and particular world-civilizations discussed in Trento the religio-historical and sociological problems raised by Martin Luther's Reformation in an inter-religious and international comparative mode. Certainly, it regards only those specialists who are willing to admit systematic and comparative questioning.

The conference location was doubly favorable, because of long years' experience of ISIG with transnational and interdisciplinary questions, and because of the *genius loci* of the city of the Council of Trent, where comparison between the double Christian Reformations—the one from Wittenberg and the Tridentine—and well beyond, is almost unavoidable.

The pages that follow pursue the double objective of offering the reader an initial orientation in the structure of the volume and its various components, and of drawing attention to certain thematic links between these latter.

2. *Balances and perspectives*

The question *Globalisation of Religion?* posed by Wolfgang Reinhard at the opening of this book confronts the reader with the historiographical and methodo-theoretical foundations, with the irradiation, with the ramifications of Max Weber's epochal work as a sociologist of religion; but it also reveals the limits of his construction.

The grand narrative of Protestant culture as the basis and matrix of what we call "modernity" or "the modern world" was born and flourished in the decade and a half between the epoch-making publication of *The Protestant Ethic and the Spirit of Capitalism* (1904/05) and the appearance of the essays *On the Sociology of Religion* (1920/21); but its effects were long-lasting. In the theory of the Axial Period advanced by Karl Jaspers, in the paradigm of the "multiple modernities" of Shmuel N. Eisenstadt, in the updatings and adjustments of the Axial Age idea by Robert N. Bellah, in the doctrines of Hans Joas that are still being elaborated, Reinhard sees as many attempts at constructing a universally applicable sociology of religion.

Although he makes a severe, indeed corrosive, analysis both of Weber's theory—criticized as Eurocentric, and for applying Western categories to non-European realities such as Asian cultures—and of the paradigm of the Axial Age as promoted by Jaspers and his intellectual heirs—criticised for the unilaterality and arbitrariness of its chronological and spatial divisions—Reinhard nevertheless does not hesitate to espouse a synthesis that demonstrates the efficacy and irradiation of the principle of Reform at a global level. The omnipresence of Luther as an icon of renewal and regeneration—the present volume demonstrates that no culture has been immune to the fascination of this myth—is only the most glaring aspect of that "distant comparison" whose methodological validity Reinhard recognizes, and which he successfully employs in tandem with "close comparison".

The essay concludes with a challenge to the imagination and flexibility of today's and tomorrow's historians. Reinhard recognizes, today, an urgency to the religious dimension of individual and collective experience that would have been unthinkable twenty years ago. That process of secularization which the historiography of the time judged to be irreversible has today become an obsolete interpretative resource. On the other hand, the present recrudescence of religion—understood also as "transcendence" or "auto-transcendence" (Hans Joas)—confers socio-cultural importance on esoteric movements that traditional historiography defined as superstitious or peripheral.

Since the scholarly itineraries of Paolo Prodi and of Wolfgang Reinhard have several times intersected and have influenced one another, the juxtaposition of their voices had been envisaged right from the first planning of the conference. Prodi, however, did not appear at Trento to read the text that he had in good time sent to the Institute he had founded[1]. *Europe in the Age of Reformations. The Modern State and Confessionalization* was his last composition. With it he entrusted to the editors of this volume a profession of faith that is at the same time a historico-political testament of great drama and pathos. It will be up to future historians to locate this testament in the context of Prodi's work and to judge whether the Bolognese master did not here reach the absolute zenith of his power of synthesis and of his intensity of writing.

To juxtapose Prodi and Reinhard means—in the economy of this volume—to put Prodi in dialogue with Max Weber. The entire work

[1] The editors of this volume thank Massimo Rospocher for his forceful reading of Prodi's paper at the conference.

of the Italian historian may be regarded as a development and a correction of the theses elaborated by the German sociologist. The very foundation of the Istituto Storico Italo-Germanico in Trento responded to the need to update and expand Max Weber's discourse—flanking Protestantism with Catholicism as an equally decisive factor in the genesis of the modern world. "The Council of Trent as the Crossroad of European politics"—the theme with which the newborn Institute launched in 1973 its program of conferences—already adumbrated that equation of Protestant "Reformation" and Catholic "Reformation" that finds its definitive codification in the title of the essay we publish here.

He bases his paper on three conceptual foundations, that is to say: 1) the theory of "confessionalization" and its corollaries[2], 2) the principle of "osmosis" or of reciprocal influence between the religious and the political sphere, and 3) the dialectic of sin and crime.

In a few pages Prodi concentrates his vision of European history from the Middle Ages to the twentieth century, while at the same time running through his own career as a scholar from the 1960s until the eve of the conference, which in his eyes must have appeared an opportunity to draw up a balance of his life's work.

This powerful synthesis is characterized by an apocalyptic tone. Historiography suffers shipwreck—we read in these pages—because history suffers shipwreck (or vice versa?); the West commits suicide; the historical cycle that generated "our" Europe comes to an end; the foundations of our society collapse. The essay is filled with metaphors of death, destruction, and defeat. It will be for future historians to decide whether and to what extent these pages document also, and especially, the diagnosis that a historian who was pre-eminently a *homo politicus* made on the nation to which he had devoted his energies, his intelligence, his faith.

In *Politics, Theology, and Religion in the Reformation* Thomas Kaufmann formulates in lucid and compelling fashion the question "why". Why

2 On the paradigm "confessionalization", which has been developed by Wolfgang Reinhard und Heinz Schilling during the late 1970s and the 1980s, cf. J.M. Headley et al. (eds), *Confessionalization in Europe 1555-1700*, Aldershot 2004, pp. 1-36; S. Ehrenpreis - U. Lotz-Heumann, *Reformation und konfessionelles Zeitalter*, Darmstadt 2008, 2nd ed., pp. 62-79; H. Schilling, *Konfessionalisierung*, in *Staatslexikon*, 8th ed., Freiburg i.Br. forthcoming.

was the Reformation? Why is the Reformation? How could a movement that defied all the European powers of the time survive and consolidate itself? The "connection between theology and politics"—what Prodi called the dialectic between religion and state structures, the osmosis between faith and power—was the concerted action that made of a Saxon monk the founder of the church that celebrates this year 500 years of life. Kaufmann's paper is the demonstration that an interpretative instrument such as Prodi feared and deplored would be rejected by historians is in fact perfectly functional.

The traditional utilitarian reasons advanced for the massive lay adhesion to the pro-Luther movement—first of all the desire of the German territorial princes to possess themselves of the lands and estates of the religious foundations—appear crude and inadequate in the face of this rigorous and differentiated analysis. We see the ranks of lay supporters enlarged and diversified: the territorial princes are accompanied by local politicians, jurists sitting on city councils, officials of princes' chancelleries, counsellors to the princes. In parallel Kaufmann evaluates, against the utilitarian considerations, powerfully involving immaterial motivations—such as the invitation to lay folk to assume spiritual responsibility in the church, and their co-opting into the sacerdotal organization—, emphasizing well documented cases in which a political role as a prince's counsellor became an intense spiritual experience (Georg Spalatin).

In the most narrowly historical and documentary sense this analysis concentrates on two turning-points of the early Reformation narrative: the appeal *To the Christian Nobility of German Nation* of 1520—"the Magna Carta of the German Reformation" (Kaufmann)—and the *Confessio Augustana* of 1530. The trump card of religious and political interaction was played, in this decade, sometimes by the Reformer himself but sometimes, more than once, by the politicians contrary to the expressed wishes of the churchman and theologian.

In *Devotion and Institutions in the Age of the Reformations* Pierre Antoine Fabre, a specialist in the history of the Jesuits and the role of Christian images in Europe and the Catholic world, addresses the theme of the Reformation from the perspective most familiar to him, that of the Council of Trent. His earlier researches induced him to question conventional historiographic understandings of an initial mission of the Council, suggesting that the Council is an exception to the rule, wherein the "rule" in question involves solutions of continuity between dogma and discipline, discourse and practice, the poles around which the Council attempted to organize theological and ecclesiastic coherence.

Fabre thus circulates in a landscape with three different kinds of reality: institutions, devotions, and the relentless inscription of Europe onto a world that Europeans have discovered and that simultaneously reveals to them what they are. On these three realities his contribution to the present volume is centered. The heart of his inquiry concentrates on the difficulty of taking into account for the early modern period what he calls the people of devotions (as opposed to "popular" devotions) and of understanding what he calls the historiographic "depression" around the study of devotional practices between the end of the Middle Ages and the end of the Ancien Régime.

According to Fabre, the joint theological presence of Catholic and Protestant Churches just after the Reformation had a double consequence. On the one hand, Protestant theologians denied to Catholic religious culture any vital articulation between its discourse and practices, considering the latter the vestiges of a faith that was extinct. Conversely, Catholic theologians rejected in Protestant theology, whose autonomy it denied, any possibility of justifying new practices. At the same time both sets of theologians simply took for granted the natural articulation of their own *doxa* and *praxis*. Hence these articulations ended up "forgotten", in a period during which they were simultaneously under challenge by the general upheaval of Christian society, of *christianitas* in its medieval definition, both by the European crisis of reforms and by the redefinition of the boundaries of the known world. The result was a series of devotional traditions for which their contemporaries did not provide key theoretical elaborations.

Pierre Antoine Fabre conveys the long-term historiographic effects of a historical denial and persists on locating in recent research ways to rediscover this world, at once "ancient" and "new".

3. *Distant comparisons, close comparisons*

The four essays in the second part of the volume verify the applicability of the basic comparative paradigm to four specific religious cultures: Greek / Russian Orthodox Christendom, Judaism, Islam, Hinduism.

In *Reform Movements in Russian Orthodoxy* Martin Tamcke traces a panorama embracing five centuries. The robust reform movements that shook the Russian Orthodox Church from the fourteenth to the nineteenth century demonstrated, on one side, the existence of aspirations and longings common to the different religious cultures of Christendom, evidencing however, on the other side, the strong internal cohesion of the eastern community of believers and the cohesive power of its devotional traditions.

Reforming ideas and watchwords that pervaded the medieval and modern Church of central and western Europe—the struggle against simony, the opposition to ecclesiastical property-owning, the aspiration to subtract the Church from political influence, even principles of precise theological connotation such as the universal priesthood of believers—successively animate groups of reformers operating within the Russian Church in the fourteenth century (the Strigolniki movement), in the earlier sixteenth (non-possessors), in the seventeenth and eighteenth century and later (Old-Believers). On the other hand, the close relationship between church and crown, and the minute attention paid by the Russian Church to ritual matters—whether to use two or three fingers in making the sign of the Cross—lend support to the author's concluding judgement: in comparing these two Christian churches, the Orthodox and the Protestant, he reveals two paths fundamentally independent of one another, despite the presence of certain influences of the latter on the former.

Placing Roni Weinstein's essay *Jewish Culture in Early Modernity. The Global Turn* next to Tamcke's essay is to juxtapose a case of close comparison to a case of distant comparison. The messianic movement, on which Weinstein focuses his attention, was strongly influenced by Protestantism, and even more by post-Tridentine Catholicism. For this reason, the paradigm of confessionalization turns out, in Weinstein's judgement, to be perfectly homogeneous and functional for the analysis of the society and political culture of the Israelite community, and also of the Ottoman Empire into which it was inserted.

The messianic movement headed by Sabbetai Zvi during the second half of the seventeenth century swept the entire Jewish world. It indicated well that by this time the Jewish culture and religious traditions acquired a marked global aspect. The major factor dominating this shift from local basis to globality was the Iberian diaspora, because of its economic, political, and cultural advantages over other Jewish traditions, and certainly because of its international networks.

The early modern period was characterized by intensified encounters between various Jewish traditions, as testified in some cities (Livorno, Amsterdam, Salonika, Istanbul, Cairo) where major Jewish communities were established. It was all the more true in the case of the small Galilean city of Safed, where major intellectual figures from the entire Jewish world were active. This multi-traditional melting pot encouraged a cultural and religious synthesis, crossing religious and political borders between Ottoman Islam and Christian Europe. In short, Safed turned into a "laboratory of modernity".

The motivation behind this wave of religious creativity, and especially the renaissance of mysticism ("Kabbalah"), was a renovation and reform and religious tradition enhancing religious devotion and piety, in a manner echoing similar changes taking place in Europe (both in Catholic and Protestant contexts) and in the Ottoman Empire.

There were several aspects of this religious reform of global dimensions, encompassing the entire Jewish world during early modernity:

- the rise of "a Jewish Saint" as a source of religious authority, alongside the classical figures of Rabbis and religious scholars;
- the printing revolution, allowing larger portions of the Jewish population access to the entire classical rabbinic canon;
- tightening control over individual consciousness and ideas;
- the appearance, unprecedented in a Jewish context, of well-structured and comprehensive theology, occupied with major themes in Jewish tradition, and especially in regard to religious practice;
- institutionalized battle against figures and ideas considered as dangerous or "heretical";
- unification of religious law, mainly in the codes of law composed by R. Joseph Karo—whose pioneering role is stressed by Reinhard—intended to be applied over the entire Jewish diaspora;
- the increasing occupation with sin and repentance, as a major component of religious devotion.

With *Renewal and Reform in Sunni Islam* Gudrun Krämer opens to the reader the horizon of the Arabic Middle East in two directions. The first is that of analogy. Between Sunni Islam and Christian Europe there exist transverse links that Krämer reveals and evaluates:

- the phenomenon of confessionalization, understood as the link between religion and state-building,
- the dialectic between faith and works—between interior conviction and exterior conduct—and the consequent applicability to Islam, by analogy, of the principle of *Lebensführung*.

On the opposite side, however, Krämer authoritatively warns against facile comparisons and superficial analogies: reference to the Protestant Reformation and its effects in the West, she observes, is more useful for evidencing the differences than the similarities between the two cultures. Among the absences that distinguish Sunni Islam from Christianity we find:

- the absence of an autonomous ecclesiastical structure, able to make binding decisions regarding doctrine and morality,
- the lack of an institutionalized clergy holding a monopoly on the exercise of the sacred,
- the rejection of the notion of "reform", since Islam is conceived by its followers as a religion that manifested itself in absolute perfection, one that in consequence cannot be reformed but only brought back to its original purity.

Among the positive principles that specifically characterize Islam, she lists:

- the coexistence of different, even opposite, interpretations of each single commandment, including concrete prescriptions such as the prohibition of alcohol and drugs;
- the absolute pre-eminence of the legal dimension and of moral and behavioral prescriptions over the doctrinal and theological dimension.

When she comes to the modern and contemporary age—from the nineteenth to the twenty-first century—Krämer introduces into her evaluation three concepts that provide three keys to interpreting the present. The encounter between Sunni Islam and the Christian West, which connotes the present time draws its explosive force from:

- the defense of Muslim identity (identity being a concept that will be closely examined by Marco Ventura),
- the watchword of resistance to western colonialism (a phenomenon that plays a key role in the essay by Brian Pennington),
- the appeal to the renewal of Islam through a return to the original purity and unity—including military force—which the community of believers knew in the time of Muhammad, and the political and educational project in which such an appeal takes form.

Krämer concludes her vibrant synthesis with a note that deserves a moment of reflection. Referring to Egypt, and in particular to the Muslim Brothers, she observes that the exponents of this reforming movement have failed in their objective "if this entailed freeing Muslims from Western hegemony in the political, economic, and cultural fields".

None of the landscapes evoked in this volume has been marked so strongly and so controversially by Max Weber's paradigm as has India in the nineteenth and twentieth century. Brian Pennington, in *Reform and Revival, Innovation and Enterprise. A Tale of Modern Hinduism*, examines the "Protestantisation of India" as a politico-educational program of profound effect. The Protestant ethic—understood as a combination of asceticism, of disciplined professionalism and of "legitimised capitalistic accumulations" (Pennington)—supplied British India with an ethico-cultural model. Out of it developed a bourgeoisie intended to assist the British in administering the subcontinent.

A program of this kind involved the imposition of western categories to Indian society and an intromission of Christian values into Indian culture—the watchword "reform" affected both the one and the other—which from the nineteenth century aroused a series of political and cultural reactions based on a program of revival. This revival promoted a narrative of an ancient golden age marked by non-idolatrous ritual practice and equitable social arrangements that became eroded as Muslim invaders and other foreigners penetrated the subcontinent.

Pennington argues that this historical framework maps a European history of reformation and counter-reformation onto India's experience of British colonialism and consequently overlooks the inventive and tactical intercessions that shaped modern Hinduism. Against a narrative of India modernizing under European influence, it proposes a reading of reforming Hinduism as social and religious innovation. Twentieth-century debates that eventually produced legislation abolishing the dedication of young girls as *devadāsīs*, or temple courtesans, illustrate the manufacture of historical narrative and social practice that works strategically in the historical present in order to fashion creative associations with the Indian past and to achieve contemporary ends. More than reformers restoring ancient practice or revivalists reasserting indigenous authority, these actors functioned as innovators and entrepreneurs in a fluid and contested present.

4. *Events of 1517, accents of 2017*

Recent history has conferred a terrible topicality on the historical memory of religions and religiosity. Religion has recaptured, unexpectedly[3], an urgency and a capacity to involve our society at all its various levels such as the earlier centenaries did not know[4]. All the contributors to this volume are marked by the shift of emphasis to the historiographical agenda. The perspective of 2017 is particularly evident in the essays that we have placed in this third and final section of the proceedings.

It was recent events that suggested to Silvana Seidel Menchi *Martyrdom* as the subject of her paper. As a transcultural and diachronic phenomenon, martyrdom lends itself to a comparative analysis because the facing-off between faiths always feeds the culture of self-immolation. In the confessional conflict to which 1517 gave rise, martyrdom acquired an imperative character and self-immolation became an omnipresent behavioral model. The author's aim is to compare the doctrine of martyrdom in the three monotheistic religions.

The essay is divided into two parts. In the first, Seidel Menchi reviews the various registers of the exaltation of martyrdom in sixteenth-century

[3] W. MONTER, *Religion and Cultural Exchange 1400-1700: Twenty-first-century Implication*, in H. SCHILLING - I.G. THÓTH (eds), *Religion and Cultural Exchange in Europa, 1400-1700*, Cambridge 2006, pp. 3-24; T. HANF - K. EL MUFTI (eds), *Policies and Politics of Teaching Religion*, Baden-Baden 2014; R. CIPRIANI (ed.), *Religions sans frontières?*, Roma 1993; J. HABERMAS, *Glaube und Wissen. Friedenspreisrede 2001*, in J. HABERMAS, *Zeitdiagnos. Zwölf Essays*, Frankfurt a.M. 2003, pp. 249-262.

[4] D. WENDENBOURG, *Vergangene Reformationsjubiläen. Ein Rückblick auf 400 Jahre im Vorfeld von 2017*, in H. SCHILLING (ed.), *Der Reformator Martin Luther 2017. Symposion des Historischen Kollegs im November 2013*, München 2014, pp. 261-281.

Europe. In a chorus of celebrations of death as the supreme form of testimony, knowing no confessional boundaries, Seidel Menchi identifies a single dissenting voice (1530). It counterbalances, and in tendency prefers, the testimony of a virtuous life to the testimony of death, cautiously placing Christians on guard against the "raptus" of self-immolation. That this was a risky operation at the level of ecclesiastical policy—and also a very farsighted intuition—appears from the fact that the author, the most famous humanist in Europe at that time, considered it opportune to publish his text under a false name, choosing as his pseudonym a personage who also acted as a protective shield: Saint Cyprian, a Father of the Church and an apologist for martyrdom, who had himself died a martyr.

In the second part of the essay, the viewpoint extends from Christianity to the other two Abrahamic religions. In Judaism, as in Islam, Seidel Menchi identifies a divarication between a culture that exalts the testimony of blood and a culture that relativizes it. In both these cultures, the supreme testimony of faith did not necessarily coincide with death. The dimension of conscience, on the other hand, which in the Christian cultures replaced the dimension of martyrdom especially in the period of the Reformation, has some parallelisms in Jewish culture, but a more controversial role in Islam. On this specific point, however, it would be necessary to interrogate the most recent results of research, and even of research that is still in progress.

Freedom of conscience already appears in the opening essay of this volume as a distinctive feature of "modernity". According to the viewpoint expressed by Wolfgang Reinhard, freedom of conscience is the long-matured fruit of a Protestantism that contrasts, in this respect, with the "Catholicism of the Pianic Age" (1791-1958), which had "deliberately emigrated from the modern world". References to the Protestant matrix of freedom of conscience appear in some of the later essays, in combination with the theme of freedom of religion. In *Faith v. Identity: The Protestant Factor in Contemporary European Freedom of Religion or Belief* Marco Ventura develops, with the rigor of a jurist, a theme that underlies this entire collection of essays. The change of emphasis from "freedom of conscience" to "freedom of religion" is imposed by the perspective that Ventura—a major contributor to the international debate on human rights—has made his own.

European jurists and public policies now use the formula "freedom of religion or belief" in preference to "freedom of conscience", because the former expression is socially inclusive—encompassing theistic as well as atheistic and non-theistic beliefs—and better responds to the socio-cultural dynamic of the post Twin Towers age. Communities or individuals who do not subscribe to the principle—of Protestant connotation—of "freedom of conscience" can invoke the neutral notion of freedom of religion or belief. On this former principle, the conclusion of the essay casts the shadow of a historical condemnation: Protestant-style freedom of conscience has functioned—Ventura suggests—as "a missionary tool, a vehicle of conversion and neo-imperialism".

Ventura's argument rests on a crucial distinction, which juridical science has distilled from today's experience: the distinction between "faith-based religion" and "identity-based religion". The former emphasizes the individual experience of the sacred, the interior journey of the individual believer, and regards only secondarily the devotional traditions and the continuity of belonging guaranteed by the profession of faith; the latter emphasizes belonging to a specific cultural community, ritual continuity, devotional practices as reinforcement of identity, and tradition as a basic existential factor. These two types of religion correspond to two models of religious freedom, the first type being a weak social binding-agent, more tolerant of altereity and of apostasy, while the second type is strongly socially cohesive, intolerant of deviations and defections. Making use of documents such as treaties and directives of the EU (2007 and 2013), and sentences of the US Supreme Court (2009 and 2014) and of the European Court (2011), Ventura argues that faith-based religious freedom and identity-based religious freedom are today in opposition with one another, indeed in conflict with one another, and that the former—and with it the Protestant-type freedom of conscience—is rightly losing ground to the latter.

In his concluding remarks *Reform, Reformation, Confessionalization. The Latin Christian Experience*, Heinz Schilling argues that the change in the German memorial culture of the Reformation from monarchist authoritarian Protestant triumphalism during the last centenaries to a democratic, ecumenical, and trans-national perspective provides an opportunity for a new evaluation of Luther's and the Reformation's impact on world history. Contrary to the nineteenth-century interpretation of Protestantism as the key player in the process to capitalism, democracy and modernity, and to Adolf von Harnack's statement in the 1920s that "modernity ... was initiated by the hammer blows to the doors of the castle church in Wittenberg", the essay extends the perspective for the year 1517 itself beyond Wittenberg into the wider world. It shows that Luther's "hammer blows" alone were not responsible for the deep changes that transferred Europe and the world from medieval to early modern and modern status. In a global perspective, Europe's departure to modernity was the result of a kind of syndrome with three leading forces at its center: the revival of ancient culture by Humanism and the Renaissance; the new knowledge of a wider world; and the reformations of Christianity, provoked by Martin Luther.

Consequently, Schilling qualifies the idea that non-Christian world religions need a Luther to keep up with Western civilization as too simple to capture the complex European experience in developing from pre-modern to modern civilization. In opening the historical perspective beyond the traditional national and European boundaries, it becomes evident that there is no reason to privilege the Protestant Reformation as 'the' key impulse for fundamental, modernizing change.

At a moment when the debate not only in Germany is focusing on Luther and his ninety-five theses, the editors are proud to offer to the international public a volume that in addition to the Wittenberg magnifying glass uses the global telescope to understand the meaning of reforms or reformations in history and present times.

5. *Acknowledgements*

The editors are most grateful to the authors, who were willing to enter into the comparative debate during the conference, especially for their generous willingness in preparing their articles for the press. In addition, they would like to thank the Auswärtige Amt in Berlin and the Generalkonsulat der Bundesrepublik Deutschland in Milan for financial support of the conference.

The Fondazione Bruno Kessler's Istituto Storico Italo-Gemanico in Trento was an amiable host and our thanks go in the name of all participants to its members and staff. We send our warmest greetings and deepest respects to the former Director of the ISIG, Prof. Paolo Pombeni, who supported the project with energy and courtesy—from the very beginning, when in the summer of 2013 we offered an initial outline of the international conference at a meeting in the Auswärtige Amt in Berlin, up to its final realization in October 2016 in Trento. Also in his successor, the present director Prof. Christoph Cornelißen, the editors have found a trustworthy ally; the same goes for the director of the publishing department Dr. Chiara Zanoni and the copy editor Friederike Oursin. Dr. Massimo Rospocher made a major contribution to the conference both by reading and reviewing Prodi's essay and by thoughtfully channeling the initial exchanges between the editors and the single authors.

The editors also have a major debt of gratitude to Mark Roberts, British Institute of Florence, who as native speaker has polished and linguistically corrected the essays collected in this volume with admirable effort and patience.

Berlin and Florence, Summer 2017

Balances and Perspectives

Globalization of Religion?

by *Wolfgang Reinhard*

When Gerhard Ritter in 1959 and Max Steinmetz in 1969 published books about the effect of the Reformation on the world (*Die Weltwirkung der Reformation*), they referred to the little world of Germany or at most that of Europe[1]. Half a century later, the semi-millennium of the Reformation can only be celebrated in a global context. Just now, even the catholic Görres-Gesellschaft organized an ecumenically attended conference on the Reformation as a basic process not only of the history of Christianity but of the history of religion in general[2]. Nevertheless, how religion in general and the Reformation in particular can be dealt with from a global point of view is still anything but obvious. Therefore, a question mark is necessary in the title of an essay that is going to test established and new perspectives of global religious history.

At a first glance, 2017 becomes a global event because of the global presence of protestant Christians. Religious globalization preceded economic and political globalization. In several consecutive waves since antiquity, Christianity has been most successful in that respect[3]. At the beginning of the twenty-first century, 2.2 billion of the 7 billion humans were Christians, followed by 1.2 billion Muslims, 900 million Hindus, 800 million a-religious mostly in China, and 400 million Buddhists[4]. One half of the Christians are supposed to be Catholics, 800 million Protestants. However, things immediately become complicated, because not more than 426 million Protestants belong to the so called

1 G. RITTER, *Die Weltwirkung der Reformation*, 2nd ed., München 1959 (first published 1941); M. STEINMETZ (ed.), *Die Weltwirkung der Reformation*, 2 Bde., Berlin 1969.

2 Combined meeting of the sections for history, religion, and ethnology at the annual conference of the "Görres-Gesellschaft", September 19-20, 2016 at Hildesheim.

3 W. REINHARD, *Globalisierung des Christentums?*, Heidelberg 2007.

4 https://de.wikipedia.org/wiki/Religion

"classical communities of the Reformation", as the traditional protestant churches have been designated by the *Evangelische Allianz Deutschland*, in contrast to the millions of members of the spreading Pentecostal communities[5]. Even if this is probably a much too general qualification, nevertheless, not more than 80 million Christians belong to the 230 churches from 108 countries, which are members of the World Communion of Reformed Churches[6], and only 70 million belong to the 145 churches from 79 countries of the Lutheran World Federation, the *Lutherische Weltbund*[7]. The rest consists of innumerable, sometimes quite unorthodox communities, especially in the case of hybridization with indigenous religious traditions. But their suspected heterodoxy may just be an effect of our Eurocentric perspective, a problem we will have to deal with at the end of our discussion.

Instead, first of all we have to comply with the subtitle of the actual conference and to consider the Protestant Reformation as just one among the many religious reforms of world history. We may suppose that repeated attempts of renewal are an essential element not only of the history of Christianity but also of other so-called "high or world religions". But I do not know if they were all continuously obsessed with the idea of reform as was the case with occidental monastic communities in particular, and with Christians in general, in accordance with Romans 12.2[8]. Under such conditions the diachronic context to some extent reduces the historic achievement of reformers, as happens to Luther, if we consider him just as an outstanding exemplar in a long series of Christian reformers.

[5] www.ead.de/arbeitskreise/religionsfreiheit/nachrichten/einzelansicht/article/weltweit

[6] https://de.wikipedia.org/wiki/Weltgemeinschaft_Reformierten_Kirchen

[7] https://de.wikipedia.org/wiki/Liste_der_Mitgliedskirchen_des_Lutherischen_Weltbunde

[8] E. WOLGAST, *Reform, Reformation*, in *Geschichtliche Grundbegriffe*, vol. 5, Stuttgart 1984, pp. 313-360, here p. 316; G. STRAUSS, *Ideas of Reformatio and Renovatio from the Middle Ages to the Reformation*, in T.A. BRADY et al. (eds), *Handbook of European History 1400-1600*, vol. 2, Leiden 1994, pp. 1-30; L. SCHILLING, *Reform*, in *Enzyklopädie der Neuzeit*, vol. 10, Stuttgart 2009, pp. 777-785; D. WENDEBOURG, *Reformation*, in *Enzyklopädie der Neuzeit*, vol. 10, pp. 794 ff.; recently on monastic reform in the Middle Ages: *Reform als Konflikt*, in "Saeculum", 66, 2016, 1, pp. 3-176.

After all, Martin Luther had some remarkable reformers as coevals. In India, the Bhakti movement, which insists on a personal relationship with divinity, has produced radical mystics such as Kabir (1440-1512) or the "doctrine of grace" of the Vishnu worshiper Vallabha (1481-1531). But perhaps most outstanding was the experience of calling made by Gurū Nānak (1469-1539), the founder of the monotheistic Sikh-religion, in about 1500[9]. They all intended to shake off the ritualistic load of traditional Indian religion. Completely different but still comparable was the activity of Wang Yangming (1472-1529) in China. He "is less known to Western readers than his contemporary Martin Luther (1483-1546), but Wang's intellectual impact was almost as great"[10]. According to his doctrine of sageliness (*xinxue*), developed under the influence of Buddhism, every human being has the capacity for spiritual advancement and should be able to overcome the sterility of traditional Confucianism. His followers, first of all Li Zhi (1527-1602), an aggressive critic of the imperial regime, created the famous Donglin Academy of the late Ming period and exerted influence on Japanese thinking[11].

In the world of Islam, the foundation of the empire of the Safavids, together with the introduction of Shiism in Iran in 1501 by the head of the Sufi order of Ardabil, might perhaps be claimed as a comparable reform initiative[12]. Probably more convincing is Gerhard Lauer's attempt to identify a new Jewish orthodoxy that claimed an immediate mystical approach to God instead of traditional religious practice. Joseph Karo's monumental *halacha* commentary of 1559, according to Lauer, even marks the starting point of a Jewish "confessionalization" in the sense of Reinhard and Schilling[13].

9 O. GÄCHTER, *Sikhismus*, in J. FIGL (ed.), *Handbuch der Religionswissenschaft*, Innsbruck et al. 2003, pp. 368-383.

10 P.C. PERDUE, *Empires and Frontiers in Continental Eurasia*, in W. REINHARD (ed.), *Empires and Encounters, 1350-1750* (A History of the World, 3), Cambridge MA et al. 2015, pp. 35-218, here p. 71.

11 *Ibid.*, p. 79.

12 S. FAROQHI, *The Ottoman Empire and the Islamic World*, in W. REINHARD, *Empires*, pp. 209-388, here p. 342.

13 G. LAUER, *Die Konfessionalisierung des Judentums. Zum Prozess der religiösen Ausdifferenzierung im Judentum am Übergang zur Neuzeit*, in K. VON GREYERZ et al. (eds), *Interkonfessionalität – Transkonfessionalität – bikonfessionelle Pluralität. Neuere Forschungen zur Konfessionalisierungsthese*, Heidelberg 2003, pp. 250-283.

All these phenomena differ completely from each other and are spatially also totally distinct. Therefore, mutual influence being excluded, the obvious similar structural tendencies identified by "distant comparison" are even more remarkable. We come across a general transcultural inclination to transcend the "works" of a ritualized tradition through a spiritualized personal relationship with God. In this respect, Luther is no singularity. Is it possible that the *Weltanschauung* of different so-called "high cultures" around the year 1500 reached a comparable level of development with similar religious needs? Is this perhaps a smaller version of the global Axial Age of Karl Jaspers when between 800 and 200 BC religious and philosophical "classics" appeared almost everywhere[14]?

In contrast, the numerous reform movements of the eighteenth and nineteenth century worldwide have to be analyzed under conditions of "close comparison" because now mutual influence and autochthonous development can no longer be separated. Quite often, some intercultural influence can be identified and is even referred to explicitly, but mainly a one-sided influence of the West in general and of Western Protestant Reformation in particular. As a "sender" of influence, Protestantism reached the culmination point of worldwide expansion during that period. Whereas Catholic missions had dominated the early modern period and had gained the major part of the New World, the end of the European Ancien Régime dealt them a heavy blow. In contrast, the Protestant side now started its successful missionary age in Africa, Asia, and Australasia with the different evangelical revival movements taking the lead. These movements were inclined to consider themselves as the accomplishment of the Protestant Reformation and may therefore be designated as the "second Reformation" which the Calvinists had once claimed for themselves[15].

The success of this second missionary age of Europe is explained by the fact that the "soft power" of the Gospel followed the "hard power" of Western colonialism exactly as in the first one, but now under Anglo-Saxon and no longer under Iberian leadership. In both cases, however, missionaries cannot once and for all be disqualified as agents

[14] K. JASPERS, *Vom Ursprung und Ziel der Geschichte*, München et al. 1949; K. JASPERS, *The Origin and Goal of History*, New Haven CT 1953, reprint Abingdon 2010.

[15] H. SCHILLING (ed.), *Die reformierte Konfessionalisierung in Deutschland – das Problem der zweiten Reformation*, Gütersloh 1986.

of colonialism. Sometimes the opposite was true[16]. Causes and effects were more complicated. Nevertheless, on the side of the "receivers" of influence, the new colonialism produced the traumatic experience of political and cultural inferiority. The obvious consequences were attempts to overcome this situation through reforms following the Western model. In the long run, this included reform of the religious or philosophical core of the traditional culture, sometimes even referring explicitly to Europe's Protestant Reformation.

Even in Germany, the Jewish reform movement of the emancipation period to some extent chose a Protestant direction when it preferred faith and ethics to the traditional religious law and employed the Lutheran invention of Catechism for that purpose[17].

The history of Islam is full of movements of revival and purification, quite often of messianic character. Already before the critical impact of Western colonialism, Muhammad ibn Abd al-Wahhab (1703/04-1792) had reduced Islam on the Arabian Peninsula to what he considered as its original rigor, and had suppressed superstitious practice such as the veneration of saints—with consequences to the present day[18]. Later reformers such as Jamal ad-Din al-Afghani (1838/39-1897), Muhammad Abduh (1849-1905), and Rashid Rida (1865-1935), however, considered the purification of Islam first of all as a necessary reaction to the challenge of the West. In contrast to traditionalists, they were not only in favor of the acceptance of Western achievements, but were convinced that a purified Islam by itself included all the values of Western culture, including its famous rationality[19]. It is significant that these men were active in Egypt, a country under a particularly strong impact of Western modernization[20].

16 W. REINHARD, *Der Missionar*, in J. ZIMMERER (ed.), *Kein Platz an der Sonne. Erinnerungsorte der deutschen Kolonialgeschichte*, Frankfurt a.M. 2013, pp. 282-293, here p. 287.

17 H.-M. HAUSSIG, *Reformjudentum*, in *Enzyklopädie der Neuzeit*, vol. 10, Stuttgart 2009, pp. 838-844.

18 R. PETERS, *Erneuerungsbewegungen im Islam vom 18. bis zum 20. Jahrhundert*, in W. ENDE - U. STEINBACH (eds), *Der Islam in der Gegenwart*, 2nd ed., München 1989, pp. 96-98.

19 R. PETERS, *Erneuerungsbewegungen im Islam*, pp. 116-128.

20 W. REINHARD, *Die Unterwerfung der Welt. Globalgeschichte der europäischen Expansion 1415-2015*, München 2016, pp. 907-910, 934-937, 1060 f.

The central category *islah* (sanification) has always been present in Muslim thought but now acquired the strategic meaning of "self-improvement". *Idjtihad*, considered as the individual understanding of the Quran and the Sunna—of scripture and tradition in Christian terminology—now became the right and duty of every believer[21]. The analogy with the Protestant Reformation is obvious. Al-Afghani explicitly claimed the part of Luther for himself[22].

Anagarika Dharmapala (1864-1933), a leader of the Buddhist revival that started at Ceylon/Sri Lanka, styled the historical Buddha as the Martin Luther of an anti-colonial "protestant" Buddhism, because he had revolted against the religious authority of the Veda and the Brahmins[23]. In British India, the pressure of modernization produced a particularly animated reform debate. A new notion of (religious) reform as (dharmic) *sudhaar* became established usage in Hindi[24]. Already Rammohun Roy (1772-1833) used the Vedanta philosophy to purify the religious life of India through suppression of superstitious idol worship and to liberate it from the tyranny of priests. In contrast, he established or rather claimed to re-establish a strictly monotheistic religion. In addition, his translation of Indian religious terminology allowed Western understanding to misinterpret Indian religious practice as one single "religion" called Hinduism. Internationally, Roy was considered as "the Luther of India", but refused to accept this distinction because of his Unitarian conviction[25]. Later on Swami Vivekananda (1863-1902) also used a version of the Vedanta philosophy as starting point. But after the great publicity of his self-presentation at the World Parliament of Religions at Chicago in 1893, he started a missionary movement called after his teacher, the mystic Ramakrishna (1836-1886), in order

[21] A. MÉRAD, *Islah I. The Arab World*, in *Encyclopaedia of Islam*, vol. 4, Leiden 1978, pp. 141-163, and information by Gudrun Krämer und Cornelia Schöck.

[22] S. CONRAD, *Eine Kulturgeschichte globaler Transformation*, in S. CONRAD - J. OSTERHAMMEL (eds), *Wege zur modernen Welt 1750-1870* (Geschichte der Welt, 4), München 2016, p. 604.

[23] S. CONRAD, *Eine Kulturgeschichte globaler Transformation*, p. 561.

[24] Information by Gita Dharampal.

[25] L. ZASTOUPIL, *Rammohun Roy and the Making of Victorian Britain*, New York 2010, pp. 5, 28, 31, 76.

to spread Indian spirituality worldwide[26]. The Western universalism of a Swedenborgian Free Church man had initiated that side event of Chicago's World Fair, which turned out to become the starting point of the alternative offer of Eastern universalism to the West[27].

Did the Chinese terms *gaige* (to change something) or *zongjiao gaige* (religious reform or Reformation)[28] boom at the same time? In any case, Confucianism cannot be analyzed with the same categories as the religions of other cultures. Nevertheless, Kang Youwei (1858-1927), the intellectual leader of the failed reforms of 1898, was praised by his disciples as the Martin Luther of Confucianism[29]. His universalistic utopia *Datong Shu*, the *Book of Great Unity*, that is humanity, transformed or even transcended Confucianism under the impact of Western ideas. But he still proposed the birth of Confucius instead of the birth of Christ as the era of a new universal calendar[30].

Kang's distinction of *shendao*, the "path of the gods", designating Christian and other religions, and of *rendao*, the "path of humans", including not only Confucianism but also his own program[31], demonstrates that in the nineteenth-century reforms originated under the impact of the secular European Enlightenment as well as under the religious influence of the Reformation. But these two strains of influence cannot be separated completely, because not only awakened evangelicals but also enlightened improvers claimed to accomplish the Reformation in the sense of a rational religion including individual liberty of conscience[32]. This kind of

[26] https://en.wikipedia.org/wiki/Vivekananda

[27] https://de.wikipedia.org/wiki/Erstes_Parlament_der_Weltreligionen; S. CONRAD, *Eine Kulturgeschichte globaler Transformation*, p. 563.

[28] Information by Chen Hongjie und Hu Haiyan.

[29] S. CONRAD, *Eine Kulturgeschichte globaler Transformation*, p. 604.

[30] W. REINHARD, *Die Unterwerfung der Welt*, p. 1294; K. YU-WEI, *Das Buch von der großen Gemeinschaft*, Düsseldorf 1974; L.G. THOMPSON (ed.), *Ta t'ung Shu: The One-World Philosophy of K'ang Yu-wei*, London 1958.

[31] S. CONRAD, *Eine Kulturgeschichte globaler Transformation*, p. 624.

[32] A. BEUTEL - G. WALTHER, *Aufklärung 5.1. Religion und Kirche*, in *Enzyklopädie der Neuzeit*, vol. 1., Stuttgart 2005, pp. 805-807; A. HOLZEM, *Christentum in Deutschland 1550-1850. Konfessionalisierung, Aufklärung, Pluralisierung*, 2 vols, Paderborn 2015, vol. 2, pp. 723-775, 848-850.

Protestantism could be attached to the process of modernization, which characterized the Western world, or was even historically promoted to the origin of that modernity. In the meantime, the Catholicism of the Pianic Age 1791-1958 had deliberately emigrated from the modern world[33].

The Protestant Ethic and the Spirit of Capitalism (*Die protestantische Ethik und der "Geist" des Kapitalismus*) published by the leading social scientist Max Weber (1864-1920) in 1904/05, became the grand narrative of this Protestant culture, which was proud of its own modernity[34]. Weber always defended this study, sometimes with remarkable aggressiveness[35], because he himself and many of his readers considered it as perhaps his most essential contribution. Even today it claims the almost uncontested rank of a classic or sometimes even a sacred text[36]. Weber

[33] The term "Pianic Age" ("Pianisches Zeitalter") follows P. HERSCHE, *Muße und Verschwendung. Europäische Gesellschaft und Kultur im Barockzeitalter*, 2 vols, Freiburg i.Br. 2006, vol. 2, p. 1044.

[34] M. WEBER, *Asketischer Protestantismus und Kapitalismus. Schriften und Reden 1904-1911*, edited by W. SCHLUCHTER and U. BUBE (M. WEBER, *Gesamtausgabe*, I/9), Tübingen 2014, pp. 97-425, quoted as WGA. The modestly revised texts of 1920 will be edited in WGA I/18.

[35] WGA I/9, p. 663.

[36] The following contributions to Weber research have been consulted, the list beginning with the most recent publications: C. ADAIR-TOTEFF, *Max Weber's Sociology of Religion*, Tübingen 2016; V. VETROV, *Von Schweinen im Kraut und Läufen mit Hindernissen: Ein Versuch über Ironie in Max Webers China-Studie*, in "Saeculum", 65, 2015, 2, pp. 321-348; H.-P. MÜLLER - S. SIGMUND (eds), *Max Weber-Handbuch. Leben, Werk, Wirkung*, Stuttgart 2014; L. SUNAR, *Marx and Weber on Oriental Societies. In the Shadow of Western Modernities*, Farnham - Burlington 2014; M. KAISER - H. ROSENBACH (eds), *Max Weber in der Welt. Rezeption und Wirkung*, Tübingen 2014; P. GHOSH, *Max Weber and The Protestant Ethic: Twin Histories*, Oxford 2014; D. KAESLER, *Max Weber. Preuße, Denker, Muttersohn. Eine Biographie*, München 2014; J. KAUBE, *Max Weber. Ein Leben zwischen den Epochen*, Berlin 2014; C. FLECK (ed.), *Max Webers Protestantismus-These. Kritik und Antikritik*, in "Österreichische Zeitschrift für Geschichtswissenschaften", 23, 2012, 3, pp. 5-178; L.A. SCAFF, *Max Weber in America*, Princeton NJ 2011; A. BIENFAIT (ed.), *Religionen verstehen. Zur Aktualität von Max Webers Religionssoziologie*, Wiesbaden 2011; G. PREYER, *Max Webers Religionssoziologie. Eine Neubewertung*, Frankfurt a.M. 2010; H. STEINERT, *Max Webers unwiderlegbare Fehlkonstruktionen. Die protestantische Ethik und der Geist des Kapitalismus*, Frankfurt a.M. 2010; M. BÖHL, *Das Christentum und der Geist des Kapitalismus. Die Auslegungsgeschichte des biblischen Talentegleichnisses*, Köln 2007; J. RADKAU, *Max Weber. Die Leidenschaft des Denkens*, München 2005; W. SCHLUCHTER -

tried to demonstrate with impressive scholarship and long footnotes that the professional ethic of ascetic Calvinists became transformed

F.W. GRAF (eds), *Asketischer Protestantismus und der "Geist" des modernen Kapitalismus. Max Weber und Ernst Troeltsch*, Tübingen 2005; H. LEHMANN - J.M. OUÉDRAOGO (eds), *Max Webers Religionssoziologie in interkultureller Perspektive*, Göttingen 2003; B. GIESING, *Religion und Gemeinschaftsbildung. Max Webers kulturvergleichende Theorie*, Opladen 2002; J. NEUSNER (ed.), *Religious Belief and Economic Behavior: Ancient Israel, Classical Christianity, Islam, and Judaism, and Contemporary Ireland and Africa*, Atlanta 1999; H. LEHMANN, *Max Webers Protestantische Ethik. Beiträge aus der Sicht eines Historikers*, Göttingen 1996; *L'éthique protestante de Max Weber et l'esprit de la modernité*, Paris 1997; M. SPÖTTEL, *Max Weber und die jüdische Ethik. Die Beziehungen zwischen politischer Philosophie und Interpretation der jüdischen Kultur*, Frankfurt a.M. 1997; H.G. LEE, *Eine ostasiatische Kritik an Max Webers Rationalisierungskonzept (und der damit verbundenen Modernisierungstheorie). Am Beispiel konfuzianische Ethik und ostasiatische Rationalisierung*, Frankfurt a.M. 1997; D. LIN, *Konfuzianische Ethik und Legitimation der Herrschaft im alten China*, Berlin 1997; W. HENNIS, *Die spiritualistischen Grundlagen der "verstehenden Soziologie" Max Webers. Ernst Troeltsch, Max Weber und William James' Varieties of Religious Experience,* Göttingen 1996; D. SCHELLONG, *Wie steht es um die "These" vom Zusammenhang von Calvinismus und "Geist des Kapitalismus"?*, Paderborn 1995; H. LEHMANN - G. ROTH (eds), *Weber's Protestant Ethic: Origins, Evidence, Contexts*, Cambridge 1993; H.G. KIPPENBERG, *Die Relativierung der eigenen Kultur in der vergleichenden Religionswissenschaft*, in J. MATTHES (ed.), *Zwischen den Kulturen? Die Sozialwissenschaften vor dem Problem des Kulturvergleichs*, Göttingen 1992; L. BILY, *Die Religion im Denken Max Webers*, St. Ottilien 1990; W. SCHLUCHTER (ed.), *Max Webers Sicht des okzidentalen Christentums. Interpretationen und Kritik*, Frankfurt a.M. 1988; W. SCHLUCHTER (ed.), *Max Webers Sicht des Islams. Interpretationen und Kritik*, Frankfurt a.M. 1987; F. WILHELM Graf, *Max Weber und die protestantische Theologie seiner Zeit*, in "Zeitschrift für Religions- und Geistesgeschichte", 39, 1987, pp. 122-147; M. PÜTZ, *Max Webers These vom Geist des Kapitalismus und der Fall Benjamin Franklin*, in "Jahrbuch der Universität Augsburg", 1987, pp. 193-207; M. PÜTZ, *Max Webers und Ferdinand Kürnbergers Auseinandersetzung mit Benjamin Franklin: zum Verhältnis von Quellenverfälschung und Fehlinterpretation*, in "Amerikastudien", 29, 1984, 3, pp. 297-310; W. SCHLUCHTER, *Max Webers Studie über Konfuzianismus und Taoismus. Interpretationen und Kritik*, Frankfurt a.M. 1983; J. RÖSEL, *Die Hinduismusthese Max Webers. Folgen eines kolonialen Indienbildes in einem religionssoziologischen Gedankengang*, München et al. 1982; B.S. TURNER, *Weber and Islam. A Critical Study*, London 1974; A. ZINGERLE, *Max Weber und China. Herrschafts- und religionssoziologische Grundlagen zum Wandel der chinesischen Gesellschaft*, Berlin 1972; S.N. EISENSTADT, *Die protestantische Ethik und der Geist des Kapitalismus. Eine analytische und vergleichende Darstellung*, Opladen 1971; P. BESNARD (ed.), *Protestantisme et capitalisme. La controverse post-weberienne*, Paris 1970; M.J. KITCH (ed.), *Capitalism and the Reformation*, London 1967; H. LÜTHY, *Variationen über ein Thema von Max Weber*, in H. LÜTHY, *In Gegenwart der Geschichte*, Köln et al. 1967, pp. 39-100; R.W. GREEN, *Protestantism and Capitalism: The Weber-Thesis and its Critics*, Boston MA 1959; K. SAMUELSON, *Religion and Economic Action: The Protestant Ethic, the Rise of Capitalism, and the Abuse of Scholarship*, Toronto et al. 1961 (originally published in Swedish 1957).

into secular entrepreneurial behavior and in this way contributed to the origins of modern capitalism. Confronted with Calvin's shocking doctrine of predestination, these people used their ascetic way of life and their consequential economic success to confirm their status as elect and to overcome the fear of damnation. In the meantime, however, this religious motivation became an obsession with making money as an end in itself. But the modern capitalism that resulted from this development, according to Weber, was just one central element of the unique rational world order of the modern occident, the basic phenomenon he wanted to explain.

As a kind of subsequent control-test[37] Weber began comparative research on the *Sociology of World Religions* (*Die Wirtschaftsethik der Weltreligionen*). Together with an important *Introduction* (*Einleitung*) and an equally outstanding summary in between on *The Rejection and the Meaning of the World* (*Zwischenbetrachtung: Theorie der Stufen und Richtungen religiöser Weltablehnung*), these studies were first published as papers in a journal, but finally together with *The Protestant Ethic* 1920/21 in three volumes as *Collected Essays on the Sociology of Religion* (*Gesammelte Aufsätze zur Religionssoziologie*). Weber began with Confucianism and Taoism[38], proceeded to Hinduism and Buddhism[39],

[37] P. GOSH, *Die protestantische Ethik*, in H.-P. MÜLLER - S. SIGMUND (eds), *Max Weber-Handbuch*, p. 247; J. KAUBE, *Max Weber*, pp. 336-349.

[38] M. WEBER, *Die Wirtschaftsethik der Weltreligionen. Konfuzianismus und Taoismus. Schriften 1915-1920*, edited by H. SCHMIDT-GLINTZER - P. KOLENKO (WGA I/19) Tübingen 1989, pp. 83-127; *Einleitung*, pp. 128-478, I: *Konfuzianismus und Taoismus*, pp. 479-522 Zwischenbetrachtung. Cf. *Von Schweinen im Kraut und Läufen mit Hindernissen*; T. SCHWINN - H.-P. MÜLLER - M. STACHURA, *Religionssoziologische Werke*, in H.-P. MÜLLER - S. SIGMUND (eds), *Max Weber-Handbuch*, pp. 259-275; G. PREYER, *Max Webers Religionssoziologie*, pp. 81-91; H. SCHMIDT-GLINTZER, *Zur Geltung und Aktualität von Max Webers Studie über Konfuzianismus und Taoismus*, in H. LEHMANN - J.M. OUÉDRAOGO (eds), *Max Webers Religionssoziologie in interkultureller Perspektive*, pp. 85-99; H.G. LEE, *Eine ostasiatische Kritik an Max Webers Rationalisierungskonzept*; D. LIN, *Konfuzianische Ethik und Legitimation der Herrschaft im alten China*; W. SCHLUCHTER, *Max Webers Studie über Konfuzianismus und Taoismus*; A. ZINGERLE, *Max Weber*.

[39] M. WEBER, *Die Wirtschaftsethik der Weltreligionen. Hinduismus und Buddhismus. 1916-1920*, edited by H. SCHMIDT-GLINTZER - K.-H. GOLZIO (WGA I/20), Tübingen 1996. Cf. M. STACHURA, *Hinduismus*, in H.-P. MÜLLER - S. SIGMUND (eds), *Max Weber-Handbuch*, pp. 271-275; G. PREYER, *Max Webers Religionssoziologie*, pp. 91-101; S. MUNSHI, *Revisiting Max Weber on India*, in H. LEHMANN - J.M. OUÉDRAOGO (eds), *Max Webers Religionssoziologie in interkultureller Perspektive*, pp. 53-68; H. BECHERT,

and ended with Judaism in antiquity[40], which according to him was no world religion, but through the prophets of ancient Israel made essential contributions to occidental culture. Weber wrote no separate paper on Islam, but his position in that respect can be reconstructed from other texts[41]. In contrast to *The Protestant Ethic*, he combined in these papers the study of religious history with extensive analyses of the social and political systems of the respective cultures. Therefore certain sociologists prefer these studies to *the Protestant Ethic*[42].

Because of Weber's occidentalist perspective, the result of the comparison was obvious in advance. But he demonstrated again with tremendous scholarship, based upon the contemporary state of orientalist research, why the respective civilizations with their religions and *Weltanschauungen* could not produce a modern economy and a modern rationality. In China and in the Muslim world, the lack of autonomous urban communities was a strategic defect, whereas in India development was blocked by the religious legitimation of the caste system. Rationality did exist, but in contrast to the West, it was used to produce perfect harmony with the cosmic order (in China), or to develop optimal techniques of world rejection (in India). Thus the leadership of secular occidental rationality of protestant origin was scientifically proved and legitimated.

Max Weber had a protestant background from his mother's side and had been well acquainted with protestant theology since his time as a student. But in 1909 he wrote to Ferdinand Tönnies: "I am absolutely

Zur Buddhismus-Interpretation Max Webers, in H. LEHMANN - J.M. OUÉDRAOGO (eds), *Max Webers Religionssoziologie in interkultureller Perspektive*, pp. 101-107.

40 M. WEBER, *Die Wirtschaftsethik der Weltreligionen. Das antike Judentum. Schriften und Reden 1911-1920*, edited by E. OTTO - J. OFFERMANN, 2 Bde. (WGA I/21, 1-2), Tübingen 2005. Cf. C. SCHÄFER-LICHTENBERGER, in H.-P. MÜLLER - S. SIGMUND (eds), *Max Weber-Handbuch*, pp. 279-286; S.N. EISENSTADT, *Max Weber on Ancient Judaism: Beyond a Pariah People: Sectarianism, Heterodoxy and Participation in Cultural and Political Arenas*, in H. LEHMANN - J.M. OUÉDRAOGO (eds), *Max Webers Religionssoziologie in interkultureller Perspektive*, pp. 139-174; M. SPÖTTEL, *Max Weber und die jüdische Ethik*.

41 G. PREYER, *Max Webers Religionssoziologie*, pp. 101-107; J. PAUL, *Max Weber und die islamische Stadt*, in H. LEHMANN - J.M. OUÉDRAOGO (eds), *Max Webers Religionssoziologie in interkultureller Perspektive*, pp. 109-137; W. SCHLUCHTER (ed.), *Max Webers Sicht des Islams*; B.S. TURNER, *Weber and Islam*.

42 P. GOSH, *Die protestantische Ethik*, in H.-P. MÜLLER - S. SIGMUND (eds), *Max Weber-Handbuch*, p. 247.

'unmusical' for religion, but neither am I anti-religious nor a-religious. And also in this respect I feel crippled"[43]. Today, his years in Rome from 1901 to 1903 rank higher in his biography[44], but he remained still convinced of the historical inferiority of Catholicism as well as of Lutheranism, a religion he particularly detested[45]. *The Protestant Ethic* can be considered as "a pamphlet of protestant culture in the guise of a scholarly investigation"[46]. Neither was his relationship with the Puritans, his heroes, and the rationalization and modernization, which they had unintentionally initiated, unbroken. Remember his famous statement: "Puritans decided to become professional men—we are forced to", followed by the metaphor of the "cage of steel" ("stahlharte Gehäuse") that originated from that development and the expectation of a dark future in the sense of Nietzsche, where the degenerated last men had to live in that cage[47]. But even in this secularized and tragic shape, reformed Protestantism remained the globalized religion of modernity.

However, this grandiose design of world history has to a large extent been falsified. First of all, the thesis of the protestant ethic suffered from a lack of "professional precision"[48] or even from "abuse of scholarship"[49]. To begin with, Weber adopted a faulty calculation of the dissertation of his student Martin Offenbacher[50], not to mention his

[43] "Ich bin zwar religiös absolut 'unmusikalisch' ... aber ich bin ... weder antireligiös noch irreligiös ... Ich empfinde mich auch in dieser Hinsicht als einen verkrüppelten Menschen", WGA I/9, 22-24, traslation WR.

[44] J. RADKAU, *Max Weber*, pp. 316-359; P. HERSCHE, *Der Romaufenthalt (1901-1903), und Max Webers Verhältnis zum Katholizismus*, in M. KAISER - H. ROSENBACH (eds), *Max Weber in der Welt*, pp. 145-158; J. KAUBE, *Max Weber*, pp. 134-144; D. KAESLER, *Max Weber. Preuße, Denker, Muttersohn*, p. 507.

[45] WGA I/9, 25.

[46] "Eine Kampfschrift des Kulturprotestantismus im Gewand einer wissenschaftlichen Untersuchung", H. STEINERT, *Max Webers unwiderlegbare Fehlkonstruktionen*, p. 25, traslation WR.

[47] "Der Puritaner wollte Berufsmensch sein – wir müssen es sein", WGA I/9, 423 ff., traslation WR; D. SCHELLONG, *Wie steht es um die "These" vom Zusammenhang von Calvinismus und "Geist des Kapitalismus"?*, pp. 16 ff.

[48] "Mangel an handwerklicher Sorgfalt", H. STEINERT, *Max Webers unwiderlegbare Fehlkonstruktionen*, pp. 35-171, traslation WR.

[49] K. SAMUELSON, *Religion and Economic Action.*

[50] WGA I/9, 128.

unprofessional interpretation of the respective statistics. Much worse was his arbitrary use of key documents[51]. In the books of the puritan pastor Richard Baxter (1615-1691) probation and success are not as important as Weber claimed, and the rigid control of behavior in Calvinist communities was not in favor of capitalist economic practice—sometimes the opposite was true[52]. The history of the interpretation of the biblical parable of the talents in Matthew 25:14-30 and Luke 19:11-27 by Calvinists, Catholics, and Lutherans has been thoroughly analyzed by Meinrad Böhl. In contrast to Weber's suggestions, Calvinists do not differ here from Catholics and Lutherans. They all consider the talents as a metaphor for the spiritual wealth of the *homo oeconomicus spiritualis.* Just one single Calvinist and one Lutheran include goods of this world, but on the condition that they be spent on charitable purposes. And just one single American Baptist refers to the former US development policy, which believed in the stimulation of entrepreneurship in underdeveloped countries[53]. According to Weber, Böhl's findings should have been different. In addition, when dealing with his second key document, the writings of Benjamin Franklin (1706-1790), Weber makes use of manipulated translations of an anti-American novel by Ferdinand Kürnberger and changes texts in a way that Manfred Pütz has called falsification of sources[54]. Weber's self-confident and high-handed hermeneutics shows no respect for Reinhart Koselleck's essential "veto of the sources" ("Vetorecht der Quellen")[55].

[51] D. SCHELLONG, *Wie steht es um die "These" vom Zusammenhang von Calvinismus und "Geist des Kapitalismus"?*, pp. 34-37.

[52] H. SCHILLING, *Die Kirchenratsprotokolle der Reformierten Gemeinde Emden 1557-1620*, 2 vols, Köln 1989-1992.

[53] M. BÖHL, *Das Christentum und der Geist des Kapitalismus*, pp. 166 ff., 222 ff.

[54] M. PÜTZ, *Max Webers und Ferdinand Kürnbergers Auseinandersetzung mit Benjamin Franklin*; M. PÜTZ, *Max Webers These vom Geist des Kapitalismus und der Fall Benjamin Franklin.*

[55] This attitude is not unusual. A famous German philosopher of the twentieth century, for instance, admits such practices with remarkable frankness: "I am sure that I appropriate other people's words—from the point of view of hermeneutics—in a brutal way. Quoting a lot and employing other people's terminology I still know that my usage is sometimes far from the authors' intentions". (Ich glaube, dass ich mir die fremden Zungen auf eine, hermeneutisch gesehen, brutale Art und Weise zu eigen mache. Auch wenn ich viel zitiere und andere Terminologien übernehme, weiß ich genau, dass mein Gebrauch mit dem, was die Autoren gemeint haben, manchmal

In the second place, religious convictions may indeed influence economic behavior in everyday life but never in the simple way postulated by Weber. And first of all, such influence is not a special trait of one particular religion or confession[56]. Thirdly and finally, in contrast to Max Weber's spiritual view of history[57], capitalism has no spiritual quality (*Geist*) but is characterized by aggressive facticity which simply succeeds through its inherent force and on its way produces its own appropriate legitimation. Therefore, concerning the economy religions in general tend to a critical attitude[58].

In contrast, Weber's enlarged approach in the *Sociology of World Religions*, which includes analyses of society and politics, has produced some lasting achievements. They are questioned, however, by the Eurocentric point of view he shares with contemporary research. He studied different civilizations for the sake of Western culture and asked Western questions using Western categories, which perhaps were quite often the wrong questions and the wrong categories, because different cultural traditions are used to answer their own questions and not ours[59]. In this way, Asian facts were measured by European standards such as nineteenth-century Anglo-Saxon capitalism[60] or the Italian city republics of the late Middle Ages[61].

wenig zu tun hat, J. HABERMAS, *Dialektik der Rationalisierung*, in J. HABERMAS, *Die neue Unübersichtlichkeit. Kleine Politische Schriften V*, Frankfurt a.M. 1985, p. 208, traslation WR).

56 W. REINHARD, *The Affirmation of Ordinary Life*, in H. JOAS - K. WIEGANDT (eds), *The Cultural Values of Europe*, Liverpool 2008, pp. 187-216.

57 W. HENNIS, *Die spiritualistischen Grundlagen der "verstehenden Soziologie" Max Webers*.

58 H. STEINERT, *Max Webers unwiderlegbare Fehlkonstruktionen*, p. 19.

59 R.N. BELLAH, *Religion in Human Evolution. From the Paleolithic to the Axial Age*, Cambridge MA - London 2011, p. 605. Nevertheless, we should not forget that this founding father of sociology had neither the elaborate terminology of modern social science at his disposition nor the jargon of post-colonialism. Quite often he had to create the terms himself, sometimes with a certain lack of precision as consequence.

60 S. MUNSHI, *Revisiting Max Weber on India*, in H. LEHMANN - J.M. OUÉDRAOGO (eds), *Max Webers Religionssoziologie in interkultureller Perspektive*, p. 59.

61 J. PAUL, *Max Weber und die islamische Stadt*, in H. LEHMANN - J.M. OUÉDRAOGO (eds), *Max Webers Religionssoziologie in interkultureller Perspektive*, pp. 129-137.

Possibly even the category "religion" itself is much too occidental to be applied to different phenomena of other parts of the world. In the case of China we obviously should rather use *Weltanschauung* instead. The very idea of "religion" has been denigrated as an instrument of colonialism. In British India, unambiguous membership of communities was enforced for political reasons. In this way, Hinduism became constituted as one single religion[62]. Originally, *religio* stood for the correct performance of worship, and then for a Christian monastic community. In the sixteenth century, Jesuit missionaries in Japan still employed the word in that sense whereas they used *lex* (law) for their religious system, a terminology which corresponded with the Japanese *ho* and the Sanskrit *dharma* of Buddhists. Nevertheless, in 2013 the search for adequate translations of our category "religion" into Asian languages still ended without result. The provocative thesis that "religion" cannot be translated and therefore should no longer be used at all could neither be confirmed nor discredited[63]. Even modern research is not able to provide a general definition of religion but uses a description of dimensions instead, which are present in most cases, such as an absolute, a doctrine, worship, ethics, and institutions. The insistence upon a system of beliefs in this context may be considered a consequence of the protestant Reformation[64]. Because the symbolic system of pre-modern religion obviously is the *differentia specifica* of the respective culture, it has even been proposed that the concept of "religion" be completely dissolved into the concept of "culture"[65].

Starting from the traditional occidental idea of religion, Weber looked in vain for the concepts of "faith", "grace", "ascesis", "mysticism", "sect", "dogma", "commandment", "redemption", "orthodoxy", "hetero-

62 A. MALINAR, *Religion*, in G. DHARAMPAL-FRICK et al. (eds), *Key Concepts in Modern Indian Studies*, Oxford 2015, pp. 231-237.

63 P. SCHALK (ed), *Religion in Asien? Studien zur Anwendbarkeit des Religionsbegriffs*, Uppsala 2013.

64 G. KEHRER, *Religion, Definitionen der*, in H. CANCIK (ed.), *Handbuch religionswissenschaftlicher Grundbegriffe*, vol. 4, pp. 418-425; J. FIGL (ed.), *Handbuch der Religionswissenschaft*, Innsbruck et al. 2003, pp. 62-80; M. BERGUNDER, *Religionen*, in *Enzyklopädie der Neuzeit*, vol. 10., Stuttgart 2009, pp. 1048-1062; K. VON STUCKRAD, *Religionsbegriff*, *ibid.*, pp. 1062-1064.

65 D. SABBATUCCI, *Kultur und Religion*, in H. CANCIK, *Handbuch religionswissenschaftlicher Grundbegriffe*, vol. 1, Stuttgart 1988, pp. 43-58.

doxy", "gnosis" in India. Certainly, some of these things existed there, but they were not arranged according to our categories. On the other hand, Weber did not understand Indian notions correctly. "Karma" for instance, in contrast to his opinion, has consequences already in this life and "dharma" is much more than the law of the caste system[66]. The English had selected and accepted the specific social theory of the Brahmins together with the system of castes, implemented it politically, and finally verified it empirically. Weber fell beautifully for this circular construction[67]. In China, his much too simple concept of Confucianism was the consequence of insufficient information on Song-culture and its Neo-Confucianism, including the metaphysical dimension, which—according to Weber—was missing[68]. And the ideal of harmony did not exclude conflicts between philosophical vision and cultural practice[69].

By application of his famous ideal type-methodology, Weber ontologized a comparatively static opposite. However, this artificial anti-Europe[70] was exposed to European instrumentalization in the sense of Edward Said's theory of orientalism[71], in the case of Weber by an intellectual instrumentalization. "His method is calculated to highlight the otherness in a conceptual scheme based on dualism"[72]. From the point of view of post-colonial criticism, Weber was a classic of Orientalism and of othering, with additional immunization of his theses through his ideal type-procedure. In contrast to natural sciences, general statements on culture cannot be falsified by the empirical demonstration of singular contradicting cases. They have to be disproved completely such as the Protestant ethic. Nevertheless, they may live on if they serve actual needs, which quite often have nothing to do with the original intention

66 S. MUNSHI, *Revisiting Max Weber on India*, in H. LEHMANN - J.M. OUÉDRAOGO (eds), *Max Webers Religionssoziologie in interkultureller Perspektive*, pp. 60-63.

67 J. RÖSEL, *Die Hinduismusthese Max Webers*.

68 M. STADURA, in H.-P. MÜLLER - S. SIGMUND (eds), *Max Weber-Handbuch*, p. 268.

69 G. PREYER, *Max Webers Religionssoziologie*, p. 88.

70 J. PAUL, *Max Weber und die islamische Stadt*, in H. LEHMANN - J.M. OUÉDRAOGO (eds), *Max Webers Religionssoziologie in interkultureller Perspektive*, pp. 115 f.

71 E. SAID, *Orientalism*, New York 1978.

72 S. MUNSHI, *Revisiting Max Weber on India*, in H. LEHMANN - J.M. OUÉDRAOGO (eds), *Max Webers Religionssoziologie in interkultureller Perspektive*, p. 67.

of their author[73]. In this sense, Talcott Parson's translation made *The Protestant Ethic* an almost sacred text in the US[74], because it articulates the "American Dream" in a dual way: on the one hand the predominating capitalist morality of economic success as practiced by workers and petty entrepreneurs[75], on the other hand the chiliastic ideal of the diffusion of the exceptional American way of life, which originated from puritanism and the evangelical awakening, over the entire world[76]. As a scientific concept, however, the Protestant ethic is no longer of interest. It was and remains, nothing more but also nothing less than the grand narrative of European superiority in the times of colonialism and protestant expansion.

With changed power relations and decolonization after World War II, this master narrative had urgently to be replaced by a new and more up-to-date one. This was to be the achievement of the philosopher Karl Jaspers (1883-1969), another secularized scion of German Protestant culture, who together with Marianne Weber is considered to be the most important protagonist of Max Weber's fame[77]. In 1949, he tried to transform Weber's Eurocentric universal history into a polycentric one. As a colonial "outside" no longer exists, "inside ... we are confronted by universal history as a task"[78]. His theory of the "Axial Period[79] is based on an article of faith: that mankind has one single origin and one goal", which both, however, are not known to us[80]. In the empirically accessible temporal space in between, Jaspers collected historical evidence for his universalistic assumption. In contrast to the Eurocentrism of Hegel, his philosophical idea of the unity of mankind could no longer be based upon the history of Christian faith. But he

[73] C. FLECK (ed.), *Max Webers Protestantismus-These, Einleitung* 3, 5; P. GOSH, *Die protestantische Ethik*, p. 247.

[74] L.A. SCAFF, *Max Weber in America*, pp. 211-228.

[75] H. STEINERT, *Max Webers unwiderlegbare Fehlkonstruktionen*, p. 23.

[76] E. BEYREUTHER, *Die Erweckungsbewegung*, in *Die Kirche in ihrer Geschichte*, Bd. 4/R 1, Göttingen 1963, p. 11.

[77] J. RADKAU, *Max Weber. Die Leidenschaft des Denkens*, p. 840.

[78] K. JASPERS, *The Origin and Goal of History*, pp. 140, 261.

[79] *Ibid.*, pp. 1-27, 51-57.

[80] *Ibid.*, p. XV.

discovered an "axis of world history so convincing to empirical insight as to give rise to a common frame of historical self-comprehension for all peoples". He identified it with the global spiritual or religious process between 800 and 200 BC, which—according to Jaspers—created man as we know him[81].

"The most extraordinary events are concentrated in this period. Confucius and Lao-tse were living in China, all the schools of Chinese philosophy came into being, including those of Mo-ti, Chuang-tse, Lieh-tsu and a host of others; India produced the Upanishads and Buddha and, like China, ran the whole gamut of philosophical possibilities down to skepticism, to materialism, sophism and nihilism; in Iran Zarathustra taught a challenging view of the world as a struggle between good and evil; in Palestine the prophets made their appearance (very important already for Weber), from Elijah, by way of Isaiah and Jeremiah to Deutero-Isaiah; Greece witnessed the appearance of Homer, of the philosophers—Parmenides, Heraclitus, Plato—of the tragedians, Thucydides and Archimedes ... without anyone of these regions knowing of the others. What is new about this age, in all three areas of the world, is that man becomes conscious of Being as a whole, of himself and his limitations ... he strives for liberation and redemption ... He experiences absoluteness in the depth of selfhood and in the lucidity of transcendence. All this took place in reflection. Consciousness became once more conscious of itself, thinking became its own object"[82].

But the carefully established equality of historical ranking was immediately empirically shaken because China and Greece did not know much transcendence in the supernatural sense and later on, without doubt the West has played a paramount role in shaping the world. Therefore, Jaspers insisted upon complementary achievements of Indian and Chinese philosophy unknown to the West[83].

In historical reality, worldwide equal political and religious ranking was still quite a distance away after World War II. For this reason, Jaspers's theory, not serving urgent needs, was not very popular for about 30 years[84]. But when the model of a modernization led by the West lost its attractiveness, the social scientist and Max Weber expert Shmuel N. Eisenstadt (1923-2010)[85] revived the Axial Age perspective

81 *Ibid.*, p. 1.

82 *Ibid.*, p. 2.

83 *Ibid.*, p. 68.

84 P. Wagner, *Palomar's Question. The Axial Age Hypothesis, European Modernity, and Historical Contingency*, in J.P. Arnason et al. (eds), *Axial Civilizations and World History*, Leiden et al. 2005, pp. 87-100.

85 S.N. Eisenstadt, *Die protestantische Ethik und der Geist des Kapitalismus.*

as an alternative, but in a modified and extended way. On the one hand, he focused upon the tension between transcendental visions and social reality, including the attempts to realize such visions. On the other hand, he more and more decentered the theory referring to the extremely complex and contradictory results of historical research since Jaspers's time. Japan for instance, a country that was irrelevant during the Axial Age, had nevertheless achieved a leading role in world history. For Eisenstadt was also the "inventor" of "multiple modernities", which are meant to replace the single modernity generated and propagated by the West[86]. Thus a historical role during the Axial Age became, according to him, the precondition of comparatively independent successful modernization, "multiple axialities" corresponded to "multiple modernities"[87].

But confronted with this historical reality, the theory of the Axial Age became empirically unsustainable and dissolved into nothing[88]. First of all, it proved an arbitrary construct already from the temporal point of view. Why these 600 years and not more? Why was pharaoh Akhenaten excluded, why Jesus Christ or Muhammad, who had messages at least as "axial" as those of the Buddha or of Socrates? In addition, the dates of Buddha's life are anything but certain and those of Zarathustra vague. The same can be said of the spatial perspective. Why were there no Mesopotamian civilizations, why was there no mention of Japan? An attempt has been made to circumvent all those difficulties through replacing the Axial Age by a timeless axial kind of civilization or even by establishing axiality as a mere quality. But in the third place, the supposed contents of this axiality cannot be brought down to a common

[86] Cf. D. SACHSENMAIER et al. (eds), *Reflections on Multiple Modernities: European, Chinese, and Other Interpretations*, Leiden et al. 2002; S.N. EISENSTADT, *Comparative Civilizations and Multiple Modernities*, 2 vols, Leiden et al. 2003.

[87] Cf. S.N. EISENSTADT, *Axial Civilizations and the Axial Age Reconsidered*, in J.P. ARNASON et al. (eds), *Axial Civilizations and World History*, pp. 531-64; S.N. EISENSTADT, *The Axial Age Conundrum between Transcendental Visions and Vicissitudes of their Institutionalization*, in R.N. BELLAH - H. JOAS (eds), *The Axial Age and Its Consequences*, Cambridge, MA et al. 2012, pp. 277-293.

[88] This is the not intended but obvious consequence of the contributions to in J.P. ARNASON et al. (eds), *Axial Civilizations and World History*, and in R.N. BELLAH - H. JOAS (eds), *The Axial Age and Its Consequences*. Cf. in addition my unpublished essay *Achsenbruch* of 2008, a critical commentary of the papers of the Bellah and Joas conference published in 2012.

denominator. The development of a kind of theoretical world view and of reflexivity is the only common trait that can be identified. But this happened at different times and not as a linear process. In Europe, for instance, in that respect the early Middle Ages fell back behind antiquity. Other apparent common traits prove deceptive. Sometimes they originate from the confusion of the formal and the material aspects. Formally, all cultures were confronted with the same anthropological problems, but materially they solved them in different ways. Of course, the "ren" according to Confucius and "to Agathon" as used by Plato are related, but they differ in detail. Monastic orders in Japan, in Thailand, and in the Occident differ as much as they resemble one another. And transcendence also presents itself in confusing varieties[89].

Nevertheless, the outdated concept of the Axial Age is still employed to support theories of supposed global religiosity. Robert N. Bellah (1927-2013), like Eisenstadt belonging to the third generation after Weber and Jaspers, wrote an evolutionary general history of religion from the origins to the Axial Age[90]. Extended from the perspective of cultural history, his Darwinian approach proves adequate to this undertaking, because it is reasonable to assume that human nature follows the same rules in biology and in history[91]. But Bellah's main interest is the religious globality of today. According to him, the study of the Axial Age has taught us to overcome the traditional exclusivity of high religions, Christianity included, in favor of a plurality of equally ranking communities that respect each other[92]. The Axial Age gave mankind not only great utopian visions, but also the great tool of a critical approach to everything[93]. But all this still looks very much like the universalism propagated by the European enlightenment, for instance in Gotthold Ephraim Lessing's *Nathan the Wise*. Apparently similar declarations of religious equality in India and China such as "the three religions are

[89] I.U. Dalfert, *The Idea of Transcendence*, in R.N. Bellah - H. Joas (eds), *The Axial Age and Its Consequences*, pp. 146-188.

[90] R.N. Bellah, *Religion in Human Evolution*.

[91] Cf. W. Reinhard, *Reformation als Mutation? Evolution und Geschichte*, in "Zeitschrift für Historische Forschung", 37, 2010, pp. 601-615.

[92] R.N. Bellah, *Religion in Human Evolution*, pp. 603-606.

[93] R.N. Bellah - H. Joas (eds), *The Axial Age and Its Consequences*, p. 465.

one"[94] in reality are inclusive and not based upon the mutual respect of independent partners.

Hans Joas is another sociologist who is "looking for friends in history"[95]. According to him, the Axial Age debate is basically an actual religious discourse where intellectuals position themselves with regard to the problem of transcendence, one of the most fundamental questions of our orientation in the contemporary world. But "transcendental realms are not subject to disproof the way scientific theories are"[96]. They have this kind of immunity in common with Max Weber's "ideal types". Self-transcendence is according to Joas the fundamental experience in this field. It is not supernatural, but happens when we meet a strong attractive force such as love, which makes us transcend the limits of our self. All humans have access to this experience but they give it different interpretations following their respective cultural traditions[97].

Despite the apparently a-religious quality of this concept, it gives protagonists of new religiosity the chance to smuggle in religious transcendence again, which, however, does not have the same contents as before. Confronted with the recent new dynamic of religion, the once dominating theory of an irreversible secularization of the world at the expense of all religions nowadays has not many adherents left. But the enthusiastic appreciation of the renaissance of religion fails to notice that Christianity, under Enlightenment influence, has experienced a kind of silent secularization. God himself is no longer transcendent in the traditional sense of supernatural beyondness but becomes just another experience of self-transcendence. In a paradoxical way transcendence has become immanent. Nobody needs to believe in a life after death any more. Christianity is reduced either to the application of the universal love of one's neighbor—maybe even in the shape of the political theology of liberation—or of the more or less mystical experience of the presence of God in the world or the human heart. Our very future

[94] *Sān jiào yī,* abgeblicher Ausspruch des Kaisers Zhenzong 998-1023 (http://www.oai.de/en/publikationen/ostasienlexikon/49-ostasienlexikon/ddd/1205-drei-religionen.html).

[95] N. BELLAH, *Religion in Human Evolution*, p. IX. a quotation from Mencius.

[96] H. JOAS, *The Axial Age Debate as Religious Discourse*, in R.N. BELLAH - H. JOAS (eds), *The Axial Age and Its Consequences*, pp. 9-29, here p. 24.

[97] Interview with Hans Joas in "ZEIT Wissen", no. 1/2013.

may depend on the option to extend this global development to other religions, in particular to Islam.

However, despite additional problems created in former days by missionary expansion and recently by the migration of adherents of Asian religions, the global religious scenario is not limited to the internal problems of world religions and their peaceful or violent interaction. Other phenomena of the religious field are at least equally important. One is the worldwide presence of popular ideas and practices, which may disapprovingly be qualified as superstition, or in a more neutral way as esoteric. Bookshops as well as the internet provide abundant material. Despite cultural differences these offers resemble each other worldwide. Astrology could be mentioned or the belief in witches, which is still alive in the West and in post-colonial Africa has led to violent persecutions[98].

On the other hand, innumerable new communities of more or less hybrid character compete with the established world religions[99]. Not only in the US but also in Nigeria, the founding of churches is a profitable business. The flourishing Afro-American religions should not be ignored, nor the international following of Indian gurus, or the booming religious market of Japan. But this phenomenon is neither new nor, as far as Christianity is concerned, a particularity of the protestant field of influence. The movement of Beatriz Kimpa Vita in the Catholic Congo of the late seventeenth century could be mentioned, as well as the Mormons in the protestant US 150 years later.

The Église de Jésus-Christ sur la Terre par le Prophète Simon Kimbangu of the lower Congo area may serve as an example. In 1969, it became a member of the World Council of Churches. Kimbangu was a Protestant catechist and at the same time a successful healer, who proclaimed himself the prophet for Africa in 1921. The dominating Catholic missionary church felt threatened and the Belgian colonial administration suspected a rebellion, because Kimbangu's numerous followers despised Catholicism, and he had declared that Blacks should become white and Whites should be black. The prophet surrendered

[98] W. BEHRINGER, *Hexen, Glaube, Verfolgung, Vermarktung*, 5th ed., München 2009.

[99] K. RÜTHER, *Religiöse Interaktion, globale*, in *Enzyklopädie der Neuzeit*, vol. 10, Stuttgart 2009, pp. 1165-1188.

himself like Jesus, was sentenced to death, but pardoned and kept in prison until his death in 1951. Despite or because of persecution, his followers increased. Finally, the colonial powers France, Belgium, and Portugal had to acknowledge the church, which now was governed by Kimbangu's family. Today it claims 10% of the Congolese as members and 17 million believers worldwide. At great expense, Kimbangu's birth and burial place, Nkamba, has been transformed into a New Jerusalem. Besides other things the church runs a university and a television station. In theology, it combines an extremely puritan Christianity with elements of African origin. For Holy Communion, for instance, liquid honey is used instead of wine because of the strict prohibition of alcohol and instead of bread, a cake made of potatoes, maize, eggs, and bananas. But first of all, since the 1970s Kimbangu has been considered the Holy Spirit incarnate, in accordance with Christ's promise in John 14:16-26, and his three sons have been considered as incarnations of the Holy Trinity since 2002. The World Council of Churches had a problem[100].

Nevertheless, such a creative indigenization and transformation of Protestant Christianity, which is absolutely legitimate from the point of view of those concerned, should enjoy equal rights in interreligious communication as proclaimed by Robert Bellah, because it is just another way of globalizing the message of the Reformation.

[100] www.kimbanguisme.net; J.-L. VELLUT (ed.), *Simon Kimbangu 1921, de la prédication à la déportation. Les sources*, 2 vols., Brüssel 2005-2010; M.L. MARTIN, *Kirche ohne Weiße*, Basel 1971 (English edition 1975).

Europe in the Age of Reformations

The Modern State and Confessionalization

by *Paolo Prodi*

1. *Foreword: The end of confessional history or history-writing?*

The approaching centenary catches us on the hop. This is a commonplace, of course: history is one long transition—a phrase this venue has heard many times. And as with all civilizations handing over the baton, it is not outside agencies that are killing the West, but the West killing itself. But what is specific to our times and this centenary is that we have lost sight of the shore from which we set out: at most, through a thick fog we glimpse heaps of rubble which we have shed in the last century or so, from the Decalogue to the atomic bomb and the Shoah. On a lighter note, you will smile to hear (if it doesn't make you weep) how a third-year university student of our colleague Claudia Pancino answered a question on the distinction between *de praesenti* marriage and *de futuro* marriage (a contractual promise to celebrate a wedding at some other date):

"Even after the Council of Trent and its attempt to regulate marriage, people failed to observe the distinction between verbs in the future and those in the present. This was partly because people were poor and ignorant and didn't know their tenses".

But joking apart, the problem may be that today's millennium youth—not just students but western society as a whole—doesn't 'do' past tense and future tense but only sees and understands a timeless present of 2.0 images. In a previous publication I tried to show how we have been involved these last few decades in an anthropological crisis: the crisis of *homo europaeus*[1], far more than just another passing transition. The

This article was previously published in "The Catholic Historical Review", 103, 2017, 1, pp. 1-19. *Translation by R. Nisbet*

[1] P. Prodi, *Homo europaeus*, Bologna 2015. For a general bibliography, see P. Prodi, *Il paradigma tridentino. Un'epoca della storia della Chiesa*, Brescia 2010.

historical argument I wish to develop today is that as the strands linking confessional churches and modern states unravel after a five-century cycle dating from the 1517 protest, our whole surroundings are changing, not just in terms of religion, but politically and institutionally as well.

Much has been said in recent decades as to where institutions are heading, most of the time seeing it as a one-way process of "secularization". It has been argued that modernity is basically just that, for politics and society as much as for science and culture at large: throwing off the theological and donning the human and worldly. By contrast, the point I have been laboring to make is that modernity stems from dialogue and osmosis between the two poles—call it dialectic or dualism, or what you will—and in various ways this has hinged on the process of confessionalization: Churches and States are tied in life and death to this common process. Historians—and still more analysts and political commentators—go very wrong when they overlook this point in tackling the present-day aspects of crisis: the issue of secularism, of multiculturalism, our daily tragedy of migration and the uprooting of peoples. The problem is that their analysis is boxed inside the modern period and its time-frame. What changes with this century is not that our view of history is better than our forefathers', but simply that now—in 2017—we can see this pattern from outside and above the viewpoint of the masters who came before us.

The claim I start from and intend vigorously to uphold is that over the last fifty years the historian's perspective has changed enormously, just as daily historical events have changed with globalization and mushrooming technology. We now stand outside the long historical cycle that generated the Europe my own generation was born into. We have thrown off confessional-ecclesiastical historiography, but we are far from having acquired a historically appropriate awareness to guide our research and the divulgation of its insights.

As for the unfolding of historical events these last fifty years, everything has changed around us. In the 1950s, the panorama in which western man grew up had been splendidly captured by Gabriel Le Bras in a short study that I hail as one of the best things written in our field: *L'Église et le village*. As though from a satellite, he viewed the common identity of our plains and villages, from Sicily to Scotland: the parish church, the Town Hall or seat of government, the market square. I have elsewhere described the course of the last half-century's history in the making (and in the writing), bringing us to this satellite viewpoint, released from the force of gravity, which was the modern era. But from the observation post or satellite we have now reached, that landscape no longer exists. Viewing the historical course of modernity in the long term, my starting contention is that we cannot understand the history of Europe without an overview of all its bearing columns: state, church, and market. The sovereign nation-state (town hall) has vanished (not the state in a generic sense, which still holds many powers and functions); the market has evaporated from the stock exchanges and condensed into 'sovereign' funds that cannot be geographically pinpointed or politically controlled; the churches of all Christian creeds (Catholic, Lutheran, Calvinist, and so on) are daily being sold and converted to mundane uses, while churches (with a capital 'C') seek other bonds with their remaining congregations and sects are springing up on all sides.

2. *Territorial churches and the modern state*

What has happened over the last fifty years or so is the collapse of three pillars supporting European society these last five centuries. We have learnt that we cannot separate religious understanding from political understanding, and vice versa. If that is so, we cannot separate the analysis of events inside European Christendom, whether in its ascending curve—the genesis of modernity and the rise of denominational states—or its descent through the great European civil wars, the process of decolonization and globalization. My claim is that, whether we observe from the standpoint of church history or modern state history, the focus of our historian's telescope must be on Europe. That is the issue propounded by Hubert Jedin in 1973 as the subject of the first seminar held at the fledgling Istituto Storico Italo-Germanico in Trento: "The Council of Trent as the crossroads of European politics". The European theater and its scenery had been well-known for decades: the abuses of the medieval church, the conflict between feudalism and modernity, a hard-won balance, with its aftermath of religious wars: from the *Confessio Augustana* of 1530 to the *Professio fidei Tridentina* of 1564, from Charles V's 1548 *Interim* to the mid-seventeenth-century Peace of Westphalia.

That historians' gathering was important, I feel, a step forward from the prevailing position of modern European historiography, whether ecclesiastical or secular. There were various different interpretations, of course, lightly touched on by Jedin in his introduction to the concept of Catholic reformation: a Europe that was about to be outmoded and defeated by the incoming Age of Reason and the Enlightenment.

Of the three pillars that gave rise to the process of confessionalization, church history naturally tended to put the spotlight on how the territorial churches formed. When the world of medieval *christanitas* entered into crisis, a number of roads beckoned towards the modern era, roads which can be conveniently summarized, as long as one remembers that they were strictly interlinked across the centuries of the modern era, and ran simultaneously, not in isolation but in varying combinations as they explored a range of concrete solutions to the vexed relationship between power and the sacred: the road of republican-civic religion; the revival of monarchy as a sacred principle; the road of the territorial churches; the road of Roman Catholicism[2]. Naturally these are only vague hints as to the territory that needs exploring. But quite clearly if one fails to connect the declaration of the rights of man and the citizen to the Revolutionary reign of terror, the ensuing concordat and Napoleon being crowned by Pope Pius VII, etc., one will understand nothing about European history. Out of such contradictions was modern Europe born.

As far back as the fourteenth century, behind the crisis of the Western Schism, the movement towards creation of the territorial churches coinciding with the new monarchies and principates is plain to the naked eye, written across the map of Europe. Gallicanism is obviously the best-known, most highly developed form, but the trend is widespread. The sovereign tends not only to rid himself of church surveillance and becomes the *dominus beneficiorum*, controlling the economy and thereby the ecclesiastical hierarchy, but also to take over the social and political functions previously pertaining to the church. From control over culture and the universities, to the development of grammar and the vernacular, down to the reorganization of welfare functions, the fifteenth century takes the form of a great laboratory ushering in the confessional age through the shaping of identities that are at once political and religious, as well as transforming politics from an exercise of jurisdiction

[2] P. Prodi, *Dalle secolarizzazioni alle religioni politiche*, in G.E. Rusconi (ed.), *Lo Stato secolarizzato nell'età post-secolare*, Bologna 2008, pp. 55-92.

and administration of justice into a tool for training and molding and regulating people's lives from birth until death. Over and above its intrinsic theological content, the Reformation in this sense becomes the most consistent and extreme manifestation of a process that was driven to compromise and ambiguity in Catholic lands: *cura religionis* became one of the prime functions of the new sovereign and his *raison d'état*, while the principle of *cuius regio eius et religio* became the main forge of collective identity in that early gestational phase of the modern state. All in all, perhaps the most interesting phenomenon was the 'ideologizing' of politics: a theological ideology gradually growing to the point where it could cast off the robes of theology and embark on the new religion of the nation, supplying the temporal and spiritual needs of the subjects. When the solution afforded by the territorial churches began to come unstuck and the pressure of indirect papal power grew—this being the new strategy of the papacy—the debate over the divine right of kings came to a head in James I's England, causing a maelstrom of conversions and disillusionment embracing a whole cast of actors. It is usually described as irenical waverings or a Nicodemite revival; though I think the drama of those characters (men such as Giordano Bruno and Marcantonio de Dominis) popping up in various European countries and religions of the age is the quest for a solution to the vexed relation between the new-style sovereign and the religious dimension entailing some re-employment of materials that the papacy had already devised on the subject more than a century previously.

The rebirth of the papacy out of the council crisis—the 1440 'solstice'—is well-known for its two salient features: in order to salvage its universal role as best it could, it developed a new kind of center-to-periphery relationship, hinging no longer on the traditional top-down connection with individual churches, but on political relations with states via concordats and nunciatures. By such devices, and at the cost of major sacrifice, the popes managed across broad swaths of Europe to limit state appropriation of local churches and to preserve their own universal standing. But beneath the diatribes and agreements betweenstates and the Church of Rome I think we should detect a subterranean flux embodying the phenomenon of osmosis that is central to our interest.

One process that should be noted is the ensuing politicizing of structures inside the church which, belatedly of course, was in its turn forced to assume concentrated sovereign power like modern states. In imitation of these, and in a kind of inverted secularization as it were, it styled itself the *societas perfecta* right down to the *Codex juris canonici* promulgated in 1917. The modern era process of confessionalization caused a deep-seated alteration in church structures as compared to the medieval era: it borrowed an internal system of faithfulness from the political sphere: Christians became faithful no longer by sharing a common faith but by adopting a *professio fidei*, an ideologically defined creed or 'confession'.

Another phenomenon central to this process of the church assuming the trappings of a state was the development of spiritual jurisdiction over people's consciences; a system of rules was created paralleling the expansion of the state's positive law with which it competed especially in the seventeenth century. I have gone into this process elsewhere, but here wish to draw attention to its two-way quality: the secularizing of the moral order and the 'philosophication' (so to speak) of positive law form one of the central features in our analysis of osmosis.

The wholesale demise of this process set in around the mid-eighteenth century. Not only did a series of concordats restrict the scope of spiritual jurisdiction left to the Church of Rome and the local churches, but the Catholic world reached a high point of internal compromise with the powers of the epoch. When Clement XIV suppressed the Society of Jesus in 1773 across the globe and even within the Pontifical State (reflected worldwide in the abortive attempt to separate 'spiritual conquest' and the missions from state colonization, following the dispute over Chinese rites and abolition of the *reducciones de indios* in Latin America), it was a far from marginal episode or simple secularization such as occurred with other religious orders, but a measure accepted and conceived by the church herself so as to enable the two jurisdictions, temporal and spiritual, to converge in the new state. The fact is that in the eighteenth century the politicizing of the church was one of the main factors leading, on the one hand, to a crisis in the church principates (besides the decline of the Pontifical State) and, on the other, to the open sore of the 'worldly' church reduced to a puppet of the state, which forms the central point in Antonio Rosmini's denunciation after the first fury of revolution had subsided.

I by no means wish to demean the importance of radical Christian movements, which between the sixteenth and eighteenth centuries rebelled against confessionalization and the creation of territorial churches, as well as against Rome's proposal to co-govern these last; but if there is any truth in the above argument, we have to examine those movements both from a political and from a religious angle. Politically, we are interested above all in those that revert to the age-old principle of the *sect*, rejecting the idea of a worldly church with its ensuing compromises, in the belief that a society of *perfecti* may be set up on earth, saints for whom God's justice entirely coincides with earthly justice. The connections between millenarian and apocalyptic movements and the development of modern revolutionary doctrines are well known and covered by a huge bibliography. But what seems to me to have been left in obscurity or rendered obscure is the very real osmosis, of men and institutions, within the political bid to change human nature and proclaim the possibility of collective historical salvation inside the fabric of the modern state.

Historians are well aware of the importance of radical religious minorities in developing the principles of liberty and democracy in the West. But when we examine these modern theological-cum-political utopias we should duly note the element of discipline and repression that goes along with the 'fundamentalist' ideal: on the one hand, the claim to religious freedom, freedom of conscience and speech, and tolerance quite unlike the line of the official churches; on the other, repression of all internal deviation, denial of any gap between political life and religious life, morals and law, conscience and group behavior. The contradiction clearly felt throughout the centuries of the modern era between the demand for state and church to be separate, and the creation of communities where religious obligations quite outweighed political obligations, needs to be analyzed in detail if one is to avoid the prevailing stereotype of theological faith simply secularizing into revolutionary faith. The idea, in a nutshell, is that during the modern era we do not just have secularization of prophecy and transformation of it into utopia, but the 'end' of prophecy: for prophecy presupposes a hiatus between ethical command (holy or divine) and political power; but that hiatus is totally removed by the modern revolutionary extension in which the two commands are unified and historically grounded in the will of the people[3]. This process of osmosis thus leads to a parting

[3] P. Prodi, *Profetismo e utopia nella genesi della democrazia occidentale*, in G.C. Garfagnini (ed.), *Savonarola. Democrazia, tirannide, profezia*, Firenze 1998, pp. 199-211. (The essay

of the ways in the mid-eighteenth century: one way—let us call it civic religion—takes its cue from Montesquieu, while the road of political religion derives from Rousseau and leads (somewhat circuitously) to the political religions of the twentieth century, especially the secularized 'salvationist' ideals of Communism and Nazism.

3. *Conscience and the law*

Such was the view of the West, states, and churches when my own generation set about studying history in the aftermath of World War II, the Shoah, and the atom bomb. While the post-Vatican II Catholic Church and the Reformed Churches did come to terms with modernity theologically, it must be said that, like all attempts at Ecumenism, this remained within the denominations, although dogmatic disputes had largely died down over the major issues that had unleashed the tempest of the Reformation: that on divine grace and free will, the church and the universal priesthood of the faithful, the relationship with Holy Scripture, the meaning of the sacraments, the Eucharist[4].

I am well aware that I lack the competence to enter the theological arena on which the meetings to celebrate the fifth centenary of 1517 will open, beginning with the forthcoming Lund conference to be held on an ecumenical plane. But to an artisan of history like myself, the interweaving of history and historiography on the issue of confessionalization was one of the most exhilarating sensations of the last fifty years, and a personal fillip for the practicing historian, owing to the spur imparted by witnessing a world in rapid evolution yet also a persisting past upon which our current social and church structures were grounded. It was that conviction which prevented me from siding either with those who saw Vatican II as innovation and reconcilement with the modern age, or (still less) with those who were tackling the problem of confessionalization.

would be incorporated with other Savonarolean texts in the vol. *Profezia vs utopia*, Bologna 2013.)

[4] For a fuller summary, see the jointly edited document drawn up within the Commission for ecumenical questions at the US Conference of Catholic Bishops (USCCB) and the Evangelical Lutheran Church in America (ELCA), published in Italian by "Il Regno. Documenti", 13/2016, pp. 409-456.

As a neo-graduate, I had my first dawn of awareness in 1956/57 with an apprenticeship at the University of Bonn under Hubert Jedin, whose *History of the Council of Trent* was already out in Italian translation, together with the great inter-denominational breakthrough of his short volume, *Katholische Reformation oder Gegenreformation?*, on which hundreds of pages would be written. In that period—for me it was the decade of 1956-1966—it was fundamental that both these terms came to coexist within the Catholic world as we sought a way out of the black-and-white mentality that denominational historians had thrust upon us for centuries—though it was also necessary to extend the coordinates of time and space and incorporate the new colonies outside Europe.

When it came to the time-frame, we young apprentices went broadly along with Jedin's insights: no longer a modern history of the Church stretching from the religious rift, the Reformation and the Catholic Reformation or Counter-Reformation, but one long timespan stretching from the Great Schism in the West and the rebirth of the papacy midway through the fifteenth century and stretching down to the French Revolution and as far as our own times. This entailed reversing the traditional position to some extent. No longer the picture of a church consumed by malpractice, but a process in which Christianity, riddled with medievalism in its institutions and spirituality, had to face up to the developments of modernity on a cultural and political plane.

The great novelty lay in studying this transition in its internal complexity and its osmotic relations, quite apart from its religious wars, important though those were. Even inside the Catholic world both components were present (reform and counter-reform), while evangelical and reformed-church historians began to display a new interest in aspects of the so-called "Zweite Reformation", the second Reformation that consolidated the territorial churches between the second half of the sixteenth and the first half of the seventeenth century. That new and longer view helped us detect the parallel—though discordant and often contrary—response by the Church of Rome and the new churches to the challenge of modernity.

Within this frame of reference I was greatly influenced by Gabriel Le Bras's long-term institutional and legal coordinates embracing institutions and canon law; likewise by the major insights yawning in figurative arts and music as the fifties shaded into the sixties. I set about a comparative study of the Tridentine reform in a number of dioceses (especially Milan and Bologna with their bishops Carlo Borromeo and Gabriele Paleotti), as well as in their complex frictions with the centralism of the Roman Curia in which power struggles were waged even over interpreting the basic decrees of the Council of Trent.

A second chapter of my studies, from 1966 on, was primarily devoted to the papal monarchy. With its twofold face of spiritual combined with temporal power—until it declined and was eclipsed altogether—this seemed to me to transform the whole claim of politics to mold man down to his daily behavior from the cradle to the grave: though very different, this road ran parallel to that followed by the countries that went over to the Reformation and left it to the prince to manage the commandments of the Decalogue (second half) and church discipline.

As I have written that more than once, modern politics was not born out of secularization of theology but from a dialectical meeting between the two poles of religion and politics entailing constant friction but also a process of osmosis by which the church tended to politicize (the high point being the papal monarchy in the modern era) and the state tended to take over the church's functions of molding the citizen-subject from the cradle to the grave—an indoctrination that would culminate in the religion of the fatherland. A ferment of different currents ran right through the Catholic and the Reformation world, involving politics (cross-alliances), culture, the new science, literature, and the arts, borne on a constant exchange of people and ideas; all of which left a deep cleavage in theology itself between the various spiritual orders and movements. One has only to think of figurative art or music to cut through the stereotypes of certain historians who, for all their eminence, are nonetheless in the grip of a denominational obsession in either a negative or a positive sense of the word.

This phase paved the way for investigation of the connection between spiritual jurisdiction—with its claim to universality, as propounded by Second Scholasticism and moral theology as an independent discipline—and the positive law of the various European States making great strides on the civil and criminal plane—a twofold regulatory plane upon which seventeenth-century civilization was governed, and which opened the door to the philosophy and theory of subjective rights, as well as modern constitutionalism which took off in the eighteenth century.

In the 1980s, around the idea of a dialectic between incipient natural law and its religious and ethical norms, on the one hand, and positive state law, on the other, the most fertile and, to my mind, exhilarating period dawned at the Istituto Storico Italo-germanico in Trento: the home team, which had begun to enjoy the extraordinary contribution of Pier Angelo Schiera (he and his wife Giuliana Nobili were already linked to the classic German school of history and the great theories of Otto Brunner), joined up with the new German school of history that was propounding the theory of social discipline (*Sozialdisciplinierung*). I cannot here cite the many, many study weeks and the books we published together—though you are free to leaf through the back issues of the "Annali" ISIG—down to the pooled ideas of the 1990s on how collective identity forms. But I feel justified in claiming that that relationship went far beyond normal academic collaboration and left its mark on the thinking of both schools of history. On the one hand, it helped give rise to a less mechanical concept of social discipline, one not confined to the splicing of top-down written rules with emerging patterns of behavior on the part of society; on the other hand, it probed deeper into the subject of individual and collective conscience, and the importance of ethics in our description of that century-long process by which there grew inside the modern state a degree of participation in the idea and body of the steadily secularizing nation, and in the birth of codes and constitutions.

Without going into the major output of Wolfgang Reinhard and Heinz Schilling in particular around the turn of the last century, focusing on the modern state, the territorial churches and the expansion of that Europe across the world, one thing I can safely say: in my own research career those meetings in Trento triggered the study of the political compact; the institutional function of oath-taking in the transition from the multiple law systems of the Middle Ages to the new professions of loyalty linked to modern states and territorial churches, amid conflict, dialogue and osmosis with the secularization process; and, lastly, the transition from the multiple law systems of the Middle Ages to the modern era's dualism between law and conscience as developed in modern constitutionalism.

As we turned the millennium, the bond with our German friends grew fainter, but I sincerely believe the road we trod together enabled us to tackle the great subjects of world history and globalization in a concordant and similar way. We paid more attention than do English-speaking historians to the long-timespan factor, as well as the slow unfolding of Christianity and western civilization (whether resorting to the concept of transition or not). But above all, I feel that our common road enables us to face the forthcoming fifth centenary of the Reformation in completely new terms. For this occasion the Istituto Storico Italo-Germanico in Trento has scheduled a history conference worthy of that major event. At this present meeting I would simply like to point out that *de nobis loquimur*; likewise to suggest that the path we have trodden together may be instrumental in our rising above the old stereotypes of history-writing, and contribute signally to our approach to today's problems, not just for the churches but for our western civilization in crisis.

I realize the limits of this talk of mine; as I said at the beginning, I do not presume to address major points of historiography, or to indulge in autobiography. I merely seek to extrapolate some themes that have clearly emerged over the last fifty years from the digging and delving we have done together, if only marginally. We do have a duty to draw these themes—unfinished and unproven though they may be—to the attention of those non-historians on whom our future depends in a world where thinking and institutions are challenged by the major changes in progress. Ignorance of history is the chief danger I see in the new generation.

4. *Before and after Vatican II*

In the last half-century, which began with the conclusion to the Second Vatican council, various themes have emerged for the historian that may roughly be outlined.

a) After five centuries the age of confessionalization has sunk to rest once and for all. This applies not just to the "Tridentine paradigm" as an epoch in the Catholic Church (as a recent book of mine takes for its title) but also more broadly to the territorial churches born from the last throes of the Middle Ages. I should perhaps stress once again for the non-specialist that by "confessionalization" one means the changeover from a single creed, central to the liturgy and common faith of all the churches of Europe, to professions of faith differing from one region of Europe to the next; creeds translated into different formulas and catechisms, and linked to various symbolic and iconic manifestations of belonging. Such "confessions", beginning with the Augustan version in 1530, sprang first from the new reformed churches and not from Rome: it would take decades and the conclusion of the Council of Trent before the latter would follow suit and explore the path of catechisms and professions of faith. In the ensuing centuries, political and religious pluralism would gain ground in Europe, entailing differences of interpretation and relationship vis-à-vis the secularization process embarked upon by modern Nation-states.

One should also remember that the paradox and impotence of the ecumenical movements that have tried to unify the Christian churches in recent decades lie in the fact that, whereas rifts in creed and theology are being bridged or at least are losing importance (though five centuries ago they led to religious wars and division, as over the issue of "grace"), marked ruptures are still observed in disciplines and institutions, while even inside the individual churches the structures are more or less alike, in a crisis, from theology faculties to the training of clergy and pastors, parishes, and so on.

b) If in the five centuries since the Reformation we have had not just a process of secularization but also a dialectical process of osmosis between the religious and the political sphere, then the end of state religion or religion linked to ethnic origins has repercussions on both the institutions of the bill of rights and on democracy itself. If this dualism between political power and religious power was a basic component in building the bill of rights and democracy, the end of the age of confessionalization cannot fail to bring a devastating upheaval in the identity processes of nations and intermediate social groups. The failure of the most wide-ranging policies of multiculturalism and secularism over the last few decades is due precisely to their having their roots in the end of this era of Reformation and the Tridentine Church.

c) At the same time as confessionalization set in around 1517, movements of radical Christianity sprang up, which belonged neither to the Church of Rome nor to the new territorial churches, though in the intervening centuries down to our day they played a fundamental role in maintaining the dualism I have just spoken of. No need even to wait for events in England to unfold: the long public rise and fall of Thomas More, Henry VIII's Act of Supremacy over the Church of England, More's own death on the scaffold (1535). Utopia was strictly connected with the new religious-cum-political movements; it became transformed into ideology, branching off from the path of radical Christianity and the road that led to the founding of new territorial churches in their varying relations to princes or to up-and-coming republican communities. For its part, radical Christianity would split either into sects who believed that utopia could be attained by a new society of *perfecti*, a chosen people devoted to building the "Kingdom of Christ" on earth, or into those somehow remaining anchored to the world of Erasmus and More, but who saw themselves increasingly debarred from any kind of influence upon society except that of being persecuted and martyred: Francesco Pucci, Giordano Bruno, and Tommaso Campanella (to name but a few). They were banished from Europe in its entirety, looked at with suspicion by all in political power, whatever their creed. In persecuting them, the Holy Inquisition seemed to perform a common service in the new Europe of states (whatever their faith), preventing backsliding into the past of popes and emperors which the new denominational states viewed with aversion.

Clearly, like all model utopias by religious sects claiming to set up the City of God on earth, that model was rejected, defeated by the new State system and scattered in various channels. It might be the ideal of an archaic golden age, picking up that age-old myth but under a quite different guise by its very utopianism, there being the historical prospect of a new age of justice and equality; or it might be the myth of the "Promised Land", into which North American Puritanism and other forms of millenarianism channeled their yearning for a fresh start. Nowadays, with the end of confessionalization and the spawning of evangelical or do-it-yourself pseudo-evangelical movements, we must also reckon with the problem of losing another important binding force of western civilization: the end of all prophecy/utopia upon which to base the vision of a future society where justice may prevail.

d) Once again, let us emphasize that modern politics did not stem from the secularization of theological thinking, but from a dialectical combination of the religious and the political pole, in a process of rivalry but also osmosis whereby the church tended to politicize (the high point being the papal monarchy in the modern era) and the state tended to take over the church's functions of molding the citizen-subject from the cradle to the grave—an indoctrination that would culminate in the religion of the fatherland. When the world of medieval *christianitas* entered into crisis, a number of roads beckoned towards the modern era, roads which can be conveniently summarized, as long as one remembers that they were strictly interlinked across the centuries of the modern era, and ran simultaneously, not in isolation but in varying combinations as they explored a range of concrete solutions to the vexed relationship between power and the sacred: the road of republican-civic religion, the revival of monarchy as a sacred principle, the road of the territorial churches, and the road of Roman Catholicism (based on concordats and nunciatures). A ferment of different currents ran right through the Catholic and the Reformation world, involving politics (cross-alliances), culture, the new science, literature and the arts, borne on a constant exchange of people and ideas; all of which caused a deep cleavage in theology itself between the various spiritual orders and movements. Again, in the field of theological and philosophical speculation the frontier—thought projected into the future, the gap between prophecy/parrhesia on one side and power on the other—increasingly shifted from inside religions to the new currents of public opinion and the press, whilst carrying over certain tenets of theology and ethics that gradually extended to the newly discovered and colonized continents. This, too, is an area where we have trodden for centuries and now find it is being challenged as the era of confessionalization wanes.

What needs to be added to the above recapitulation is that this was not only a Europe still engrossed in culture and Latin, Roman law, the interweaving of new literary genres, new tonal music, melodrama, etc., but an integrated economic community, a *respublica mercatorum*, a land of new financial capitalism whose frontiers can hardly be seen as coinciding with the old religious fault-lines, even though they did assume a common *fides* at the basis of credit: the atmosphere of trust among men of different religious beliefs, which Voltaire himself noted as the air being breathed on the London Stock Exchange in the 1720s.

e) I believe that during the centuries of the age of confessionalization an essential distinction formed between 'sin', meaning disobedience to the law of one's professed religion or code of morality, and 'crime', meaning disobeying the state's positive law. At the heart of the process of the church assuming state characteristics and politics growing theological, running parallel with the expansion of positive state law but quite separate from and competing with it, there formed an area of spiritual jurisdiction over conscience, a system of norms within every community, infringement of which was likewise deemed blameworthy, though not subject to penalty: state law gradually became a defense against the outside, the frontier of a territory which was governed by domestic rules of its own that everyone recognized. The forms here diverged and contrasted, from the confession of sins, defined as a sacrament by the Council of Trent, to public airing of faults, or private conferring with pastors. A great transformation took place right across Europe, especially in the seventeenth century. I have gone into this process elsewhere, but here wish simply to stress its two-way nature: secularization of morality and "philosophication" (as it were) of positive law via a bill of human rights formed a central feature in the development of this Europe of ours. I sense that this distinction between sin as disobedience to ethical rules and crime as infringement of state or meta-state positive law is now waning or has already vanished, equally among international finance speculators and among new generations of schoolchildren (not just in the *banlieues*) blithely unaware of the Decalogue. I have already argued that this represents the collapse of one of the two pillars on which *homo europaeus* was built. Law itself now perches on one leg—as Jacques Ellul said years ago: it commits suicide when it identifies with political or economic power. Attempts by neo-Illuministes to create artificial legs by meta-law à la John Rawls or suchlike seem to me no substitute for religious support by churches, which is now on the wane. The last century's tragedies appear not to have vanished but to have spread their net in new millennium globalization.

f) The demise of the age of religious creeds, the Tridentine Church and the territorial churches, shifts the identity boundaries from the heartland of the western system to the wide world and the other universal religions: monotheistic religions born in the Mediterranean area and those of the age-old East. This has given concrete reality to the brilliant comparison that Max Weber suggested a century ago on the plane of theory, history, and anthropology. Failure to register this shift is causing terrible confusion not just in reportage of ongoing wars but even in the analyses of experts. Obviously in a few lines I cannot do justice to the complex issues that stem from this simple statement. I have tried to do so elsewhere. But amid the storms of our present times, it becomes a historian's duty to point them out. Clearly the major debate now running for decades as to the connection between monotheism and violence (which I cannot get involved in here) seems a tendentious field at this time of mushrooming killings and atrocities in God's name. To delve into past millennia for the historical roots might prove a false trail.

More and more I have come to believe that, since the founding of the Israeli State, the Jewish-Semitic world has become a prime case, the cutting edge of the West's attempt to reconcile—as some think still possible—an ongoing process of confessionalization of public life (strictly bound up with religions and ethnic belonging) with the full guarantees of a bill of rights. This formidable gamble involves us all in a welter of guilt for our past of political religions which no longer exists except for the (clearly important) memory of the Shoah.

g) As for the consequences of western de-confessionalization at the interface with Islam, if we wish to understand the rise of the latter and its attractiveness even within historical Christendom—something we would never have imagined even thirty years ago—I would mention two points that have emerged from historical research in the last few years. First, I feel that Islam stemmed from a heresy that germinated within Christianity, which then developed and diverged more and more doctrinally but contained at its heart rejection of the church as an institution; there never has been an institutional structure without its somehow identifying with political power. If, by way of a solution to the issues of secularism and cohabitation, one could create a responsible independent organization—a Church of Islam, as it were—Islam would no longer be Islam. That is why today we badly need a reminder of the long labor of war and conflict that Christianity had to go through over the centuries, as well as the process of de-confessionalization. Historically, Islam has involved many experiments with relations between political power and the religious community (*umma*); there have been countless theories purporting to solve the problems of compromise brought about by territorial expansion. In the Muslim religion, however, certain features have remained—rooted partly in Byzantine tradition or Mosaic law tailored to desert-dwellers—whereby the political chief is God's representative on earth without intermediaries or the limitation of institutions, while legally there is no positive canonical legislation separate (or nearly so) from the radical or moderate positions of the faith.

The second point is that Muslims living inside this Christendom identified with the West, but now witnessing the demise of creeds, cannot perceive the difference between right and wrong. Of course, we should not ignore the causes due to social and economic conditions in the *banlieues* and inner jungle of our cities, or the perhaps more widespread instances of personal pathology; but the attraction of Islam, especially among the younger generation, can only be explained by a void in the path of salvation caused by a breakdown in the scheme of redemption that the Christian Churches used to represent.

h) The complexity increases—and, with it, the superficiality of my present treatment—when it comes to the effects of the end of confessionalization at the interface with religions of the Far East. The loss of dualism between religion and politics, and hence Europe's inability—via permanent revolution, pluralism and dynamism—to outline a world different from the present, comes up against the various contentions of Confucianism, Buddhism, Hinduism, Taoism, etc.: viz. that in an unchanging cosmos heavenly and earthly power coincide to form a universe where every creature has its appointed place. As regards China in particular, until a few years ago the problem could be seen in the perspective of the two churches: the church remaining faithful to Rome, and the church controlled by the party. Nowadays, with the extraordinary development of neo-Confucianism, the problem has broadened onto the cultural and spiritual plane to the point of involving the civilization of the Middle Empire in all its dimensions. The old system largely inherited from European Marxism has dissolved, but in the megalopolises and the countryside are we glimpsing a change of civilization going beyond the new technology? As I experienced for myself as president of the Giunta Centrale per gli Studi Storici, when Italian and Chinese historians got together to prepare the international conference held last year at Jinan, the main concern of the Chinese delegation was to show China's perfect continuity from the empire 3,000 years ago down to the turbo-capitalism of today. The watchword was the alleged harmony of tradition and modernity, past and present; there was a pronounced tendency to ignore all points of conflict, rupture, contradiction, or history as a process of becoming. The problem is whether it is possible to alter the "heavenly mandate" and whether man, European or otherwise, can choose between good and evil, and a personal road to salvation.

5. *New paradigms for the historian*

The first motion I put forward today for discussion from the observatory of religious history is that the Second Vatican Council did not open a new era but closed the Age of Trent by reconciling the churches with modernity. That does not detract from its importance, but makes the debate sterile between the proponents of continuity and those of the clean break, such as characterized the ensuing decades.

The second motion is that the whole edifice of the West is collapsing, pace those who claim that with the end of the age of confessionalization the whole edifice of European civilization can stand upon the single platform devised by secularization during the Age of Enlightenment: the constitutional bill of rights. Let there be no misunderstanding. We cannot put the clock back, but multiculturalism has proved itself impotent and it remains to be seen if, and with what, we can replace the dialectic and distinction of powers which gave the West its identity during the confessional era.

2017 is hence not just a fifth centenary. These notes can be thrown overboard, but the impression remains that in recent decades we have been through a most unusual experience in which the history of events and the historiography of pondering them have interwoven as rarely happens. On a small scale, that applies to Trento, the place where the great crossroads of modern Europe was negotiated at the outset of this cycle of centuries.

Going back to my opening quotation from a student, it is perhaps we who have lost the ability to speak *de futuro*. We are quite unable to predict the future, any future. Not a situation of war such as we witnessed in centuries past, when hostilities were declared, armies were ranged against each other, etc. We continue to speak of war, but we are well aware that the daily assaults on our complex society go beyond all frontiers, physical or ideological. New technology has not only brought conflict into daily life but, by media coverage, has also cancelled the distinction between real death and imaginary death, especially among individuals whom loss of collective identity has rendered psychologically fragile. Belonging to a class, a nation, a religious community is as nothing, for all the (no doubt legitimate) arguments of the sociologists, anthropologists, and psychiatrists as to the reasons behind each suicide bomb attack—a jumble of claims that confound the traditional Islamic line of thinking upon which our specialists expend their breath.

What is unleashing youngsters against the West is the future void. It is also the point at which the mono- and multicultural approaches collapse in contradiction. The old coordinates have come adrift, not only in the West but also within Islam. We historians should be the first to say that if we are unaware of our denominational past these last five decades, we cannot build our own future; but the opposite is also true: without a guideline linking past to future we are unable to survive. If there is any truth in all of this, then it is quite mistaken to harp on about terrorism alone, and try to distinguish moderate Islamism from extremism. Of course we must fight with every weapon we have against attacks on our democratic institutions and our civil rights. But the central issue is for the young to be able to glimpse an identity and a future for themselves, a story of redemption, a forum inside which their *arbitrium* (in its various meanings) can be drawn upon, over and above the law in accordance with Luther's appeal: the call of conscience, of the right to find one's own road to salvation, is certainly the greatest legacy the Reformation bequeathed to Europe, and which we are expected to carry over into the scenarios of the future.

Politics, Theology, and Religion in the Reformation

by *Thomas Kaufmann*

In any epoch of earlier Latin European history, the relation between theology and politics, between religious and social dynamics, has probably never been closer than during the Reformation. The theological objections expressed by the Wittenberg Augustinian monk Martin Luther against the papal Church's system of indulgences, which resulted in his denouncement as a heretic, nevertheless had a positive resonance across class and social lines: among clerics and laymen, citizens and peasants, knights and imperial princes. The theological convictions of Luther and his fellow campaigners gained historical influence because they became a factor in politics. Town magistrates and territorial rulers attended to these convictions, in many cases motivated by reforming movements. They provided a home for reformation theology and its protagonists, supported them, and consequently began to work against existing church law, striving within their respective communal and territorial contexts of responsibility for a reform of the church.

To a critical degree, the Reformation owes its survival and its success to the dedication of the political powers responsible. Without the commitment of the territorial princes, their privy counselors and political experts, without the actors of municipal politics, the town clerks, jurists, and council members, the Reformation would hardly have had a sustainable success. Without all the "ghosts" called forth by the Wittenberg sorcer-

The following notes are restricted to what is inevitable: the form of a talk. This was initially a public lecture. As a result, the following notes are limited. More general aspects of the history of the Reformation in Germany and my conceptional ideas on it are treated in T. KAUFMANN, *Geschichte der Reformation in Deutschland*, rev. ed., Berlin 2016; on issues of the Reformation in Latin Europe cf. T. KAUFMANN, *Erlöste und Verdammte. Eine Geschichte der Reformation*, München 2017. On Reformation and politics cf. e.g. L. SCHORN-SCHÜTTE, *Gottes Wort und Menschenherrschaft*, München 2015; M. HECKEL, *Martin Luthers Reformation und das Recht*, Tübingen 2016. *Translation by Alyssa Evans*

er's apprentice in the moment of his denunciation in his appeal *To the Christian Nobility of the German Nation*[1] in summer 1520—without the laymen of all estates taking part in worldly rule—without all these, the theological proposals coming from Wittenberg after 1517 would have become nothing more than another episode of the history of heresy. From a theological point of view, Luther's appeal *To the Christian Nobility* is his least impressive writing. Politically, however, it became his most important publication and achieved a critical significance to the further process of the Reformation. There is no doubt, from the very beginning, that the Reformation owes its success to the inseparable connection between theology and politics.

It is true that Luther's theology of humility[2], existentially deeply rooted in and fed by his probing penetration into the Biblical text, motivated him to condemn the doctrine of indulgences as an intolerable exoneration of the seriousness of the repenting sinner that was demanded by God. This sparked the sequence of events that we are accustomed to regarding and remembering as the beginning of the Reformation: the indulgence controversy, his trial at Rome, the Electoral Saxon diplomacy of negotiation, and the threat of excommunication. But a Reformation, that is, a transformation of the traditional church in accordance with certain biblical norms, theological doctrines, and liturgical standards, only took place after Luther had succeeded in mobilizing the "Christian Nobility of the German Nation". It was not Luther's theological "discoveries", but the interaction of theology and politics, of religious insights and concrete creative impulses that triggered the Reformation and shaped it.

An historical concept of Reformation history that claims to describe the Reformation primarily as a consequence of certain theological root causes, as for example Luther's so-called "theological discovery",

1 My interpretation of this tract has been given in detail in the commentary T. KAUFMANN, *Martin Luther. An den christlichen Adel deutscher Nation*, Tübingen 2014; Studienausgabe 2016. The only contemporary translation into a vernacular language was the Italian one, published in 1533: *Libro de la emendatione & correctione dil stato Christiano*, printed clandestine in [Strasbourg] with [Ulricher]; VD 16 L 3765 (Bayerische Staatsbibliothek München), digitized.

2 For Luther's theology in general and his beginnings cf. B. HAMM, *Der frühe Luther. Etappen reformatorischer Neuorientierung*, Tübingen 2010; R. SCHWARZ, *Martin Luther Lehrer der christlichen Religion*, Tübingen 2016; for general orientation see R. KOLB - I. DINGEL - L. BATKA (eds), *The Oxford Handbook of Martin Luther's Theology*, Oxford 2014.

over-simplifies the complex layers of the problem and tries to reduce the Reformation syndrome to an initial event in Luther's biography. It attempts to reduce the whole meandering variety of the period's events and thoughts to the basic cause of Luther's challenged conscience as a theologian, thus reducing the *initia reformationis* to the *initia Luther*[3]. But if one interprets the Reformation as the process of reshaping the existing church through the creative participation of lay actors, leading to the introduction of communion under both kinds, to services centered on a sermon, the abolition of the mass, of convents, vows, pilgrimages, and many more issues, you will have to attribute the significance of a Magna Carta of the German Reformation to the appeal *To the Christian Nobility*. I would argue that there is hardly a greater misunderstanding of the history of the German Reformation and the appeal *To the Christian Nobility* than the judgment by MacCullouch: that Luther had only wanted to address an "elite audience"[4], and that his text did not convince it. Luther addressed not only the emperor, the imperial princes and the lower nobility; he also appealed to the municipal magistrates, although basically all were laymen, each one in his place, to take into their hands the responsibility for the reform of the church which he saw now as irreversibly corrupt. With the territorial and municipal reformations, and not lesser, with the communal and peasant reformations, the ghosts he had called up came to the fore. The concept of the priesthood of all believers, unfolded for the first time in the appeal *To the Christian Nobility*, was no less than a theological enabling of faithful baptized Christians to interfere creatively with church reform and not to leave it to the clerics. It was the theological basis for the fact that laypersons of all estates became active agents of change; it was even the root cause for its facilitation. I see a kind of key to the understanding of the German revolution as a whole in the entanglement of theology and politics as it is first found in Luther's appeal.

Only because Luther succeeded in connecting the substantiation of salvation in justification, in baptism, and in the faith to the empowerment

[3] For the discussion on the question of whether the Reformation can be seen as an epoch/time period cf. the survey in S. EHRENPREIS - U. LOTZ-HEUMANN, *Reformation und konfessionelles Zeitalter*, Darmstadt 2002.

[4] D. MACCULLOCH, *The Reformation. A History*, New York 2003, p. 132, cf. p. 125.

to do reformation acts, did the theological movement triggered by him become a political force that changed the church in Germany and in other European countries more deeply than anything or anyone before.

This line of interpretation, of an intense and derivable entanglement of theology and politics, can be proven from the sources and groupings of the early Reformation movement. It stands in a twofold opposition: on one side, it is opposed to the view favored by theologians—the predominance of theological ideas over political effects. On the other, it stands against the quasi "utilitarian" conception, favored by historians, according to which theological thoughts were only a means to achieve certain worldly aims, especially the realization of the construction and expansion of municipal and territorial church regimes that had already set in before the Reformation.

The first concept, primarily aligned to the history of theology, follows a pattern of cause and effect. It claims that certain theological ideas, such as the priesthood of all believers, had a certain effect in the reforms introduced for political reasons. Because of the normative theological foundation in this approach, it is possible to distinguish between appropriate and inappropriate actualizations of the reformatory doctrine. In this way, it can be clearly decided if the princes had understood Luther correctly, or if the peasants, on the other side, had understood him incorrectly. The danger of this option is obvious: because of an interest in the normativity and legitimacy of a certain interpretation of the *theologoumenons* of the "priesthood of all believers", the horizon of interpretation, which was still open in summer 1520 when the appeal *To the Christian Nobility* was published, is narrowed to the position of the late Luther, which was clearly subservient to authority.

The second concept, the utilitarian position, feeds on a basically secularist pathos of authenticity: the princes and the patrician magistrates were essentially interested in an expansion of their financial and political power at the expense of the church. Religion was only a pretext in order to achieve aims that were political. I want to stress explicitly that this line of interpretation could perfectly refer to contemporaneous ideas of political theory and is not simply anachronistic. To Machiavelli, for example, it was self-evident that rulers behaved quite adequately if they used religion as a way of enhancing their reputation; power interests—veiled and disguised by religion—could be justified, such as those, for instance, in the case of the Jews and Moors, who had been forcibly converted to Christianity, the so-called "Marranos", by the "Catholic Kings" of Spain[5].

However, both lines of interpretation—the line of theological history and the utilitarian line—have one thing in common. Both separate theology and politics, although with a respectively special interest in one of them, and both view them hierarchically. According to the theological-historical option, Luther naturally had his focus on religion and theology; the fact that he mobilized the noble laypersons was only due to the desperate situation of the mendicant friar who was threatened by papal excommunication and had given up all hope for an interior reformation of the church. According to the utilitarian position, the princes had employed a theological main idea in order to reach worldly aims, admittedly without inner conviction.

At the same time, and rightly so, both interpretations presuppose that under the conditions of pre-modernity there can be no question of any autonomy of the political; to the theological-political line, politics are basically instrumental to theology, while to the utilitarian theology is mainly a camouflage for politics.

In opposition to this, interpreting theology and politics in the sense of an intense and underivable interpenetration of both, is to have faith in the language and the imagination of the sources and to advocate for their alterity. But of course, this cannot be to ignore the political significance of theological arguments or to misrepresent political actions linked to theological arguments as acts of pious confession without any political calculation. On the contrary, Luther states in his appeal *To the Christian Nobility* that laypersons "have to be allowed to be priests and bishops, and their office should count as an office that belongs to a Christian community and is useful to the Christian community"[6]. This is a fundamental theological statement that had the highest possible political impact at the time it was uttered. In saying this, Luther authorized the laity to take over spiritual responsibility in the Church. "What crawled out of the baptismal font, may claim that it has already been consecrated as priest, bishop, and pope"[7]. Consequently, no cleric

[5] Cf. MACHIAVELLI, *Il Principe* (1532), chap. 21, pp. 92 f.

[6] WA 6, p. 408, 9-11; T. KAUFMANN, *An den christlichen Adel*, pp. 93 ff.

[7] WA 6, p. 408, 11-13.

can claim the prerogative of a higher qualification through consecration. This theologically revolutionary act was grounded in the respective biblical guidelines and overcame the fundamental separation between clergy and laity that had existed since late antiquity. As such, it had great political significance. The church itself had become a political factor in the highest degree, and this was exactly what the Wittenberg mendicant friar found deeply repulsive. Luther held only contempt for the successful military and territorial policies of Pope Julius II, who appeared in battle fully armed. He called Julius a "blood drunkard" (*blutseuffer*)[8]. Machiavelli, on the other hand, admired the energy (*virtú*) of specifically this pope, who had conquered Bologna, defeated Venice and driven the French out of Italy—and all this "only to increase the power of the Church, and not the power of some private man"[9]. By denouncing the political entanglements of the Church while simultaneously stressing the obligation of all the baptized, especially the worldly authorities, to stand by their reforms, Luther politicized his basic ecclesiological conviction that the "worldly authority [*weltlich hirschafft*] had become a member [*ein mitglied*] of the Christian body"[10]. It became an urgent course of action for the spiritually emancipated laity. Further, the imperative of the worldly authority in favor of the Church reform did not derive from their political office as such, but from their affiliation to the *corpus christianum*. This means they were supposed to act out of "Christian Love 'as they are not obliged as the worldly authority' and in the name of God / in favor of the Gospel and the miserable Christians ... and for their benefit and salvation"[11], as Luther wrote in the foreword to the *Unterricht der Visitatoren* (1528), quite in line with the appeal *To the Christian Nobility*. The doctrine of the three estates[12], deeply rooted in the Latin European tradition and taken up by the Reformer since 1519, distinguished between the three estates of house, instruction, and war (*oeconomia*, *ecclesia*, *politia*).

8 WA 6, p. 406, 2.

9 MACHIAVELLI, *Il Principe*, chap. 11, p. 48.

10 WA 6, p. 410, 3 f.

11 WA 26, p. 197, 25-27.

12 T. KAUFMANN, *An den christlichen Adel*, pp. 49 f., 216 f., 501 f., *passim*; cf. L. SCHORN-SCHÜTTE, *Die Drei-Stände-Lehre im reformatorischen Umbruch*, in L. SCHORN-SCHÜTTE, *Perspectum. Ausgewählte Aufsätze zur Frühen Neuzeit und Historiographiegeschichte anlässlich ihres 65. Geburtstages*, München 2014, pp. 251-280.

At first, it served to define functional differences within the Christian body that was constituted by baptism and faith, while at the same time stressing the unity of the construct "church", which was distinct in mutual service. In this sense, the *politia* was part of the Christian body. The most comprehensive systematic elaboration of the doctrine of the three estates can be found in Luther's great confession of 1528[13]. It is hardly a coincidence that this belongs to the historical context when the establishment of a Protestant church in Electoral Saxony began to proceed rapidly in the course of the visitations.

Luther spoke of the three estates in connection to his interpretation of the second article of the Apostolic Creed. After discarding the regulations of the old Church and its devilish "hordes" (*rotten*),[14] such as congregations, monasteries, foundations—that is, systems of distinction and separation that had been invented by human beings—he explained the order of creation constituted by God which, according to him, was coordinated and synchronized, but not hierarchically structured: "The state of the priest, the state of marriage, the worldly authority"[15]. Each of these estates is sacred, but none of these "orders" (*orden*) is "a path to salvation"[16]. Salvation can only be achieved through faith in Christ. The "common order of Christian love, where you do not serve the three orders only, but also generally every needy person with various benefactions"[17] is above and before these three estates. According to Luther, the pope is interfering with the gospel, intending to rule over the worldly authority that has been instituted by God, and is in this way threatening the entire good order of creation. He is a "monster" (*monstrum*)[18], and not part of the order of the three estates. His rule is no "office, neither of the Church nor politically" (*magistratum, neque ecclesiasticum neque politicum*)[19]. More than that, he destroys all *politia*.

[13] WA 26, p. 504, 30 ff.

[14] WA 26, p. 503, 17.

[15] WA 26, p. 504, 31.

[16] WA 26, p. 505, 16.

[17] WA 26, p. 505, 11-13.

[18] WA 39/2, p. 42, 24.

[19] WA 39/2, p. 42, 1. For the following remarks in the text above, this disputation on Mt 19:21 from 1539 stands in the background.

To Luther, therefore, the doctrine of the three estates offers a theological interpretative pattern that identifies the coherence of spiritual and worldly estates within the body of Christ, and their specific tasks as well as the diabolical powers outside of God's order: the pope, who has perverted the worldly estate, and the Turk, who has perverted the matrimonial estate[20]. The application of the doctrine of the three estates does have consequences: as an interpretation of reality, it offered possibilities for political actions, such as the right to resist the emperor seduced by the papal devil, or the right to an armed struggle against the armies of Sultan Suleiman[21].

However, alongside his coordination of the *politia* in relation to *oeconomia* and *ecclesia*, Luther also uses phrases that push towards discriminating the two, to place the church and worldly rule into a hierarchical relation. This happens when he states that our works in the church relate to the salvation of the soul, while the works in the household and in *politia* relate conversely to the body. It also happens when he separates them in terms of aims (the *finis politiae* relates to peace in the world, while the *finis ecclesiae* relates to eternal peace), and when he insists that *politia* and *religio* should not be mixed, as they are as far apart as heaven and earth. Only those who have the gospel know what *politia* is, as the gospel alone is the power to distinguish rightly in the face of the law. This means that Luther based his political theory in a special way on his theology and its immanent categories of distinction between law and gospel, and the spiritual and worldly rule of God. The extent to which he succeeded in doing this was controversial among his contemporaries, as is generally known—one needs only to think of the Peasants' War. But it is not controversial that Luther's utterances of 1525, which became so politically disastrous, were of a decidedly theological nature: to Luther, the appeal to slaughter the peasants ("Stab, beat, strangle, whoever can" ["Steche, schlahe, würge hie, wer da kann ..."])[22] was a consequence of the authorities' God-given right

[20] WA 30/2, p. 127, 13-17; cf. T. Kaufmann, *"Türckenbüchlein". Zur christlichen Wahrnehmung "türkischer" Religion in Spätmittelalter und Reformation*, Göttingen 2008, p. 162; cf. A.S. Francisco, *Martin Luther and Islam*, Leiden - Boston MA 2007, pp. 131-141.

[21] Cf. T. Kaufmann, *Konfession und Kultur. Lutherischer Protestantismus in der zweiten Hälfte des Reformationsjahrhunderts*, Tübingen 2006, pp. 29-66.

[22] WA 18, p. 361, 25.

to the sword. It implied the unconditional right to defend their rule, bestowed upon them by God[23].

To the political elites, the powerful attraction of reformation theology can certainly be seen in the fact that, at least after the Peasants' War, there could be no serious doubt that the leading reformers stabilized existing political structures and power relations and fought against every form of rebellion and disobedience against legitimate worldly authorities. Because of Luther's ingenious and extremely momentous opening up towards politics, and its basis based in the center of his theology, political actors slowly recognized that a reformation held the promise of courses of action and chances, even profits. Reformation theology's openness to commitments from the political elites in the sense of multi-voiced calls for a reform of the church from top to bottom had become more and more unmistakable during the fifteenth and sixteenth century, and experienced a concretization in the humanism north of the Alps. This corresponded with the tangible interests of the worldly authorities. Already by the early policy of protection granted to Luther by the administration of Electoral Saxony, political and theological motifs could not be separated or played against each other. First, there was the dynastic competition of the Wettin branch against the Brandenburg who, after the rapid rise of Margrave Albrecht to the Archdioceses of Magdeburg and Mainz, now possessed two of the seven Electoral dignitaries. Luther's attack on the Saint Peter's Indulgence sold under the responsibility of Albrecht could even be sure of the sympathies of both Saxonies. Then there was the imperial political interest to fence in the influence of Habsburg and to include Rome in the political calculations. Further, there was the territorial political objective to promote the newly founded University of Wittenberg that had been recognized throughout the empire because of Luther, and to which larger numbers of students were beginning to flock. Its reputation could be enhanced, and it could also be distinguished as a factor of regional economy. Finally, a man like Spalatin, the most important adviser, confessor, court chaplain, and secretary of Prince Elector Frederick of Saxony, had been won over to the Reformation because of the intense theological impressions he had received through personal contact with the Wittenberg professors of theology, Luther and Karlstadt, and their writings. And there was

[23] WA 11, pp. 229 ff.

certainly Frederick himself and his co-ruling brother, Johann, with their highly intense piety, conventional in its outer appearance, but focused on the internalization of faith and the word of the Bible, and characterized by a sense of dependence on God's help and the responsibility for the salvation of their subjects. This made them susceptible to the theology of the Augustinian monk who wooed them intensely. And there was an increasingly discernible opportunity to make efforts to establish a territorial church regime more effectively with the help of the theological convictions of Luther and his disciples, something that had already been initiated during the decades before the beginning of the indulgence controversy. These earlier efforts had included a focused promotion of the reform-oriented and observant orders, the filling of key spiritual positions, resistance against personal-political Roman demands, and an enhancement of religious and moral standards within the territory. All this could now be realized with a territorial church that became a pillar of the state. In the towns, similar developments can be observed. Here also, the reform order of the early 1520s could directly take up pre-reformation efforts to fence in the influence of episcopal town rulers, to place the filling of pastorates under the rule of the magistrate, to control ecclesiastical finances, to domesticate the clergy and enhance their morality, to adapt the educational level of the clergy to the enhanced needs of a citizens' culture, and to integrate the community socially and morally by concentrating on normative municipal-communitarian values such as justice, common good, and concord.

Further, it can be observed on the municipal and territorial level that the enhancement of theological lay competence, emphatically demanded by reformatory publications, took place in reality. Municipal politicians, town clerks, princely counselors, knights, even territorial princes of both sexes came forward, not only as readers, but also as authors of theological texts, as had probably never been the case in such intensity in any earlier period of church history[24]. Since his excommunication and interrogation at the Diet of Worms in 1521, Luther had seen

[24] Cf. e.g., P. MATHESON (ed.), *A People's History of Christianity*, Minneapolis MN 2007; R.W. SCRIBNER, *For the Sake of Simple Folk*, Oxford 1994[2]; M. USHER CHRISMAN, *Conflicting Visions of Reform. German Lay Propaganda Pamphlets 1519-1530*, Boston MA 1996; T. KAUFMANN, *Die Zwickauer Propheten*, in STADTVERWALTUNG ZWICKAU (ed.), *"Martinus halbenn …". Zwickau und der reformatorische Umbruch*, Zwickau 2016, pp. 53-62; T. KAUFMANN, *Erlöste und Verdammte*, p. 411 ff.

his cause obtain a political disposition. Consequently, political actors who viewed Luther's cause positively were obliged to explain—or let somebody else explain for them—with theological arguments why they did not prosecute the heretic and his disciples, why they did not execute the Edict of Worms, and why they did not stand up against the rapid spread of the reformation movement. The fact that Luther had been banned and outlawed, without an attempt to disprove him theologically, fueled an awareness of deep injustice and strengthened the conviction that his theology must be true. Because of the reformation translations of the Bible, which were soon available, the political elites could form their own opinions[25]. There is no doubt that many of them became involved in the risks of the Reformation out of deep religious convictions, that they were even convinced that an affiliation with the Protestant doctrine was opportune not only in order to appease the masses of the people, but also for the salvation of themselves and their subjects. A theologization of the political debate dominated the 1520s and motivated worldly authorities to publish confessions. For example, the upper German imperial towns decided during the Diet at the imperial town of Ulm in December 1524 to allow the Word of God to flourish, which "their subjects are eager to know" ("unterthonen … begirig sein")[26], or in their famous *Protestation of Speyer*, the Imperial Estates denounced the ban to further spreading the Reformation by invoking "God's Glory and our salvation and the beatitude of our souls" ("Gottes ere und unser heil und selen seligkeit")[27] and confirmed the accountability of each individual before God. All this marks a state of affairs that is entirely new in its intensity. Just as the Reformation did not come into effect without theology, corporatist or territorial politics had become impossible without theological legitimation. This becomes most evident with the fact that it was the Protestant powers, the towns and territories, which conclusively debated, approved, finally signed and took responsibility for the most important doctrinal text of the

[25] Cf. for Luther's translation of the New Testament, especially in relation to Erasmus' demand to translate it into the vernacular on behalf of the lay people T. KAUFMANN, *Der Anfang der Reformation. Studien zur Kontextualität der Theologie, Publizistik und Inszenierung Luthers und der reformatorischen Bewegung*, Tübingen 2012, pp. 68-101.

[26] G. PFEIFFER, *Quellen zur Nürnberger Reformationsgeschichte*, Nürnberg 1968, p. 309.

[27] *Deutsche Reichstagsakten*, Jüngere Reihe, vol. 7/2, no. 167, pp. 1345 ff.; T. KAUFMANN, *Erlöste und Verdammte*, p. 571.

Reformation—the *Confessio Augustana* of 1530. It was not a theologian but a politician, the Saxon Chancellor Christian Bayer, who read the German version before emperor and empire[28].

The close interactions between politics and theology can also be illustrated by some of the more burdensome aspects. The unfortunate dispute concerning the interpretation of the Lord's Supper, which finally led to an irreparable rift within the Protestant camp, placed great strains on the plans for an alliance among the adherents of the Reformation. Since the abolishing of the Imperial Recess of the first Diet at Speyer in 1526 that had provided that each imperial territory should treat the *Edict of Worms* in the way that it was "hoped and trusted to be responsible before God and His Imperial Majesty" ("gegen Gott und Kayserliche Majestät hoffet und vertraut zu verantworten"[29]) it became clear to the "Protestants"—as they were called since the Protestation of Speyer in 1529—that they would only be able to meet the threatening danger of the forces of the old faith if they joined forces in a military-political alliance. But Luther and his adherents did not agree. To them, the confession was prior to the alliance, meaning that an alliance was ruled out with all those forces that stood with Zwingli of Zurich, with Oecolampadius of Basel, or with Bucer and Capito of Strasbourg when it came to the question of the bodily presence of the human nature of Christ in the elements of the Lord's Supper. After the Imperial Recess of Augsburg in November 1530, in which Charles V had inculcated the commitment to the "ancient true Christian faith and religion, passed on for a long time" ("den alten wahren lange herbrachten Christlichen Glauben und Religion")[30], had forbidden all changes in the church before the *concilium*, and had demanded implementation of the *Edict of Worms*, the danger to the protestant imperial territories became imminent. However, with the Schmalkaldic League of December 1530, they succeeded in forming a defensive alliance to protect the Reformation that abstained from a narrowly interpreted conformity of confession. There are even some factors that suggest a certain taming of the theological conflict,

[28] *Ibid.*, pp. 581 ff.

[29] Citation following R. KASTNER, *Quellen zur Reformation 1517-1555*, Darmstadt 1994, no. 154, pp. 493-495, here pp. 494 f.

[30] R. KASTNER, *Quellen zur Reformation*, p. 507; cf. T. KAUFMANN, *Erlöste und Verdammte*, p. 601.

compelling the Protestant territories to cooperate politically because of the external threat to Protestantism in the empire. The resolution of the Wittenberg Concord (1536) or the rejection of Luther's Schmalkaldic Articles (1536) as the confessional basis of the league points in this direction. In any case, in the aftermath of the Augsburg Diet, the specific logic of the political came more and more to the fore. Concerning the question of the territories' right to resist the emperor, as far as issues of conscience are concerned, Luther and the Wittenberg theologians finally had to give in to the arguments of the lawyers and to recognize such a right[31]. In summer 1532, Luther complained at the dinner table:

> "Now, my highest annoyance is the *politia*, as the devil can't win over me, he now wants to put politics onto me and to perturb my conscience. If I give advice, people don't follow me and accuse me of wanting to rule; if I don't give advice, it has to go conform to my conscience. I do not know what to do!"[32].

The impasse that he speaks of probably corresponded to a structural change within the framework of reformation history: a phase of theological dominance of politics in the 1520s was followed by a phase in the subsequent decade when politics was paramount. But now it had become obvious that it was the stability of the political system of the empire that secured the Reformation in the long run. Because of the simultaneity of imperial-centralist and statist-federative moments that constituted Germany's specific statehood, it became possible to accept religious differences, after a hard struggle, without destroying the unity of the empire. The legal-political suspension of the question of religious truth on the level of the empire and the release of the theological dispute over the truth on the level of the territories constituted the tension-filled relation between theology and politics in the long run. Because of the principle *cuius regio eius religio* of the Religious Peace of Augsburg[33], it was ensured for decades that, on one side, confessional

[31] Cf. E. Wolgast, *Die Wittenberger Theologie und die Politik der evangelischen Stände*, Gütersloh 1977; E. Wolgast, *Die Religionsfrage als Problem des Widerstandsrechts im 16. Jahrhundert*, Heidelberg 1980.

[32] "Jetzund ist mein hochste vexation die politia, den den Teufl kann mir nichts abgewinen und will mir nun politiam auf mein hals laden und mein concientz damit pertubieren. Rath ich, so folgt man mir nicht, und sprechen, ich will regiren; rat ich nichts, so muß ich ein concientz dazu haben. Weiß nicht, wo aus damit", WATR 2, no. 1715, p. 191, 24-28.

[33] Cf. several studies of Martin Heckel, for instance: *Deutschland im konfessionellen Zeitalter*, Göttingen 2001[2].

theologians built citadels of doctrines, broke into wild polemics and drove forward their controversies on the truth of Christianity with ever more subtle arguments, and on the other side, the external peace of the empire was maintained. The religious-legal system of Augsburg had put limits to the politicization of theology as well as to the theologization of politics—to the benefit of both!

Let me come to an end. In the time of the Reformation, politics and theology were inseparably entangled, but the intensity of this interaction was subject to historical change. In the decisive decade of the German history of Reformation, that is in the years between Luther's appeal *To the Christian Nobility* in 1520 and the *Augsburg Confession* in 1530, an immense theologization of politics took place. Every decision in favor of the Reformation had to legitimate itself with ultimate liability—to the salvation of the prince and the subjects, to the gospel as an irresistible force, and to the word of God as an infallible norm. Even the views of politics of the so-called "radical reformers" were shaped by these normative charges, but did not last due to motifs of imminent apocalyptic, eschatological expectations[34]. The reform-minded municipal magistrates, the urban diets, the princes of the Reformation and their coalition partners—they all acted as confessors. After 1530, the logic of arguments and actions came to the fore—especially the legal, political, and military-strategic ones. Now it became important to secure sustainably the successful urban and territorial reformations of the 1520s. To do this, all those instruments were needed with which conflicts and interests were fought out this side of heaven.

[34] Cf. T. KAUFMANN, *Radical Political Thought in the Reformation Era*, in B. HEAL - A. KREMERS, *Radicalism and Dissent in the World of Protestant Reform*, Göttingen 2017, pp. 27-35.

Devotion and Institutions in the Age of the Reformations

by *Pierre-Antoine Fabre*

1. *Introduction*

Any synthetic reflection on the denominations and churches of the long European Renaissance, of which the Catholic Council of Trent (1545-1563) constitutes a chronologically central episode, necessarily confronts profoundly heterogeneous realities, of which it will nonetheless be necessary to attempt to describe one or more historiographical principles: on the one hand, the institutional colossi, governed by their own laws, but fractured by shocks which had broken the continuity of their historical supports; on the other hand, devotional realities, rituals the articulation of whose doctrinal foundations were undergoing a profound crisis, if we may understands by "crisis" at once a historical upheaval and the questioning of the theoretical conditions of possibility of the set of practices that they explained and legitimated; thirdly, the irresistible entry of Europe into a wider world which Europeans had discovered and which, at the same time, was in the course of revealing to them their own realities. This series of phenomena, in part merely contemporaneous, in part interconnected, permit us to sketch out the three fields in which the following discussion will develop. We will refer to the main works that treat these different fields, privileging the most recent publications.

2. *The broken circles of ecclesiastical control*

As a result of the stratified accumulation of institutional formations, which had begun in Late Antiquity, in the Renaissance the notion of a

I should like to thank my colleague and friend Yves Hersant for the precision shown in his reading of the French version of this text. *Translation by Korshi Dosoo*

"church" encompassed three different realities that were, in theory or in practice, in conflict with one another: the church in its strict sense, a material institution devoted to the supervision of human society, with the threefold mission of controlling secular political authorities, confecting the sacraments, and guaranteeing the execution of cultic practices rendered to God; religious orders, constituted as reified models of a human world fully "ordered" in service of the divine; and lay congregations and confraternities, which were mixed groups, on the one hand because they contained (male and female) monastics and (male and female) laypeople, and on the other hand because they strove to build in the world of secular life—that is to say, in the world of the church, whose parish system constitutes the most modern medieval achievement—zones of higher religious intensity, comparable in this respect to monastic spaces[1].

These three types of institutions, marked of course by numerous intersections, nevertheless represent three specific modalities of the relationship between the church and religious practice: the first consecrated secular life (through baptisms, weddings, and offering first, regular, and final communion) and placed the divine service of created beings directly into lives lived within the sphere of human affairs; it made worship social, not only through the fundamental ritual of Eucharistic consumption, but also through the whole range of sacraments—in particular marriage—which justified sexual relationships. The second institution, that of religious life, on the contrary, made the social bond itself religious, in every sense, making of the religious vow the indissoluble interweaving of human convention and divine alienation, by which, before God, one abdicates one's freedom for the benefit of others; this is, in effect, worship as the offering up of the subject by itself, as subjection[2]. The third operates what might be termed the "delimited sacralization of the social condition": the member of a confraternity does not enter an area of higher religious intensity as a man or a woman (as a monastic would), but as a blacksmith, a baker, or as the inhabitant of a particular neighborhood or of a particular city,

[1] Mario Rosa has proposed—as a heuristic—a geographical distribution of these three types of institution in the modern period, Italy privileging the renewal of the religious orders, Spain the role of the episcopacy, and France that of lay congregations. Cf. M. Rosa, *Clero cattolico e societa europea nell'eta moderna*, Roma 2006.

[2] P. Prodi, *Il sacramento del potere*, Bologna 1992.

etc. He or she brings a defined aspect of his or her human existence into the sacred world. This third type of institution is thus defined as existing in an unstable equilibrium between the first and the second types, between the socialization of the sacred and the sacralization of social relations. One might say that, from this perspective, church, monastery, and confraternity divided the social world into spaces that might be separate and neighboring, or else brought into opposition by their intersections. This social space was global and pervasive. The rigorously circumscribed parish framework could only be fully realized by the weakening of other boundaries, in France, for example, by the French Revolution and the dissolution of regular religious orders. This space was also dense and—in part—removed from the ordinary rules of reproduction and exchange; particular, and also temporal, that of a society dedicated to its present. While the church, in its universality, necessarily looked back to the origin of its mission, that of the long-awaited end of times, and while monasteries attempted to anticipate a society pared down to its ultimate function: the glorification of the creator, the world of the confraternities was, on the contrary, also a world of fragmented cults: not of God, but of his saints, from the protector of the carpenters to that of the plague-stricken from the patron of the grooms to that of the pilgrims[3].

Any local history of this period, urban or rural (the development of the three institutions is of course inseparable from the progressive urbanization of the European territory between the end of the Middle Ages and the seventeenth century) will bring into relief the composition of these spaces, nuancing and complicating any overly abstract presentation[4]. It might also testify to a strong continuity of this institutional

[3] In an excellent recent book, D. HERVIEU-LÉGER, *Le temps des moines*, Paris 2017, has demonstrated both the power and the limits of this model of monasticism over the course of its history. He demonstrates in particular the tension between the anticipation of the Kingdom of God and the reconquest of the world in the monastic reforms of the nineteenth century. The crisis of this monastic model in sixteenth-century Europe would be measured by the yardstick of this tension: on the one hand an increase in mysticism, on the other social reform, and sometimes both within the same religious institutions; cf. P.-A. FABRE - F. RURALE (eds), *Claudio Aquaviva SJ (1581-1615). A Jesuit Generalship at the Time of the Invention of the Modern Catholicism*, forthcoming.

[4] S. PEYRONEL RAIMBALDI, *Speranze et crisi nel XVIe modenese*, Milano 1979; F. RURALE, *I gesuiti a Milano*, Roma 1992; A. TORRE, *Il consumo di devozione, Religione e comunitai nelle campagne dell Ancien Regime*, Venezia 1995; J.D. SELWYN, *A Paradise Inhabited*

geography throughout the period. However, the European Renaissances were marked by three upheavals—not all equally visible, but today recognized and studied as such—of the secular, regular, and lay institutions, which together constituted the ecclesiastical framework of the "Christian community".

First, Christendom experienced the second great schism in its history, after the separation of the churches of the East and the West[5], the break of the Reformation, begun in the first decades of the sixteenth century. Not only did this break clearly shatter the apparent unity of the Western Church, the medieval *christianitas*, for the first time since the earlier schism, but these fractures multiplied throughout the following period, for two principal reasons. On the one hand, the insurrection against the hegemony of Rom made no place for an alternative hegemony within the world of the Reformation; the Protestant churches were thus from the beginning (and up to the present) multiple churches, precisely because of their refusal of a governing principle, which transcended regional specificities and, on the political level, the different relationships between churches and states. This is what historiography has recognized as "confessionalization", that is to say, the responsibility of political power to protect denominations, a corollary of

by Devils. The Jesuits' Civilizing Mission in Early Modern Naples, Burlington VT - Roma 2004.

5 The history of the repercussions of this schism in the modern West, and in particular the limits of the separation of the Orthodox Churches and the Roman Church, remains largely to be explored, from the attempts at reconciliation between the two churches (the Council of Florence, in 1431-1439, must be understood as the prehistory of the Council of Trent), to the persistence of the Byzantine icon and its inventive tradition, long underestimated in Western Christian art history, in the culture and inheritance of Western European. To take only two examples, from two different spheres: the argument in defence of the cult of images in the last decades of the sixteenth century draws heavily on the heritage of late Byzantine literature, that of the fourteenth and fifteenth centuries; the sanctuary of Loreto, founded on the miraculous translation of the Santa Casa from Nazareth to Italy after the fall of Acre in 1294, is also founded on the enshrinement of an apotropaic icon of Mary, which preceded the arrival of the Santa Casa and gives her first localization. On this point see G. CRACCO, *La Santa casa di Loreto*, in *Loreto crocevia religioso tra Italia, Europa e Oriente*, Loreto 1992, and more generally A. CHASTEL, *Byzance et l'Italie*, Paris 1999, whose course, taught at the Collège de France in the last years of his life, remains ground-breaking. The work of Ovidiu Olar on the western diplomacy of the Patriarchate of Constantinople, in the process of being published, will provide new insights.

the renunciation on the part of these same cults of religious authority in the forms, in which the Christian Church had hitherto exercised it, through all of its ideological and coercive tools, especifically the Holy Office of the Inquisition, and through the sacrament of confession. At the same time, the disappearance of the regular religious orders in Protestant Europe led to an exacerbation of the dissident dynamics of the Reformed Churches, dynamics that until then had been largely absorbed by the proliferation of orders, the emergence of which had always corresponded to reform movements within ecclesiastical institutions. These two logics led not merely to the separation of Europe into two antagonistic blocs but to the emergence of a multiplicity of formations—from the Lutheran Church to the Calvinist Church and to all of those that followed and combined them—the result of which was the religiously plural Europe of the sixteenth century[6].

Secondly, at the heart of what had become the Catholic Church, the Protestant Reformation provoked, but also accompanied[7], the flourishing of new religious movements, taking most often, according to the general principle of medieval Christendom, the form of new religious orders. These new orders disguised their novelty under a principle inherent to Christianity, the "bonne nouvelle"[8]. But they were, nonetheless, really new, and singular in their attempt to rethink the relationship between secular clergy and monastic orders. This led to the flourishing of regular clerics in the middle of the sixteenth century: members of the religious

[6] See, for a spectacular journey across this plural Europe, the long voyage of Jean de Labadie, variously described by L. KOLAKOWSKI and M. de Certeau (P.-A. FABRE - N. FORNEROD - S. HOUDARD - C. PITASSI [eds], *Lire Jean de Labadie*, Paris 2016).

[7] Hence the debate, which marks all the historiography of the twentieth century, between the idea of a Catholic Reformation and that of a Counter-Reformation, a debate whose stages we do not have time here to even briefly recount. See P. PRODI, *Christianisme et monde moderne*, Paris 2006.

[8] The contradiction between the entrenchment of Christianity in its long tradition, upon which depended its claim to authority, and its need to proclaim its novelty, is coterminous with Christian history throughout the entirety of its duration; S. ELM - E. REBILLARD - A. ROMANO (eds), *Orthodoxie, christianisme, histoire*, Roma 2000. See, on this point also an extremely useful work, now republished, by P. DE LABRIOLLE, *La réaction anti-païenne. Etudes sur la réaction anti-païenne du Ier au VIe siècle*, Paris 2004 (1st ed. 1934). This contradiction accounts, at least in part, for the challenge of Christian humanism in its attachment to philology as a tool for the rediscovery of its ancient heritage, and as an instrument for the manifestation of its living sources.

orders who dwelt in the world, or priests who lived in communities, of which the best known, for both their geographic and temporal extent, are the Jesuits, members of the Society of Jesus founded by Ignatius of Loyola in 1540[9], but similar groups proliferated at the same period—from Oratorians to Theatines and Barnabites, Scolopi and Mercedarians, and to which must be added the reform movements within ancient and medieval orders, such as the Capuchins, an offshoot of the Franciscans, or the Recollects, which grew out of the Augustinians.

Finally, the secular confraternities were also subject, in the same period, to two contrary tendencies that contributed to a strong differentiation in their morphologies (their modes of recruitment, organization, and activity). On the one hand, in the wake of the new precariousness of the ecclesiastical magisterium, linked to the rupture of the Reformation, these nodes of piety and discipleship became increasingly secularized, now atomized and connected to new hierarchical formations. On the other hand, there was also an inverse tendency towards the restoration of a highly clericalized Christian society. These two trends could be found within the same groups[10], and the same individuals[11], and they overlapped the porous borders that bounded, in practical terms, Catholicism and the Reformation[12].

How should we conceive of these dynamics within the institutions of the "Churches", in relation to the evolution of religious practices?

Concerning the Reformation, it is quite obvious—and yet true—that the Protestant rebellion swept away a whole series of traditions that were hitherto indissociable from the life of the church, and which were closely connected with the mediation of priests and monastics, from the cult of the saints to the cult of relics and of images, invested with thaumaturgical powers by their guardians as well as by their clients. The iconoclastic episodes were but the most spectacular face of a revolt,

9 J.W. O'Malley, *The First Jesuits*, Cambridge 1993; F. Motta, *Bellarmino. Una teologia politica della Controriforma*, Brescia 2005.

10 B. Dompnier (ed.), *Confréries et dévotions dans l'Europe moderne*, Roma 2008; L. Châtellier, *L'Europe des dévots*, Paris 1987.

11 S.-M. Morgain, *Pierre de Bérulle et les carmélites de France*, Paris 1995.

12 S. Seidel Menchi, *Erasmo in Italia 1520-1580*, Torino 1987; J. Le Brun, *La jouissance et le trouble*, Genève 2005; M. Bataillon, *Les jésuites dans l'Espagne du XVIe siècle*, Paris 2009.

and of a doubt, that destabilized the innumerable supports of divine intercession by removing the links between faith and these material practices. At the same time, this destabilization extended to the attitudes of the "Catholic" population, who in reaction called for a revision of what the post-Tridentine church itself persecuted as traces of paganism, which had infiltrated the body of Catholicism. More profoundly, the discovery of the historical character of Christian rituals—and the texts, which legitimated them—in the sense of an admission of their mortality, gradually prepared for the birth of an abstract deity in a world that has been described as "disenchanted". God or nature: we increasingly find between the two contrivances linking them by means of objects, acts, and effects inappropriate for either God or nature. To all of these matters we must later return, but without forgetting either the liberating power of this sweeping-away or the force, which might impose it.

Concerning the emergence of new religious orders, it is perhaps equally clear that none was able to sustain new cultic forms comparable to those which had been established in previous centuries, except perhaps in those places—and we will return to this question too—where the past reinvented itself by necessity 'within' modernity: in the world of the new Christianity of mission territories. From this point of view, it is no coincidence that, within the Society of Jesus, the cult of Francis Xavier, a missionary in Asia, developed much more steadily and profoundly than that of Ignatius of Loyola, who never left Rome[13].

The third term, the confraternities and teaching orders, confirms this diagnosis, whatever the secularizing or restorative orientation which directed them: the development of the Marian congregations throughout the seventeenth century shows how far the multiplicity of particular mediating figures—this or that saint for this or that guild or place—could give way to infinite variations on a single figure, that of Mary (even if it was also opposed by contrary impulses); ceasing to define specific modes of devotional address, paradoxically, led the believer to follow the modalities of his own desire, and his own way, a tendency strongly marked also in the modern Confraternity of the Holy Guardian Angels[14].

[13] I.G. ZUPANOV, *Disputed Mission: Jesuit Experiments and Brahmanical Knowledge in 17th-century South India*, Oxford 1999.

[14] C. OSSOLA, *Gli angeli custodi*, Milano 2004.

3. *Theology and religion between Reformation and Counter-Reformation*

We cannot, however, stop at this first evaluation, whose ultimate convenience derives from its convergence with a common appraisal, conforming to a long-established historiographical tradition, largely inherited from the progressive ideology of the Enlightenment, of the "de-sacralization" of societies during the long Renaissance, or, according to the division found in of anglophone literature, "Early Modern History". We must ask why the history of cultic practices presents such difficulties that it alone can account for this evaluation, here not solely due to an appreciation of the historical processes involved, but because of an epistemological obstacle arising from an understanding of the real contemporaneous relations underlying the evolution of the churches and denominations.

Let us begin with one case, that of John Calvin's pamphlet published in 1543 on the subject of the cult of relics, known under the title *A Treatise on Relics*[15]. A little-known text, for reasons easily understood: Catholic historiography has been unwilling to investigate this virulent, albeit admirably refined and penetrating, attack on what is surely one of the most conspicuous cults of the Catholic Christian tradition, by reason of its double reference to the saints that it preserves and to the churches that preserve them. Protestant historiography, for its part, has not used this work as a primary text, relegating it to a position of secondary importance. Nonetheless, Calvin did write it. But if we cross the first polemical threshold—inherited from earlier pamphlets—on the proliferation of false relics, the worship of the breath of the ass, etc., and investigate it more closely, we see that this text conflates true and false relics, making of the "relic" in general, in its intimate relationship with the most venerable antiquity, the stake in a radical criticism of the pretensions of the Roman Church, which held a monopoly over this antiquity, transferring the value accorded to antiquity to a new value accorded to Christian origins, a value of which the Reformation, dusted free of all relics, would be the bearer. In doing so, Calvin actually transformed the relic into a pure object of discourse, since it was no longer a matter of separating wheat from the chaff, but of denying the

[15] P. BOUTRY - P.-A. FABRE - D. JULIA (eds), *Reliques Modernes. Cultes et usages chrétiens des corps saints entre Réformes et révolutions*, Paris 2008.

postulates of the veneration of relics. In this way, the Genevan destroys all possible space for practice.

Why is this difficulty in accounting for what one might call the "people of the cults" (rather than the "popular cults")? This question is central. It is based on the observation of a historiographical "depression" in the study of worship practices between the end of the Middle Ages and the end of its monarchic systems. How should we understand it?

Here I sketch only one hypothesis. The theological competition between the Catholic and Protestant churches in the aftermath of the Reformation had a double consequence: on the one hand, Protestant theology denied Catholic religious culture any living connection between its discourse and its practices, describing them as vestiges (or "superstitions", monuments, remains) of an extinct faith; on the other hand, Catholic theology denied Protestant theology the theoretical autonomy to justify new practices; and both theologies simultaneously presupposed for themselves a natural relationship between their *doxa* and their *praxis*. Thus, we find buried, in a period when they were also tested by other events, a whole series of religious traditions, essentially connected with material forms of mediation and intercession between individuals and the source of their hope, to which their contemporary theoretical elaborations did not give them the keys.

If we take the hypothesis of this double misunderstanding seriously, the next step is to identify the signs of vigor, resistance, adaptation, and transformation of Christian cults in the course of the long renaissances[16]. Let us place three landmarks.

[16] The meeting organized in 2006 by the French Historical Mission in Göttingen on the subject of confessionalization advanced this idea by proposing another notion, that of "confessional culture", which allows us to reintroduce religious practices into the discussion, which crossed territorial and political divisions, cornerstones of the historiographic notion of "confessionalization", see P. BÜTTGEN - C. DUHAMELLE, *Historiographies religieuses croisées, France-Allemagne (XVI-XVIIIe siècles)*, Paris 2007. It is also necessary to highlight the ongoing contributions of Dominique Julia, which have a certain continuity with those of Alphonse Dupront, on modern practices of worship, on the project—carried out on such diverse subjects as pilgrimages, relics, and shrines—to define a "religious modernity", cf. A. DUPRONT, *Genèses des Temps modernes, Rome, les Réformes et le Nouveau Monde*, Paris 2001; D. JULIA, *Réforme catholique, religion des prêtres et "foi des simples". Études d'anthropologie religieuse (xvie-xviiie siècles)*, Genève 2014; D. JULIA, *Le Voyage aux saints. Les pèlerinages dans l'Occident moderne (XVe-XVIIIe siècle)*, Paris 2016. See also, on the concept of sacredness between Reformation and Counter-Reformation,

The practice of pilgrimage has long been considered an exclusive concern of the Middle Ages: the transit of men and women to distant shrines seemed, through something of an exaggeration, to have been checked with the growth of states, with their borders, policies, and passports. But recent research has shown that modern pilgrims were not daunted by these constraints, and that the impingement posed by frontiers was but one of many obstacles, characteristic of all pilgrimages: states of emergency, of policing, and of panic[17]; it has shown that the parish framework within which long-distance pilgrimage might have been checked did not prevent the pilgrim from pushing against its boundaries, and that there was no expectation that he would not search for breaches[18]. But it is true that the spiritual literature of the seventeenth century tends to transform material pilgrimage into the fiction of a spiritual itinerary, and that it tends to do so not only as part of a certain retreat on the part of cultic practices faced by modern "civilization", but also because, for this body of literature (as, in a slightly different way, for Calvin), it serves as a way of bridging the gap between discourse and practice[19].

But it is doubtless necessary to close this rapid tour with the cult of "holy images". On the one hand, because very recent work in historiography, anthropology, and art history has succeeded in revealing the visual and ritual aspects of the cultic image[20], but also because, in late Renaissance Europe following the Reformation and the Council of Trent, there is an extraordinary eclipse in the discourses devoted to praising the creation of works of painting and of sculpture, and this habit was

J. Beyer - A. Burkardt - F. von Lieburg - M. Wingens (eds), *Confessional Sanctity*, Mayence 2004. A great deal of work remains to be done here, especially in the field of evangelizing missions, whose trans-confessional history, from America to Asia and from the first period of globalisation to decolonisation, remains to be written.

17 P. Boutry - D. Julia (eds), *Pèlerins et pèlerinages dans l'Europe moderne*, Roma 2003; P. Boutry - P.-A. Fabre - D. Julia (eds), *Rendre ses voeux. Identités pèlerines dans l'Europe moderne*, Paris 2002.

18 P. Martin, *Une Religion des livres*, Paris 2003.

19 M.-C. Gomez-Géraud, *Le crépuscule du grand voyage. Les récits des pèlerins à Jérusalem (1458-1612)*, Paris 1999.

20 H. Belting, *Likeness and Presence: A History of the Image before the Era of Art*, Chicago IL 1997; G. Didi-Huberman, *L'image ouverte*, Paris 2007; F. Cousinié, *Le Peintre chrétien. Théories de l'image religieuse dans la France du XVIIe siècle*, Paris 2000; F. Cousinié, *Images et méditation au XVIIe siècle*, Rennes 2007.

marked in two otherwise radically different types of text. First, in apologetic texts, which could praise images only by ignoring their material aspect, in order better to affirm their mediating transparency; and secondly in prescriptive texts, which, signifying under what conditions the Christian image, legitimate in principle, could remain lawful in its material realization, virtualized the image in the twofold meaning of a force (*virtue*) and of a power, or of a potential force in that power. The écrit was inscribed between images, propounding what they were, and designating what they must be, since it gave as examples images that it set up as models, but which preceded it in their creation; the text thus asserted its theoretical autonomy through this conversion of a real image into a possible image[21]. A third category of texts should furthermore be brought into the discussion, those discussing the use of the image in the Christian practice of spiritual meditation[22].

Thus we are justified in thinking of the cult of images in the European churches at the end of the sixteenth century as the most secret and intense place of articulation between theology and religion, between Reformation and Counter-Reformation.

4. *Christian faith between old and new worlds*

It would be impossible today to reflect on the western churches and their denominations in the first centuries of the modern era without looking beyond the borders of Europe, not in order to build precarious synchronies between the histories of cities, courts, artistic patronage, or systems of exploitation in Europe and Asia or in the kingdoms of Africa, but because the expansion of the West towards its western limits, on the one hand, and towards the east, on the other, deeply and directly changed the areas we have already traversed, the identity of the churches and the perceptions of the denominations. Only a paradoxical lack of knowledge of the consequences of this epoch of European supremacy for Europe itself can explain the often peripheral character of its entry onto the world-stage in the syntheses of modern history,

[21] P.-A. FABRE, *Décréter l'image? La XXVème Session du Concile de Trente dans le texte*, Paris 2013; L. SAVIUCCI INSOLERA, Lydia, *Immagine e arte sacra nel Concilio di Trento*, Roma 2016.

[22] P.-A. FABRE, *Ignace de Loyola. Le lieu de l'image*, Paris 1992.

with a few significant exceptions[23]. To conclude our presentation let us open three windows onto these metamorphoses of the Christian faith, and onto the conception of its social organization and its ritual acts.

For the first window, let us resume the course of our enquiry: the regular and secular institutions of the "Universal Catholic Church" did not cross the oceans without interference—what, indeed, is a foreign mission? An apostolate in the world? Did it bring the regular clergy closer to the secular clergy, with whom the competition would be as lively as the proximity was close? Or was the foreign mission rather a superior form of withdrawal from the world, of contemplation, of "estrangement" from the age? It would then make of those who were by vocation regular clerics, but who were yet engaged in the world, aspirants to the most withdrawn chartreuses, exiles to the limits of the world. The debate that recurs throughout the history of evangelizing missions, between the imperatives of "work" and of "study", coupled with a second tension between intellectual work and spiritual life, is testimony to this[24].

Our second window: the administration of the sacraments, which are the strict correlates of the worship rendered to God, since God recognizes his subjects by the various signs and anointings, which he gives to them. Christian literature of the sixteenth and seventeenth centuries, as demonstrated by important ongoing research, recharged in all its power the sacramental "act" as the passage from a before to an after, by way of the act, which was in some manner both necessary and self-sufficient for the accomplishment of divine recognition[25].

Our third window, opening inwards: the construction, by Western missionaries in China, of rites of reverence to Confucius and the ancestors as "civic rites" and consequently compatible with the observance of Christian rites, which relied upon the definitional criteria of these

[23] M. de Certeau, *Le lieu de l'autre*, Paris 2008; P. Prodi, *Christianisme et monde moderne*; A. Prosperi, *America e Apocalisse, e altri saggi*, Pisa - Roma 1999.

[24] A. Romano, *Rome and its Indies: A Global System of Knowledge at the End of the Sixteenth Century*, in S. Burghartz - L. Burkart - C. Göttler (eds), *Sites of Mediation: Connected Histories of Europe, 1350-1650*, Leiden 2016; A. Romano, *Impressions de Chine. L'Europe et l'englobement du monde (16e-17e siècles)*, Paris 2016.

[25] C. de Castelnau-L'Estoile - G. Pizzorusso, *I sacramenti cristiani nel nuovo mundo*, in "Mélanges de l'École française de Rome", 2008.

civic rites, particularly in their material abstraction, which cannot fail to have as a consequence—and this is undoubtedly one of the fundamental reasons for the failure of the "adoptionist" strategies in Chinese missions—a corresponding effect in the spectacular admission of the "civility" of the religious practices prescribed for European devotees by the post-reformation Catholic Church, and the threat posed by this "civility" to the religious intensity of the rite itself[26].

Or, again, in the form of a conclusion, let us examine the long delay taken by Claudio Acquaviva, General of the Society of Jesus from 1581 to 1615, in responding to the insistent demands of the Jesuits sent to the highlands of Peru, in dealing with what they called the "idolatry" of the Indians[27]. What was to be done with these cults? How should they be transformed? Did they, or did they not, contain some degree of sacredness? The Roman head of the order finally took an interest in the concerns of his subordinates dwelling at the ends of the earth only when the struggle for the defense of the cult of Catholic "holy images" had intensified in Europe, and when it had therefore become an urgent matter to demarcate the proper veneration of icons, and to distinguish this from the adoration of material things. Were not the idolaters of the Andean *altiplano* merely an imported luxury, like wood or silver or spices, to adorn the arguments of the European casuists by persuading them of the authenticity of their own cults? Or did they manage to convince the clergy of Italy, France, or Spain that the worship of things participated, at the most profound level of human experience, and within the opaque night of matter, in a necessary appeal to the forces of the spirit?

[26] D. MUNGELLO, *The Great Encounter of China and the West*, Oxford 1999; P.-A. FABRE - I. ZUPANOV, *Controversy on Rites*.

[27] J.C. ESTENSSORO, *Del paganismo a la santidad*, Lima 2005.

Distant Comparisons, Close Comparisons

Reform Movements in Russian Orthodoxy

by *Martin Tamcke*

1. *Introduction*

When liberal-minded German Protestant theologians celebrated L.N. Tolstoy (1828-1910) as a new Martin Luther towards the end of the nineteenth and beginning of the twentieth century, this rather had a telling effect on the theologians who fought for more freedom and was less of a statement on Tolstoy[1]. Although the German legal proceedings in Leipzig accusing Tolstoy of blasphemy showed superficial similarities to the actions of the Russian Church, the actual procedure was distinctly different. In Leipzig, only one plaintiff stood against the publication of Tolstoy, whereas in Russia he was the victim of Church regulations and state censorship. Tolstoy's reasons for translating the Bible were entirely different from Luther's. Tolstoy recreated the text of the Old Testament to emphasize the teachings of Jesus with a clear disregard for every aspect of historicity or miracles[2]. Soon other theologians, among them Adolf von Harnack, realized that Tolstoy was in fact promoting some approaches that essentially went against those of Luther. Harnack referred in particular to Tolstoy's ascetic ideals, which were more characteristic of Russian monks than of Lutherans in Russian clothing[3].

[1] E. HANKE, *Prophet des Unmodernen. Leo N. Tolstoi als Kulturkritiker in der deutschen Diskussion der Jahrhundertwende* (Studien und Textezur Sozialgeschichte der Literatur, 38), Tübingen 1993; M. TAMCKE, *Tolstoi, Lev Nikolajevitsch*, in *Biographisch-Bibliographisches Kirchenlexikon*, 12, 1997, pp. 304-317; M. TAMCKE, *Protestantische Theologie*, in M. GEORGE - J. HERLTH - C. MÜNCH - U. SCHMID (eds), *Tolstoj als theologischer Denker und Kirchenkritiker*, Göttingen 2014, pp. 608-619.

[2] M. TAMCKE, *Tolstojs Religion. Eine spirituelle Biographie*, Berlin 2010; M. TAMCKE, *Religija Tolstogo. Duhovnaja biografija*, Moscow 2015.

[3] A. VON HARNACK, *Das Wesen des Christentums*, Gütersloh 1999, p. 54 (here he sees Tolstoy near Gnosticism), p. 109 (here he criticizes the ascetism and escapism which characterizes Tolstoy's work), p. 112 (affirmation about Tolstoy's point of view about money and power), p. 129 (positive reception of the position in Tolstoy's ethics that

But let us not dwell on Tolstoy and the Tolstoyan movement and instead turn our attention towards the main topic: the reform movements in Russian Orthodoxy. It is the preposition 'in' that I am particularly concerned with in the title of this lecture. I am interested in the movements that originated within the Russian church, and not in the reasons that led to the excommunication of one particular member who had already left the common practice of his confession behind.

In all churches around the world, be it in Russia or elsewhere, ideas of reform and new beginnings take hold now and again. Often the objectives of these reforms point in opposite directions.

Since the baptism of Vladimir the Great, the Russian church had followed the Byzantine model of church-state harmony. The Bishop of Novgorod stipulated that orthodox Russians serve God first and their ruler second[4]. Ilarion, the first Russian metropolitan, considered Vladimir an apostle among rulers, a new Constantine, and an *isapostolos*—an equal of the apostles[5]. This Byzantine legacy of a close relationship between church and state has been a crucial issue and, to this day, gives impetus to reformers in the Russian Orthodox Church.

2. *Strigolniki*[6]

The first reform movement that challenged Russian Orthodoxy were the Strigolniki, who gained influence during the fourteenth century. Their name already gave reason for concern. It could have its origin in their ritual practice involving a particular haircut: "strici" means cutting or trimming. Protestant theologians often drew parallels between this movement and similar movements in the West. Hans-Dieter Döpmann refers to this correlation in his history of the Russian Orthodox Church:

one should not resist against evil), p. 222 (positive reception of the religious aggrandizement of the individual person in Tolstoy's work).

4 Bishop Luka Shidjata (1034-1054, 1057-1059), quotation: H.-D. DÖPMANN, *Die Russische Orthodoxe Kirche in Geschichte und Gegenwart*, Wien - Köln - Graz 1977, p. 15.

5 H.-D. DÖPMANN, *Die Russische Orthodoxe Kirche*, pp. 16-17.

6 J. PRINZ-AUS DER WIESCHE, *Die Russisch-Orthodoxe Kirche im mittelalterlichen Pskov*, 2004; B.A. RYBAKOV, *Strigolniki. Russkie Gumanisty XIV Stoletiia*, Moscow 1993; H.-D DÖPMANN, *Die Russische Orthodoxe Kirche*, pp. 48-51.

"although there is no proof of actual contact, there is a development of critical ideas in the Russian context that are reminiscent of the pre-reformation church critique in the West which revolved around the question whether the well-being of the church can still be guaranteed"[7].

One might be skeptical about the attempt to find parallels between the history of others and one's own, but the fact remains that reform movements in Russia had a lasting effect on the relationship between the church and the state.

Research into the Strigolniki is greatly hindered by the fact that the church destroyed their writings, which leaves only their opponent's distorted teachings as a source of information. However, certain central elements of their life and teaching can be identified: they opposed simony, as they considered the selling of church offices as unworthy and incompatible with their belief. Citing Paul the Apostle, they supported a general priesthood of laymen. They condemned the notion that churches are properties and disregarded the clergy. Instead, they subscribed to a Christianity without worship or idolization, based on the gospels alone. One branch of the Strigolniki opposed monasticism and they rejected parts of the bible although their opponents recognized that they showed an "unusually extensive knowledge of the bible" (Doepmann). Among their followers were many deacons. Their movement was particularly attractive to citizens, tradesmen, scholars, and merchants. The heads of the church dealt with them harshly. The deacons Karp and Nikita, alongside fellow members of the group, were thrown off a bridge in Novgorod and drowned in 1375. They are the only members of the movement who are mentioned by name. The heads of the church tried to limit the damage and made sure their own sinecures were secure. They advised the public not to interfere with church property. Metropolitans had such properties officially declared inviolable. The question that remains is whether it is appropriate to still refer to this movement as a "heretical movement" in western Protestant research, even though this term seems understandable in the context of Russian orthodox literature.

[7] H.-D. DÖPMANN, *Die Russische Orthodoxe Kirche*, p. 50, original citation: "Und so zeichnete sich, auch wenn sich unmittelbare Berührungspunkte schwer nachweisen lassen, eine von den russischen Verhältnissen geprägte, der vorreformatorischen Kirchenkritik des Westen sähnliche Entwicklun gab, bei der es um die Frage ging, ob das Heil in der damaligen Kirche noch gewährleistet ist".

3. *The "non-possessors" and the "Judaizers"*[8]

An entirely different case presents itself in the conflict between the monastic reform movement and the Russian Orthodox Church after the latter was granted autocephaly. Joseph of Volokolamsk promoted a strict coenobitic monasticism that included absolute obedience to the rules and close cooperation with the state. In stark contrast to this, Nil Sorsky pleaded for a complete rejuvenation from within, particularly under the Transvolga-Elders (or startsy). The movement he represented was keen on fully establishing the hesychastic practice of the "Prayer of the Heart" in the Russian Church. The monks believed a retreat into solitude to be paramount. One subject that was the cause of heated arguments between the two movements was the question of property. Joseph considered property ownership by monasteries indispensable when it came to convincing respectable men of a life in the monastery; equally, he deemed their property necessary to ensure they could provide social services. Joseph's opponent Nil Sorsky and his student Wassian advocated the ideal of absolute poverty. According to Wassian only cathedrals should be allowed to own property, provided that these properties be run by lay administrators. However, in 1503 the Holy Synod declared the church's properties inviolable, ensuring the validity of the church's claims to a considerable number of estates and lands donated to them over the previous centuries. Wassian regarded these documents as a contradiction of the gospel, of the apostles, and of the life of the fathers. Maksim Grek (Maximus the Greek), an influential advocate of Nil Sorsky's and Wassian's position, gave evidence of a Russian change in practice that could no longer be considered a continuation of established rules but constituted a new practice outside the orthodox norm. The Russian translation of the 7th Ecumenical Council in 787 concerning the permission to own farmland and vine-

[8] G. Schulz, *Die theologiegeschichtliche Stellung des Starzen Artemij innerhalb der Bewegung der Besitzlosen im Rußland der ersten Hälfte des 16. Jahrhunderts*, Erlangen 1980; J. Korpela, *Feodorit (Theodorit) Kol'skii. Missionary and Princely Agent*, in L. Steindorff (ed.), *Religion und Integration im Moskauer Russland. Konzepte und Praktiken, Potentiale und Grenzen im 14.-17. Jahrhundert*, Wiesbaden 2010; F. von Lilienfeld, *Nil Sorskij und seine Schriften*, Berlin 1963; H.-D. Döpmann, *Der Einfluss der Kirche auf die moskowitische Staatsidee. Staats- und Gesellschaftsdenken bei Josif Volockij, Nil Sorskij und Vassian Patrikeev*, Berlin 1967; S. Wollgast, *Russische häretische Bewegungen des 15. und 16. Jahrhunderts*, in "Deutsche Zeitschrift für Philosophie", 14, 1966, pp. 978-994.

yards extends the permission of ownership to entire villages and their Christian inhabitants. The discrepancy between the Byzantine original and the Russian interpretation of this rule was not acceptable to the reformers. In the end, the startsy were brutally removed by the state after Wassian and Maksim Grek had already been convicted.

Thus Joseph triumphed over the startsy, who only regained a foothold in the nineteenth century, and he unreservedly fought the heretics of Novgorod, who in the literature are often improperly termed "Judaizers". They emerged in the fifteenth century among the lower clergy and educated laymen in Novgorod. Their demands were similar to those of the Strigolniki in their critique of the simony. In their fight against advocates of ecclesiastical landownership they explicitly refer to the gospels. In the Judiazers' attempts to reform the church, Döpmann detects "a reference to western reformatory movements in the overall Russian context"[9]. The new-found interest in a classical humanistic education and the rational understanding of doctrines, liturgy, and sacraments posed a challenge to the church at a time when the standard of education was particularly low. The church reacted by having Archbishop Gennady create a complete Slavic codex of the bible. Joseph of Volokolamsk, however, felt provoked by the Judaizers' attacks on the Russian Orthodox Church. He repeatedly wrote tracts to counteract them and to vindicate the church's teachings. A collection of his writing forms the basis of Russia's first attempt at explaining the foundation of its belief. It is worth mentioning that the Judaizers utilized classical literature as well as Jewish and Arabic scholarly writing in their arguments. This gave a strong impulse to Russian scholars and enhanced their level of theological reflection. The fight against Judaizers, once again, divided the movement surrounding Nil Sorsky from the one that followed Joseph of Volokolamsk. While Nil referred to the salvation prayer for the Judaizers and trusted in God's judgment, Joseph insisted that the group be persecuted by the state. He envisaged an equivalent of the Catholic Inquisition. Joseph's ideas took hold and developed into religious worship of the Tsar as the sole orthodox leader who could steer the church to safety just as Noah did his ark (Filofey of Pskov). The idea of Moscow as the third Rome was born. This also meant that the state could now legitimately interfere in matters of religious belief

[9] H.-D. DÖPMANN, *Die Russische Orthodoxe Kirche*, p. 66; original citation: "trotz aller russischen Spezifik einen Bezug zu abendländischen reformatorischen Strömungen".

and life style, and impose its measures by force. The elder Artemy was installed by the Tsar as the abbot of the Trinity Lavra of St Sergius for six months in 1551. Thus, one of the spiritual centers of the Russian Orthodox Church was controlled by a supporter of the non-possessors. He was the last memorable representative of the movement that opposed the rigid demands of the Josephites. The fight against him began after he left his office and retreated into solitude. He was suspected of heresy, banished to the Solovezky Monastery in the White Sea in 1553/54, and fled to Lithuania whence he defended the orthodox faith. Artemy became one of the main representatives of the non-possessor movement. In his declarations and demands he refers to the bible and replaces Nil Sorsky's plea for the "Prayer of the Heart" with a call for an ascetic life in the form of spiritual love. He describes his life in Christ as a practice of the Cross. But despite his resistance and the astonishing effect it had, the alliance between the church and the state instigated by Joseph (among others) was extremely successful in fending off adversaries. In the end, the writings of Joseph of Volokolamsk were accorded normative validity at the Synod of 1553/54 and silenced the voice of the non-possessors for the time being.

4. *The Old Believers*[10]

The conflict surrounding the reform led by the Patriarch Nikon bears similarities to previous reform movements, but at the same time it sparked new tensions on a different level. The close relationship between state and church that Joseph of Volokolamsk had established to fight his theological and religious adversaries was destroyed with regard to the church leadership. In the early seventeenth century, a group called the Circle of the Zealots of Piety (*Kreis der Eifererfür die Frömmigkeit*) aimed at reviving the practice of preaching. The members of this group were commonly known as "Friends of God". Among their members

[10] P. HAUPTMANN: *Rußlands Altgläubige*, Göttingen 2005; P. HAUPTMANN, *Altrussischer Glaube. Der Kampf des Protopopen Avvakum gegen die Kirchenreformen des 17. Jahrhunderts*, Göttingen 1963; S.A. SENKOWSKY, *Russia's Old Believers*, München 1970; F.I. MELNIKOW, *Kurze Geschichte der altorthodoxen (altritualistischen) Kirche*, Barnaul 1999 (an important source from the point of view of a former persecutor of the Old Believers who later came to see in them the positive representation of Russian religiosity).

was priest Avvakum of Nizhny Novgorod. In the beginning they were also close to the abbot of the Novodevichy Convent who would later become Patriarch Nikon. Nikon became abbot of the monastery under Tsar Alexej in 1646. The upcoming reforms concerned not only the practice of preaching; they aimed at standardizing liturgical forms that had diversified due to various outside influences. One prominent aspect of the reform, led by the patriarch himself, was the issue of religious rites. The patriarch of Jerusalem, Paisios (1645-1660), who was in Moscow in 1649, pointed emphatically at a Russian practice that he considered a renunciation of orthodoxy, namely that, since the synod of 1551, the Russians crossed themselves with two instead of three fingers. For Paisos, this was an unacceptable alteration. This left two opposing reformatory approaches irreconcilable. One sought to bring the Russian practice of piety to the standard of the Greeks, the other adhered to the Russian reforms. The arguments on both sides lacked historical accuracy, but nonetheless reinforced irreconcilable differences. The supporters of Russian reforms argued that they had learned the two-finger crossing from Andrew the Apostle, while the Greeks had taken their three-finger crossing from the Germans. With the Tsar's consent, patriarch Nikon set out to harmonize the Russian customs with the Greek traditions. This entailed the use of three and not two fingers to trace the cross. Nikon is claimed to have said that despite being Russian, his faith and church service were Greek. He fought to reconcile the Russian practice with the faith of the entire orthodoxy. He banished his adversaries from the reformist Zealots of Piety, disregarding a warning by the patriarch of Constantinople to not take overly drastic steps and to be understanding of the unique Russian forms.

Alongside these internal ecclesiastic conflicts over reforms, a power struggle between the patriarch and the Tsar ensued. The Tsar changed traditional laws that were drawn up by laymen which drastically limited the church's influence. He forbade monasteries to accept donated lands and estates. Nikon's ideas pointed to a very different direction: he wanted to establish ecclesiastical hegemony and called himself "great ruler". The disagreement became irreconcilable and in 1658 Nikon resigned his position. Nikon, the Zealots of Piety, and their rites were spared at first, but in the synod of 1667 Nikon was officially convicted by his church and relieved of his position. The leaders of the Zealots of Piety, among them Avvakum, had already been convicted by the synod the previous year. Despite Nikon's conviction his reforms remained effective and the rites and practices of the Zealots of Piety were deemed improper alterations. The fact that the synod of 1555 had come to a different conclusion was explained by lack of education. The Zealots of Piety as a whole were left to the authority of the state, which used brute force on its opponents. The Solovezky Monastery put up resistance against the Tsar and his troops, thus remaining a place of refuge for the members of the Zealots of Piety until the monastery was conquered through betrayal in 1676. At this point, the leader of the Zealots of Piety, Avvakum, saw Tsar Alexej and the deposed patriarch Nikon as the Antichrist from Revelations; for him they corresponded to the two horns of the apocalyptic beast in Revelations 13:11. The clear separation of the ruler and Nikon led new parts of society to join the Zealots. The Cossack and peasant uprising under Stepan Razin in the region between the Don, the Volga, and the Urals had numerous Zealot-supporters who no longer felt obliged to follow their ruler after Avvakum had identified the Tsar as the Antichrist. During these fights the two-finger crossing served as a symbol of orthodoxy among the Zealots, who regarded the three-finger crossing as a sign of the Antichrist. This subtle difference became the epitome of the conflict. The Old Believers held on to old Russian customs and traditions: they were forbidden to shave their beards, or to wear modern clothing or make-up, and they refrained from non-religious art and from the theater. The fight against theater productions in particular was aimed at the Lutheran priest in Moscow who staged plays at the Tsar's court. The Old Believers had no bishops who could ordain a priest, thus they organized themselves without priests. Services were held by laymen who also performed baptisms, while the other sacraments were not practiced. The iconostases disappeared from these priestless churches. Avvakum's account of his life in exile introduced the genre of autobiography into Russian literature. Previously only hagiographies had existed, and although Avvakum was influenced by these narratives he created his own individual account of his life. His letters and his book of interpretations have been preserved. Avvakum's writings are considered outstanding and illustrate the exceptional literary abilities of a man who was ruthlessly persecuted by the church. His suffering ended on April 14, 1682, when he was burned at the stake. The following centuries were characterized by persecution and marginalization. The Old Believers were not allowed to appear in court and swear an oath against a member of the church. In 1722 the Old Believer's baptism was declared a punishable offence. It is conspicuous that the literature of those who opposed the Old Believers shows a complete ignorance of their views and opinions. Eventually, one branch of the Old Believers attempted a reconciliation with the established church. Young men had to pay a fee if they wanted to avoid performing their military duty. They still considered the Tsar the Antichrist and refused to pay their taxes. Their leader was burned with his followers after he was surrounded by soldiers in 1743. His orientation, however, had already spread throughout the movement. When the Old Believers opposed the claim of Catherine I to the throne, refusing to accept a female sovereign, the edict of toleration (1762) was revoked and Catherine had 20,000 Old Believers deported to Siberia in 1764. The metropolitan of Moscow attempted to convince the Old Believers to join the church, allowing them to keep their rites as long as they recognized the authority of the episcopate of the Russian Orthodox Church. This attempt led only very few Old Believers to return to the established church. This group of former Old Believers exists to this day. They are called the Old-Ritualists or Edinoverie ("those of the same faith") and they emphasize that they share a common faith with the established church. Their center is the Church of Presentation of Mary on the Moscow cemetery, since 1800 with the permission of the Tsar.

The fight surrounding the Old Believers shows opposing reform plans. There is the attempt to bring the Russian Orthodoxy closer to the entire orthodoxy, which would probably have granted them a leading position among the orthodox. This reform was one that was instigated by the head of the church and faced strong opposition by the people. The Old Believers supported a reform that was based on the inclusion of Russian culture into Christian practice and could be understood as an independent Russian orthodox culture. They were not backward thinking or conservative in their ideas, and it is rather symptomatic that their attempt to reform the practice of preaching was an early ambition. In some ways, the Old Believers are an example of reform movements that felt the state and church working against them. And, of course, the redrafted laws passed by the Tsar to limit the church's power signified a reform that would later lead to the abolition of the patriarchy. The reform of the Tsar was, again, a reform from above. Only the movement of the Old Believers was an actual movement.

And they took up demands from previous reforms when they opposed ecclesiastical landownership, enabled the community to act on their own without a priest, limited the number of sacraments, and—in addition to ethical and purist demands—promoted a consciously biblical path in life.

5. *Reform ideas, but no reform movements*[11]

The reforms of the nineteenth century were considerably influenced by religious reforms in Western Europe, since Napoleon's adventures in Russia had brought Russian Orthodoxy into contact with European religious movements. Additionally, they were faced with growing secularizing tendencies. Among the influential thinkers was the Protestant Heinrich Jung-Stilling, to whom Tsar Alexander I was particularly close. Minister for Religious Affairs and Public Education Prince Golitsyn, adopted the idea of an enligthened Christianity. A Christian fear of God was supposedly the basis of true enlightenment. A Russian bible society was founded to translate the bible not into Church Slavonic but into Russian. The non-orthodox Johannes Evangelista Gossner was also part of the board of directors. However, ultra-conservative circles managed to stop the reforms. The ministry was abolished, and in 1876 so was the bible society. The publication of the Russian bible was stopped and the translators returned to Church Slavonic: it was not until 1876 that the first Russian translation of the bible was published. Although these reforms counteracted the secularization under Peter the Great and Catherine the Great, which had led to a considerable number of monastery expropriations of the monasteries, they were still instigated by the Tsar and they never reached so many people as to be considered a reform movement. Protestant impulses had a lasting effect on the development of a diverse range of Russian free churches, traditionally called "sects" in Russia, which were opposed to military service and had their individual customs. For example, they might allow drinking milk during Lent. These reform movements were, again, not aiming at reinventing the Russian Orthodox Church. It should be mentioned that since the eighteenth century, the seminaries used Protestant textbooks to teach dogmatics which required the Russian students to learn Latin.

[11] Extensive commentary in M. TAMCKE (ed.), *Filaret von Moskau. Ausführlicher christlicher Katechismus der rechtgläubigen, katholischen, morgenländischen Kirche*, Berlin 2015.

The reception of the theology and philosophy taught at the University of Göttingen in particular led to alienation and disagreement. Pushkin's comment on the "spirit of Göttingen" (*Göttinger Geist*) is based on the Russian reception of scholarship in Göttingen. But these Protestant impulses did not spark serious reform movements. Similarly, efforts of individual progressive and liberal circles to re-establish the patriarchy and free the church from state intervention could not be considered widespread movements, which explains why they did not face opposition from within the church. Although the ecclesiastical council of 1917/18 took up some of the demands of the aforementioned reform movements—one of which was the re-establishment of the patriarchy—these efforts were merely following political developments by then[12]. The separation of church and state that was introduced by the state was not appreciated by the council mentally still very much rooted in the old system of tsardom. The new state rules signified the beginning of an era that saw the church as an institution under pressure. This left little room for reforms from within the church, when soon after, the church had to fight for its survival in Russia.

6. *Conclusion*

Reform movements are a part of the ecclesiastical history of Russian Orthodoxy, just as they are part of the history of all other churches. However, unlike reform movements found in the Syrian Orthodox Church of the Saint Thomas Christians in India, the reforms in Russia remained unsuccessful at first. In India, the reform led to a split within the church that resulted in the formation of one of the most agile churches in India: the Mar Thoma Syrian Church, which outwardly upholds orthodox traditions but is Protestant within. The Old Believers who only faltered in the face of a revoked edict of toleration in the early twentieth century could no longer be overcome by state force, nor could the Russian Orthodox Church convince them to return, because they were too polemic and lacked the willingness to integrate their demands. The phenomenon of the Edinoverie (Old-Ritualists) illustrates the impossibility of re-integrating Old Believers into the

[12] G. SCHULZ, *Das Landeskonzil der orthodoxen Kirche in Rußland 1917/18. Ein unbekanntes Reformpotential*, Göttingen 1995.

church after almost one and a half centuries, expecting there to be no consequences for the entire church. It would not be advisable to draw hasty conclusions when it comes to parallels between reform movements within the Russian Orthodox Church, as it is often done in research on Eastern Christianity. Proof of connections between Russian reform movements and western Reformation cannot be established. The Russian reform movements should be analyzed in the context of Russian culture and its counterpart in the Byzantine tendency of piety that helped in the resistance against strict ecclesiastical organization in unison with the state. Reform movements could only count on the state in a few instances and only for a limited amount of time, because the state and the church were in themselves part of the secular construct the reformers set out to challenge.

Jewish Culture in Early Modernity

The Global Turn

by *Roni Weinstein*

I.

A messianic movement, certainly one of the most significant ones in Jewish history, swept the Jewish world along the second half of the seventeenth century[1]. It encompassed communities and individuals in Morocco, the Iberian Diaspora and ex-conversos from Spain and Portugal, Italy, northern Europe—mainly Amsterdam, the eastern part of the Mediterranean basin (the Sham area of the Holy Land and Syria of today), the Ottoman Empire in Europe and Anatolia, Iraq, and as far east as Kurdistan and Yemen—in short, the entire Jewish world. It mobilized the support and enthusiasm of simple people, men and women[2], as well as members of the rabbinic and political elite. When the entire move failed, the supposed messiah converting to Islam and followed by a substantial portion of his close followers, a major effort took place, of silencing and erasing any scrap of memory of the Sabbatean movement, the major events, "heretical" compositions, and of its major figures. In spite of this effort of *damnatio memoriae*, the Sabbatean figures and tracts continually inspired Jewish religious life along the coming centuries. As a historian of religion with a leaning to

[1] M.D. GOLDISH, *The Sabbatean Prophets*, Cambridge MA 2004; J. BARNAI, *Sabbateanism – Social Perspectives* (Heb.), Jerusalem 2000; Y. LIEBES, *Studies in Jewish Myth and Jewish Messianism*, New York 1993; C. ŞIŞMAN, *The Burden of Silence: Sabbatai Sevi and the Evolution of the Ottoman-Turkish Dönmes*, New York 2015; A. ELQAYAM, *The Mystery of Faith in the Writings of Nathan of Gaza* (Heb.), Ph.D. thesis Jerusalem, 1993. See also the classical G. SCHOLEM, *Sabbatai Sevi: The Mystical Messiah, 1626-1676*, Princeton NJ 1975.

[2] The participation of women in Sabbatean prophetic enthusiasm was a completely exceptional trait in Jewish context and was justly emphasized by historians; see A. RAPOPORT-ALBERT, *Women and the Messianic Heresy of Sabbatai Zevi: 1666-1816*, Oxford 2011.

social history, I find this messianic wave all the more fascinating as it marked all the significant and problematic spots of Jewish culture during early modernity: changes in power and legitimacy of political control, gender issues, crisis in rabbinic authority, social discipline over the young and women, the new and important role of Kabbalah in shaping Jewish society, shaping body and sexuality (a "Jewish civilizing process", to borrow a term from Norbert Elias)[3], the role of young people, the need for religious reform not only among the elite but reaching out to popular parts of Jewish population, the crucial role of seventeenth century Ottoman Empire, a new definition of messianic tradition and the role of the Messiah, the contribution of ex-conversos from Iberia in transferring basic concepts from the Catholic world into the Jewish milieu, ritual innovation, the importance of religious enthusiasm and of inspired and charismatic figures. As much as the quantity of recent research on the figure of Sabbetai Zvi and his messianic movement increases, it still appears to me as an unresolved enigma, as to its motivations and its later deep impact. Yet it supplies an irreplaceable map of all the significant trails of Jewish modernity. The messianic enthusiasm at its height reached the entire known Jewish Diaspora of that period. In other words, it provides an invaluable indication of the global turn, and the deep infrastructure common to various Jewish traditions, in spite of geographical and deep cultural variations. It marks the passage from locality to unity. In the mid seventeenth-century, the global dimension (or global turn?) was well present in the Jewish culture.

The global perspective seems highly adequate to understanding Jewish Diaspora, where the sense of dispersion and exile play such an imminent role, especially during late antiquity and medieval periods[4]. Exile entailed interaction with political, cultural, and religious aspects of several civilizations among which the Jewish minority lived and adapted, as well as easily crossing religious borders between Islam and Christianity. It is surprising all the more that such a perspective was hardly followed in modern research. Even now when the domain of "global

[3] R. Weinstein, *The Rise of the Body in Early Modern Jewish Society: The Italian Case Study*, in M. Diemling - G. Veltri (eds), *The Jewish Body. Corporeality, Society, and Identity in the Renaissance and Early Modern Period*, Boston MA - Leiden 2008, pp. 15-55; R. Weinstein, *Corpo e sessualità ebraici nella prima età moderna*, in "Contemporanea. Rivista di storia dell'800 e del '900", 14, 2011, 4, pp. 711-716.

[4] Y.F. Baer, *Galut*, Lanham MD 1988.

history"—or its parallel terms, "connected history" or "world history"—turned significant in historical research of the last twenty years, or so, its application in "Jewish studies" is rather limited in Israel, Europe, or the United States[5].

Yet as much as the global view is relevant for understanding medieval Jewish culture and history[6], it became even more urgent and pertinent in regard to early modernity[7]. The period is characterized by massive immigration, either voluntary or forced: the total expulsion of Iberian Jews from Spain (1492) and Portugal (1497); their spread in several north European locations and mostly in the Ottoman Empire; the progressive expulsion of Jews from German cities and the shift to east and central Europe; the enforced city quarters for Jews in Italy ("ghetto" is the known term) leading to the evacuation of smaller communities. Jews started to arrive in new places, well beyond the horizon of past settlements. And so during the sixteenth and seventeenth centuries, Jews and Conversos (Jewish converts to Catholicism) were found all along the Mediterranean basin in Catholic and Muslim traditions, in England[8], northern Europe, the "New World" in either North and South America, as well as south-east Asia—following the Spanish, Portuguese, and Dutch expansion, and the expanding Ottoman Empire. In short, a wide and unprecedented geographical vista.

Geographical extension was not enough in itself to produce a new cultural phase. It provided the material arena for the dominant agent of change in contemporary Jewish history: the Iberian Diaspora[9]. Even

[5] I would mention some exceptional works adopting the global perspective, such as R. WEINSTEIN, *Jewish Thought in Early Modern Period: Major Themes and Currents* (Heb.), in Y. MALI (ed.), *History of Ideas*, vol. 2: *The Early Modern Period*, forthcoming; D.B. RUDERMAN, *Early Modern Jewry: A New Cultural History*, Princeton NJ 2010; D. SOROTZKIN, *Orthodoxy and Modern Disciplination: The Production of The Jewish Tradition in Europe on Modern Times* (Heb.), Tel-Aviv 2011.

[6] B.-Z. DINUR, *Israel BaGolah* (Heb.), Tel-Aviv 1958, "Introduction", pp. V-LVI.

[7] J. BELICH - J. DARWIN - M. FRENZ - C. WICKHAM (eds), *The Prospect of Global History*, Oxford 2016; S. CONRAD, *What is Global History*, Princeton NJ 2016.

[8] D.S. KATZ, *The Jews in the History of England, 1485-1850*, Oxford 1996.

[9] On the long and impressive Jewish-Spanish heritage, see R. WEINSTEIN, *Kabbalah and Jewish Modernity*, London 2016, chap. 7: "Catholic Traditions in Safed Kabbalah. Sephardim and Conversos", pp. 142-165; H. BEINART (ed.), *Moreshet Sepharad: The Sephardi Legacy*, 2 vols., Jerusalem 1992.

after the massive killings of Jews during the 1391 riots, and again prior to their final expulsion, alongside the massive forced conversions, the Iberian Jews remained the leading demographic component of the Jewish people at the dawn of the sixteenth century[10]. The Iberian Jews were well aware to their superiority in respect to other contemporary Jewish communities, and they stated it proudly and openly:

> "It is well known that the Sephardi people and the sages in the [Ottoman] Empire are more numerous in comparison to other communities, the land is theirs, and they are its glory and brilliance ... and the minority who previously occupied the land [the *Romanioti* Jews] need to follow the Sephardi traditions of Torah ... Glory to the creator, that the Sephardi are the clear majority in this land, both in quantity and in quality, and the *Romanioti* Jews are like two cresses at the top of the tree and two out of hundred"[11].

It entailed a sense of uniqueness and glory of their *nación* or *nação*, intended to be maintained distinct and separated from other Jewish groups. So much so that members of the Sephardi origins were not allowed to marry others from either Ashkenazi (German) or Italian origins, and excluded non-Iberians from any political position within the community[12]. Wherever they immigrated they imposed their cultural and political heritage upon indigenous communities. Their might relied on a distinct cultural past and their economic activity; unlike most Jewish communities in medieval Europe, which favored local traditions and a local perspective, Jewish-Spanish politics relied mainly on supra-communal powers, managed by a small number of elite families. This Jewish aristocracy was affiliated to Spanish kings, both politically and economically, and adopted a distinct lifestyle and religious attitude. Its political horizon and contacts were wider than anything known in other late medieval Jewish communities, so that Jews (and later con-

[10] On changes in early modern Jewish demography, see D.Ph. BELL, *Jews in the Early Modern World*, Lanham MD 2008, pp. 35-57.

[11] R. Moses of Arokis, cited by J.R. HACKER, *The Sphardim in the Ottoman Empire in the Sixteenth Century*, in H. BEINART (ed.), *Moreshet Sepharad*, vol. 2, pp. 109-133, the citation appears on p. 115.

[12] C. GALASSO, *"Nasce questa aversione da un punto di religione per una parte e di superbia per l'altra". Ebrei italiani e sefarditi a Livorno tra Sei e Settecento*, in "Annali dell'Istituto storico italo-germanico in Trento", 29, 2003, pp. 119-153; Y. KAPLAN, *An Alternative Path to Modernity: The Sephardi Diaspora in Western Europe*, Leiden 2000; M. BODIAN, *Hebrews of the Portuguese Nation: Conversos and Community in Early Modern Amsterdam*, Bloomington IN 1999.

versos) in Spain were deeply involved in court politics, diplomacy, and even espionage. This worldly acquaintance and self-assurance is even reflected in the famous biblical commentaries of R. Isaac Abravanel (1437-1508), scion of a renowned Abravanel court-family in Spain, where he provides theoretical commentaries on political regimes in general[13]. These court families at times combined financial and political power with cultural and religious knowledge, enabling them to exert control over the rabbinic milieu. The Spanish communities had their own legal and mystical traditions as well that had evolved over the centuries of local *convivencia* in Spain. Their sense of superiority relied on a clear economic basis. Through the early modern period, the Iberian Jews wove an international commercial network—extending from Spain and Portugal, the Italian cities, Amsterdam, the Ottoman Empire—and relied heavily on family ties as well as on the cooperation of both Jews and conversos[14]. With their innate sense of superiority and natural honor, cultural distinction of a separate *nación*, aided by wide political experience and connections as well as an international commercial network transcending the lines of Islam and Christianity, the Jews of former Spain and Portugal offered a connecting link to the entire Jewish collective, a link of global dimensions and perspective.

The early modern immigrations in Europe contributed to what Paul Hazard characterized as a "crisis of European consciousness" among the intellectual elite[15]. The case was not much different in the Jewish

[13] Z. BAR EITAN, *Abravanel's World of Torah: A Structured Interpretation*, Park City UT 2014.

[14] F. TRIVELLATO, *Il commercio interculturale; la diaspora sefaradita. Livorno e i traffici globali in età moderna*, Roma 2016; F. TRIVELLATO, *The Familiarity of Strangers: The Sephardic Diaspora, Livorno, and Cross-cultural Trade in the Early Modern Period*, New Haven CT 2009; F. TRIVELLATO, *Marriage, Commercial Capital, and Business Agency: Transregional Sephardic (and Armenian) Families in the Seventeenth and Eighteenth-Century Mediterranean,* in C.H. JOHNSON - D.W. SABEAN - S. TEUSCHER - F. TRIVELLATO (eds), *Transnational and Transregional Families in Europe and Beyond*, New York - Oxford 2011, pp. 107-130; J.I. ISRAEL, *Diasporas within a Diaspora: Jews, Crypto-Jews, and the World of Maritime Empires (1540-1740)*, Leiden 2002. The interface between politics and economic power of the Sephardi Diaspora was well illustrated in the case of the commercial boycott organized on the city of Ancona, after the burning at the stake of former conversos, accused as Judaizers (*Judaizantes*); see M. SAPERSTEIN, *Martyrs, Merchants and Rabbis: Jewish Communal Conflict as Reflected in the Responsa on the Boycott of Ancona*, in "Jewish Social Studies", 43, 1981, 3-4, pp. 215-228.

[15] P. HAZARD, *La crise de la conscience europeene 1680-1715*, Paris 1985.

context. Immigration led to encounters between various Jewish ethnic traditions and local heritages and necessitated a restructuring of Jewish culture beyond the local level. This was an especially acute issue in relation to religious heritage, which was claimed to originate from divine revelation and shared by all Jewish believers. Larger syntheses were needed once the Sephardi, Italian, and Ashkenazi traditions of law, mysticism, and rituals came into unprecedentedly closer contact[16].

In the Jewish *orbis terrarum* several cities housed Jews from various local-ethnic traditions: Italian cities north of Rome, Amsterdam with its particular Iberian dominance, Edirne and Istanbul in the Ottoman Empire, or Prague in central Europe. These were all places resonating with economic and religious activities. But more exciting and pertinent to this discussion was a small and peripheral city, in the eastern part of the Mediterranean basin, the city of Safed in the Galilee. Safed harbored Jews from all ethnic and local traditions: northern Africa (Morocco, the Maghreb), Iberian conversos, Italy, Provence, Ashkenaz (Germany), eastern Europe—mainly Poland, Sephardi people, Romanioti (ex-Byzantine communities), and Musta'arab (Jews living with Muslims in the Holy Land for centuries). In no other city did such an encounter take place.

Due to economic and religious incentives for immigration, Safed turned out to be the leading Jewish city in the Holy Land during the sixteenth century, overshadowing the city of Jerusalem. Even so it remained a peripheral place in respect to Damascus, Cairo, Edirne, Salonika, and certainly Istanbul, where Jewish communities prospered. Yet its place in Jewish cultural and religious history was parallel to the role of Paris in medieval theology in the Catholic context, or the city of Baghdad during the Abbasid Caliphate for Medieval Islam. The religious innovations and reforms issued in that city during less than half a century inspired the Jewish world for centuries, and it continues to do so. The leading intellectuals and rabbis of the Jewish world lived in this rather small city. Their number reached a critical mass, enough to produce a

[16] I am currently working on the various traditions reflected in the codes of law composed by R. Joseph Karo, as a response to the encounter of various legal-Halakhic traditions as well as European and Ottoman legality. For an important discussion on the encounter of Jewish religious traditions and their deep impact on Kabbalistic writing, see M. IDEL, *Italy in Safed, Safed in Italy: Toward an Interactive History of Sixteenth-Century Kabbalah*, in G. VELTRI - D.B. RUDERMAN (eds), *Cultural Intermediaries in Early Modern Italy*, Philadelphia PA 2004, pp. 239-269.

religious Renaissance in almost every aspect of Jewish culture: legality, Talmudic studies, judicial processes, mysticism, religious poetry, biblical hermeneutics, confraternal activity, and new religious practices and rituals[17]. Seen in retrospective Safed became a tumultuous "laboratory of modernity"[18], elaborating the social, theological, and ritual elements that would later evolve as Jewish orthodoxy.

Managing such an internationally composed city demanded resolving two issues: the first one, of more practical character, according to what legal, political, and cultural criteria would the city be managed? This would concern the internal matters as well as the encounter with Ottoman authorities. The second one, would there be a dominant tradition prevailing over the others, of no less precedence and prestige?

The first challenge was tied not only to the presence of various Jewish ethnic traditions but also to the arrival of their distinguished representative members. Once they encountered each other in this relatively small urban space, they could not avoid the question of what the unifying factors of Jewish tradition were, beyond the immense variety of ethnic and local heritage. Put differently, what were the lines of cohesiveness and collective identity, beyond which lay danger, heresy, and social exclusion? These concerns were not much different form those occupying the rising modern states in Europe during the confessionalization process[19], or for that matter in the Ottoman Empire, during these years of constituting a wide empire[20] . Safed was the key scene of "Jewish

[17] An extensive description of this process see R. WEINSTEIN, *Kabbalah and Jewish Modernity*, *passim*.

[18] On the term "laboratory of modernity" in the Jewish-Italian case, see R. WEINSTEIN, *De la Halakha à l'anthropologie*, in *L'Italie, laboratoire de la modernité* [Special issue], "Les cahiers du judaisme", 22, 2007, pp. 103-113.

[19] W. REINHARD - H. SCHILLING (eds), *Die katholische Konfessionalisierung*, Münster 1995; H. SCHILLING (ed.), *Kirchenzucht und Sozialdisziplinierung im frühneuzeitlichen Europa* (Zeitschrift für historische Forschung, Beiheft 16), Berlin 1994.

[20] T. KRSTIĆ, *Illuminated by the Light of Islam and the Glory of the Ottoman Sultanate: Self-Narratives of Conversion to Islam in the Age of Confessionalization*, in "Comparative Studies in History and Society", 51, 2009, 1, pp. 35-63; T. KRSTIĆ, *Contested Conversions to Islam: Narratives of Religious Change in the Early Modern Ottoman Empire*, Stanford CA 2011; D. TERZIOĞLU, *How to Conceptualize Ottoman Sunnitization. A Historiographical Discussion*, in "Turcica", 94, 2012-2013, pp. 301-338; D. TERZIOĞLU, *Where 'İlm-I hal' Meets Catechism: Islamic Manuals of Religious Instruction in the*

confessionalization", whose ramifications in major Jewish religion I will later present.

The second issue was clearly resolved in favor of Iberian tradition, as should be clear by now. Safed was not an isolated city, but part of the wide and international Sephardi network. What happened in Amsterdam, Livorno, Edirne, or Istanbul (large communities of Jewish-Iberian immigrants) directly affected the small Galilean city[21]. It affected the cultural and religious creativity of local intellectuals, and their intentions of reforming the Jewish religion in concrete historical settings. From the early sixteenth century on, the Sephardi immigrants reached demographic prominence, and their dominance was expressed by their leading rabbis. They imposed their will either in synagogue liturgy or in dividing charity money coming from abroad for the support of the local poor. Their prominence was mainly expressed in the study of religious law (*halakhah* in Hebrew) in advanced religious schools (*yeshivah*, or the Spanish version *Midrash*) and its enforcement in local courts of law. No wonder, as the leading religious scholars and innovators originated from Iberian origins. Most of the mystical innovation revolved around the exegesis of the *Book of Splendor* (*Sefer HaZohar*), considered a component of Spanish heritage in the sixteenth century.

The models serving the Sephardi people in regulating the major issues in the city of Safed derived from three components in their particular heritage. The first one, by nature, was the internal Jewish heritage carried by Spanish and Portuguese refugees to their new destinations. It enabled a *translatio scientiae* of culture formed in southern parts of Spain since the early Middle Ages, where the three monotheistic religions had a deep cultural interaction—in spite of political and military violence—until the final phase of the Reconquista[22]. Unlike the fragmentary community life in Ashkenaz, the Spanish communities obeyed the centralistic rule of several elite families, and their religious issues

Ottoman Empire in the Age of Confessionalization, in "Past and Present", 220, 2013, pp. 79-114; G. BURAK, *Faith, Law and Empire in the 'Ottoman Age of Confessionalization' (Fifteenth-Seventeenth Centuries): The Case of 'Renewal of Faith'*, in "Mediterranean Historical Review", 28, 2013, 1, pp. 1-23.

21 Y. KAPLAN, *The Sephardim in North-Western Europe and the New World*, in H. BEINART (ed.), *Moreshet Sepharad*, vol. 2, pp. 240-287.

22 Y. BAER, *A History of the Jews in Christian Spain*, Philadelphia PA 1978; E. ASHTOR, *The Jews of Moslem Spain*, Philadelphia PA 1978.

were often managed by a "Court Rabbi" (*Rab de la corte* in Spanish), backed by royal authority and the community leaders' support. Under such conditions the Sephardi culture evolved with its own particular traits either in the legal-Halakhic domain[23] or in mystical creativity—such *Sefer HaZohar*, composed in the thirteenth century by R. Moses de Leon (in Spain), and later served as fundamental inspiration and canonical text for early modern Kabbalistic renaissance[24]. The second component was the Spanish-Catholic culture with which the local Jews were well acquainted after centuries of cohabilitation. It the pervaded the Jewish culture of the common people and not only of the erudite elite, interested in refined literature, science, and philosophy. Add to this the intriguing component of Jews converted to Catholicism through the centuries forming a mediating bridge between both religions. Prior to the general expulsion, some of these converts were highly immersed in monastic orders and local universities and contributed to reform Catholic religious life and erudition[25]. Those of them, quite numerous during the early modern period, who "turned back to their forefathers' religion" carried this Catholic baggage to the Jewish milieu mostly unnoticed. Spanish communities formed in northern Europe—Holland and partially Germany—increased the Sephardi exposure to Protestant religiosity. Yet most important was the third component, the Ottoman Empire, where most Iberian refugees arrived and settled. As other non-Muslim minorities, such as the Greeks and Armenians, the Jews constructed a linguistic, commercial, and cultural bridge between the Muslim Ottomans and Europe. It was a period not only of military and political expansion of the Ottoman Empire, but also of absorption of large numbers of converts to Islam from Christian populations along the Mediterranean basin, and of experimentation in legal thought and practice, military practice, administration, finance and land reform,

[23] On R. Isaac Canpanton (1360-1463) "The Luminary of Castile", whose disciples held a central place in major Talmudic and legal schools after the expulsion, see A. DAVID, *On the Biography of R. Isaac Kanpanton. A Mojor Sephardi Scholar of the Fifteenth Century* (Heb.), in "Kiryat Sefer", 51, 1976, pp. 324-326. R. CANPANTON renovated a scholastic-like method of Talmudic studies, see D. BOYARIN, *Moslem, Christian, and Jewish Cultural Interaction in Sefardic Talmudic Interpretation*, in "Review of Rabbinic Judaism", 5, 2002, 1, pp. 1-33.

[24] B. HUSS, *The Zohar: Reception and Impact*, Portland OR 2016.

[25] S. PASTORE, *Un'eresia spagnola. Spiritualità conversa, alumbradismo e inquisizione (1449-1559)*, Firenze 2004.

in cooperation with Sufi orders, refined architecture, and life-style[26]. The contact with the particular Ottoman mode of Sunni Islam revived dormant Muslim elements of Sephardi culture surviving from their life in Andalusia.

The double expulsion from Iberia was often accompanied by atrocious acts of violence and death, experienced along the departure. What could ease the trauma to some extent was the fact that the passage from Spain and Portugal eastward to the Ottoman area was not that dramatic. In both contexts, they lived within leading empires of international power, during their best years of military and financial expansion, as well as religious renovation. In the European case, the rising and centralized states increased cooperation with and control over religious institutions. The confessionalism thesis indicated the similar processes taking place in both Catholic and Protestant states, in spite of marked theological contestation. The result was an increasing disciplining and control over individuals and families, over their bodies and minds, exerted by heads of family, communities, and state institutions[27]. As time passed, the lines between the normative and correct, on the one hand, and the deviant and heretic, on the other, were firmly established and enforced. These processes are well known in the European context, but hardly referred to in European historiography regarding Ottoman culture. Recent research revealed a deepening interest shown by Sultanic authorities in the faith and beliefs of their Muslim subjects. The need to deepen the Islamic practices and beliefs in recently Islamized populations and the theological-political tensions with the Safavid kingdom during the late sixteenth century led to what Derin Terzioglu termed "a sunnitization process of the Ottoman Empire". Guiding literature was composed

[26] G. VEINSTEIN (ed.), *Soliman le Magnifique et son temps*, Paris 1992; G. NECIPOĞLU, *A Kanun for the State, A Canon for the Arts. Conceptualizing the Classical Synthesis of Ottoman Art and Architecture*, in G. VEINSTEIN (ed.), *Soliman le Magnifique*, pp. 195-216. See the general synthesis in D. GOFFMAN, *The Ottoman Empire and Early Modern Europe*, Cambridge 2002. On the high rate of Christian converts to Islam in the Ottoman context, see T. KRSTIĆ, *Contested Conversions to Islam, passim*.

[27] P. PRODI (ed.), *Disciplina dell'anima, disciplina del corpo e disciplina della società tra medioevo ed età moderna* (Annali dell'Istituto storico italo-germanico in Trento. Quaderni, 40), Bologna 1994; A. PROSPERI, *Tribunali della coscienza. Inquisitori, confessori, missionari*, Torino 1996; C. PANCERA, *Educazione dei costumi e insegnamento delle virtù*, in G.-P. BRIZZI (ed.), *Il catechismo e la grammatica*, vol. 1: *Istruzione e controllo sociale nell'area emiliana e romagnola nel '700*, Bologna 1985, pp. 287-346.

with the Sultan's encouragement and patronage, initially guiding the new Muslims to correct beliefs and ritual behavior. Towards the close of the century, these tracts—composed in Turkish rather than Arabic as customary in religious matters of belief—addressed educated city dwellers. Some of the popular books were composed by adherents of religious-reform oriented persons (the Kadizadeli movement), aiming to advance stricter adherence to religious law (*Shari'a* in Arabic). The attendance at Friday prayers was enforced by "lay" authorities in big cities, as part of adherence to the community. Even legal authorities were involved in drawing the lines between the orthodox belief and "heresy". Legal-opinion literature (*fetva* in Turkish) in this regard showed an increasing between external signs—verbal expressions, physical acts—and internal beliefs. The range of "heresy" increased and included further cases that necessitated "a renewal of faith" (*Tecdid-i Iman* in Turkish), and returning to the pale of the Muslim community, or even re-validating marriage. The list of forbidden acts against the faith was updated and expanded to include new acts, considered harmful to correct religious life, and loyalty to the Ottoman regime.

Globalization, so it seems from recent historical works on various parts of the globe, was certainly one of the fundamental features of the early modern period. Exchanges and contact between various zones increase significantly during the long period stretching from the fifteenth to the eighteenth centuries. Concretely it manifested itself in the increasing trade of precious metals and the use of bullion and money, the exchange of animals and plants, the spread of diseases, social unrest leading to popular rebellions, the transfer of military techniques, the rise of centralized political units, and certainly commercial networks[28]. Some insightful works of recent historians were devoted to the religious changes, and their contribution to the formation of larger ethnic and political units[29]. If modernization in the Jewish case-study evolved on a supra-local stage, then a global perspective is essential. The new

[28] C.H. PARKER, *Global Interaction in Early Modern Age*, Cambridge 2010; J. FLETCHER, *Integrative History: Parallels and Interconnections in the Early Modern Period, 1500-1800*, in "Journal of Turkish Studies", 9, 1985, pp. 37-57.

[29] S. SUBRAHMANYAM, *Connected Histories: Notes towards a Reconfiguration of Early Modern Eurasia*, in "Modern Asian Studies", 31, 1997, 3, pp. 735-762; C. ŞIŞMAN, *Transcending Diaspora: Studies on Sabbateanism and Dönmes*, Istanbul 2016, chap. 2: "Global Crisis, Puritanism in the Early Modern World", pp. 23-55.

and wide geographical dispersion, with which I started my discussion, exposed the various Jewish settlements to religious currents of reform and to apocalyptic trends on the rise in Europe, the Ottoman Empire, the Moghuls, the Safavid in Iran, and even further east in Japan and Korea. The usefulness of this perspective could be demonstrated in regard to the rise of a new source of religious authority, considered as of the sixteenth century as legitimate as the classical rabbinic ones: the "Jewish Saint"[30]. It could be interpreted in three seemingly different aspects: first, as continuing the tradition of charismatic and inspired Jewish figures of late antiquity and the Middle Ages[31]; to continue, it certainly relates to the cult of saints in Catholic Europe and especially Spain and Italy (one of the important immigration destinations of Sephardi refugees), and its increasing role during the counter-reformation[32]. Early modern Kabbalah has a multi-layered response to the Catholic attraction, including the role of saints. Thirdly, the Sufi saints or the "Friends of God" (*Awliya* in Arabic) have grown in number in Islam from its early history, and were later mobilized by the Ottoman sultans in converting indigenous populations and in enforcing the Sunnitization of the empire[33]. The rise of Jewish saints happened in an Ottoman-ruled city (namely Safed), where several meeting-places of Sufis (*Zawiya* in Arabic, *Tekke* in Turkish) were active. Their music and confraternal meeting around a Sufi guide were adopted by Jewish Kabbalists. Without getting into details none of these perspectives suffices by itself and their separation is a matter of analytic convenience. Only by considering the various elements and their global horizon can we fully understand the deep contribution of the saintly figure and its innovative role in Jewish religious tradition of this period.

[30] R. WEINSTEIN, *Kabbalah and Jewish Modernity*, chap. 2: "The Rise of the Jewish Saint", pp. 44-66.

[31] A.J. HESCHEL, *The Holy Spirit in the Middle Ages until Maimonides's Time* (Heb.), in S. LIEBERMAN (ed.), *Alexander Marx Jubilee Volume*, vol. 1, New York 1950, pp. 175-208.

[32] *Storia della santità nel cristianesimo occidentale* (Sacro/Santo, 9), Roma 2005; A. KLEINBERG, *Prophets in Their Own Country. Living Saints and the Making of Sainthood in the Later Middle Ages*, Chicago IL - London 1997.

[33] A.T. KARAMUSTAFA, *God's Unruly Friends: Dervish Groups in the Islamic Later Middle Period, 1200-1550*, Salt Lake City UT 1994, pp. 65-84.

Alongside massive migrations within the Jewish world ("massive" in respect to previous periods), the increase of cultural homogeneity was preconditioned by international networks of communication and commerce, as well dense family ties[34]. The wide horizons of activity could be used to intensify old traditions of Jewish culture and to structure it according to new needs. Such was the case of the use of the credit and banking system of Ottoman Jews (especially those of Istanbul) for transferring large sums of charity money to the poor people in the Holy Land. The charity activity was traditional, yet the financial institutions in use and the mode of charity allocation bore a global charcter. Several processes in early modern Jewish culture echo contemporary globalization and the widening contact between Christian Europe, the Sunni Ottoman Empire, and the "New World".

II.

1. *The impact of print*

By the end of the sixteenth century, the entire Jewish canon was put into print: the Bible and biblical commentaries, the Talmud, major legal codices, prayer books, *The Book of Splendor* and other mystical tracts, ethical and guidance literature. This had major implications as it defined past heritage in terms of a closed set of well-defined textual content, and—at the sametime—it progressively weakened the oral element of cultural transmission[35]. As in Europe, printing entailed a consensus regarding the "correct" phrasing of the printed text and the ensuing exclusion of a variety of alternative variations, often related to local traditions of various Jewish areas. These texts, significantly less accessible to the general public before their print, turned into potentially "open texts", beyond the direct control of rabbinical authorities. The book market followed economic rules and supplied the demands of the growing numbers of readers. This showed in the printing of books addressed to non-erudite readers (those excluded from the rabbinic elite), or addressed special sections of the Jewish population, such as

[34] F. Trivellato, *Marriage, Commercial Capital, and Business Agency.*

[35] A. Raz-Krakotzkin, *The Censor, the Editor, and the Text: The Catholic Church and the Shaping of the Jewish Canon in the Sixteenth Century*, Philadelphia PA 2007.

women in general or young men. In eastern Europe the books composed in vernacular—Yiddish and not the "Rabbinic" Hebrew—offered an alternative perspective on religion[36].

2. *Control of consciousness and ideas*

As I mentioned previously, the intensified encounters among Jewish immigrants carrying diversified and opposing cultural heritages, forced the rabbinic elite to confront the issue of correct positions, or those to be shared by the entire Jewish collective. This challenge became all the more urgent with the increasing impact of the print revolution. The battle, as in the previous century of Italian Humanism, seemingly regarded textual correctness, but that was never the main point. It revolved around the setting of limits between the correct and trusted positions and mistaken and dangerous ideas. As in the European case, the printing of Hebrew books was accompanied by mechanisms of exterior (Catholic Inquisition) and interior censorship[37]. A printed book in Hebrew had to be preceded by the approval (*Haskamah* in Hebrew) of its contents by at least three rabbinic authorities (a habit which continues in the Jewish-orthodox tradition to this day). This was both a safety precaution in view of the Catholic Church during the counter-reformation period and a mechanism of internal consensus and rejection of unwarranted ideas. It was followed by occasional lists of "recommended" books, accompanied by either explicit or implied exclusions of other books, even those composed by important rabbinic figures. These lists mainly concerned mystical or theological issues (see the next section). This period witnessed the rise of a number of famous rabbinic figures who dedicated their life-long efforts to persecuting "heretical" ideas and persons[38].

[36] C. Turniansky - E. Timm - C. Rosenzweig, *Yiddish in Italia: Yiddish Manuscripts and Printed Books from the 15th to the 17th Century*, Milano 2003; J. Baumgarten, *Introduction to Old Yiddish Literature*, Oxford 2005; Z. Gries, *The Book in the Jewish World, 1700-1900*, Oxford 2007. On the Ottoman context, see J. Hacker, *Authors, Readers and Printers of Sixteenth-Century Hebrew Books in the Ottoman Empire*, in P.K. Pearlstein (ed.), *Perspectives on the Hebraic Book; The Myron M. Weinstein Memorial Lectures at the Library of Congress*, Washington D.C. 2012, pp. 17-63.

[37] A. Raz-Krakotzkin, *The Censor, the Editor, and the Text, passim.*

[38] E. Carlebach, *The Pursuit of Heresy: Rabbi Moses Hagiz and the Sabbatian Controversies*, New York 1990.

3. *The emergence of Jewish theology*

Classical Jewish tradition is well reflected in Talmudic literature. The Talmud in its both Jerusalemite and Babylonian versions contains countless juridical and moral discussions. In practically all cases there is no ending and conclusive position following the long discussions. This is highly indicative of classical and medieval Jewish culture, in which no limits were set between correct and incorrect positions. On practically every fundamental religious issue there are several optional positions and no consensus reached. In other words, the theological aspect is practically non-existent. The attempt during the Middle Ages of a towering figure such as Moses Maimonides to offer a theological structure or interpretation (of clear Aristotelian coloring) of Jewish tradition was harshly criticized and never expanded beyond a restricted philosophical elite. All this changed at Safed in the writings of early modern Kabbalists, especially those of R. Moses Cordovero and the books attributed to R. Isaac Luria by his disciples. The Lurianic *magnum opus* is a vast and exhilarating journey through divinity and relates to every significant aspect of theological thinking in a tight and structured way. From then on, theology was part of the Jewish canon and provided a basis for every ritual practice, as much as it generated immense ritual innovation[39]. Not by coincidence R. Luria was a member of the rabbinic elite and composed a list of "recommended books" in the mystical domain for his disciples, aiming to condemn unaccepted tracts to oblivion. Early modern Kabbalah shifted the gravity center of Jewish tradition from ritual practice to the thoughts and conscious intentions (*Kavanot* is the Kabbalistic neologism) while occupied in action. They introduced an informal police force and court of law to inspect people, their moral behavior, and their consciousness. Another innovation was the use of confession in a manner very similar to the European pattern[40]. Due to the prestige of Safed Kabbalists, and especially to the sanctified figure of R. Luria, such practices started to spread in the entire Jewish world.

[39] R. WEINSTEIN, *Kabbalah and Jewish Modernity*, chap. 1: "A New God. Theological Innovation", pp. 11-43.

[40] *Ibid.*, chap. 6: "Sin and Repentance. Jewish Confession", pp. 123-141.

4. *A unified code of Law*

The growing number of political units in early modern Europe aimed at higher juridical unification. For this reason, various rulers initiated the collection of local customs producing more general and homogenous codes of law: in Portugal (*Ordenações afonsinas*, 1467; *Ordenações manuelinas*, printed, 1512), and later in France (collections of *Coutumiers* in shortened and harmonized versions, the project of Antoine Loisel), in Imperial Germany (the *Carolina* of Charles V), and in Spain (*Leyes de Montalvo*, the edict of Philip II regarding the criminal law). Padoa-Schioppa persuasively describes how the state moved from putting limits on local/particular laws to a phase of producing the law and presenting itself as the source of law and legality, from which all other legal traditions of corporate bodies were derived. Regarding the vertical axis, it took the place of God as a source of justice and legitimized positive law on relativist and lay/national ground serving community and political utility[41]. Once the ethos on the devine origins of human law was denied, another motivation took its place, which is the consolidation of centralized states in Europe. One of the crucial components of the states' political machine—alongside a standing bureaucracy, increased armies and enforced order by police, new school systems, and finally a taxing apparatus—was the production of laws and accumulation of existing local laws in broader codes of law as a sign of power and sovereignty. The law, under such perspective, was to be derived from local "national" and ethnic traditions and not from the Roman heritage; The contemporary needs (the legal terminology was *lex odierna*) and ethnic heritage were considered as sources or roots of modern law[42]. Therefore the use of national languages rather that Latin was to serve in the production of laws. The need for clarity and lucidity seemed more urgent in order to make law present and active in increasing segments of the population. It increased the critical tone in regard to massive books of theoretical writing in favor of legal

[41] P.A. PADOA-SCHIOPPA, *Storia del diritto in Europa. Dal medioevo all'età contemporanea*, Milano 2007, pp. 356-366.

[42] I. BIROCCHI, *Alla ricerca dell'ordine. Fonti e cultura giuridica nell'età moderna*, Milano 2002, *passim*, exposes the increasing interest in teaching contemporary law and "national law". In such a context, Canon law lost much of its prestige and role to the utilitarian tools of *ius comune* as a basis for state-law.

compendia and shortened versions of law-books[43]. A similar process of codification under state patronage took place in the Ottoman context especially during the sixteenth and seventeenth centuries[44]. The Sultan Suleiman ("The Legislator" as he was known, *Kanuni* in Turkish) advocated the promotion of the *Hanafi* school of religious law (*Shari'a* in Arabic) at the expense of others, thus deviating from a long tradition of legal pluralism within the Muslim tradition. At the head of the legal establishment he nominated a state-official (*Şeyhűlislam* in Turkish) in charge of composing several codes of law (*Kanuname* in Turkish) valid in the entire empire. This series of codes was intended to be applied in courts of law, serve in the practical work of judges, and have precedence over the local traditions. The rule of great ruler such as Suleiman, who had apocalyptic aspirations, was presented as legitimized by concepts of justice and an efficient legal system no less than by military and political power[45]. Precisely at this time, in Safed, R. Joseph Karo (1488-1575) finished composing his double codes of Law *House of Joseph* and its abridged version *Set-up Table* (*Beit Yosef* and *Shulchan 'Aruch* in Hebrew)[46]. Several Jewish codes of law preceded this project, but Karo's work was unique in the way it combined legal-Halakhic traditions from both Sephardi and Ashkenazi traditions and benefited from the advantages of print in order to spread it to major Jewish diasporas. The intention behind this project was implicitly stated in R. Karo's introduction to Beit Yosef, which is to provide a sole legal reference to the entire Jewish people. The inspiration from both European and Ottoman legal history of this period are unmistakable; Unification of Jewish law was a fundamental issue in making Jewish

[43] On early modern critique of over-writing in legal field, see A.M. Botelho Hespanha, *Cultura giuridica, libri dei giuristi e techniche tipografiche*, in M.A. Visceglia (ed.), *Le radici storiche dell'Europa. L'età moderna*, Roma 2007, pp. 39-68; I. Birocchi, *Alla ricerca dell'ordine*, pp. 159-165.

[44] G. Burak, *The Second Formation of Islamic Law: The Hanafī School in the Early Modern Ottoman Empire*, New York 2015; S. Buzov, *The Lawgiver and his Lawmaker: The Role of Legal Discourse in the Change of Ottoman Legal Culture*, Ph.D. thesis Chicago, 2005.

[45] C.H. Fleischer, *The Lawgiver as Messiah: The Making of the Imperial Image in the Reign of Süleymân*, in G. Veinstein (ed.), *Soliman le Magnifique*, pp. 159-177.

[46] R. Weinstein, *Research of Jewish Law (Halakahah) between Yeshivah and Academy. The Case-Study of Rabbi Joseph Karo* (Heb.), in R. Felday - G. Hertz (eds), *Migrating Knowledge: Selected Articles*, forthcoming.

legality relevant to contemporary circumstances. This book was hailed mostly with enthusiasm by both rabbinic and erudite authorities, and it went on to become a dominant reference in the Jewish legal system.

5. *Messianism and religious reform*

Messianic and apocalyptic visions are too often identified with the monotheistic traditions of Judaism and Christianity. Yet recent research pertaining to new global perspectives has indicated apocalyptic fermentation in various parts of the globe: early modern Europe: in both Catholic and Protestant contexts; the Ottoman Empire: especially during the period of Sultan Suleiman "The Legistlator"; the Safavid kingdom: during the reign of Shah Isma'il, Moghul India, and Orthodox Christianity[47]. Apocalyptic visions originated in political settings and suited the intentions of great military and political leaders (such as the Spanish kings in relation to colonial expansion or Sultan Suleiman as part of extending the Ottoman rule to almost the entire Arab world). Such figures orchestrated and controlled religious reform, either in religious institutions, mystical traditions, or rituals practices. Messianism was not confined to marginal groups of "heretics" or disruptors of political order. In many cases it originated from the hard core of political leadership and served its long-term plans.

The wish for religious reform was stated explicitly by major figures active in the early modern city of Safed[48]. They initiated a major change in Jewish culture by turning the Jewish mystical heritage (*Kabbalah*, literary tradition handed over along the generations) from a highly secretive and esoteric lore confined to a restrained elite into public discourse. The mechanisms of change were the ethical literature of Kabbalistic coloring, religious confraternities, hagiographical literature (again practically unprecedented in Jewish context) around the figure R. Isaac Luria, and new ritual practices. The new Kabbalistic revival in early modern Safed was clearly motivated by an intention to reform every aspect of Jewish religion, including the figure of the Messiah.

47 See the articles by Subrahmanyam, Fleischer, Goldish, and Şişman, mentioned above.

48 R. WEINSTEIN, *Kabbalah and Jewish Modernity*, chap. 6: "Sin and Repentance. Jewish Confession", pp. 123-141.

Some of these Kabbalists—such as R. Joseph Karo or R. Isaac Luria—hinted that they were intended by some divine plan to undertake this role, while others—such as the ex-converso Solomon Molcho—were probably considered as such by their enthusiastic adherents. Yet in all cases, interest in the messianic figures was not derived from the roles they were supposed to play according to classical rabbinic tradition—i.e., leading the Jewish people back to the Holy Land and erecting the holy temple as a symbol of salvation—but from the fact that they were to enhance and lead a process of spiritual revival, religious reform, and the concurrent revelation of divine secrets of the *Torah* (a metonym for Jewish heritage). The dissemination of such concepts in the entire Jewish world prepared the ground for the eruption of the Sabbatean movement in the later seventeenth century.

6. *The battle against heresy*

The "confessionalization" of Europe and the Ottoman Empire and its impact was mentioned previously. The printing of the Jewish canon during the sixteenth century marking the written law (*halakhah* in Hebrew) as the backbone of Jewish culture and its codification by R. Joseph Karo, the suggestion of a structured and elaborated theology—have all contributed to the formation of a structured tradition with much clearer lines of identity. Under such new conditions the lines between the tolerated and the endangering became not only clearer, but more important to protect. Theology, in the Jewish case study as well, could only be suggested if it could be enforced upon the believers by some monitoring of police institutions (such as the Inquisition in the Catholic case, or religious officials in the Ottoman case). Heresy and the battles to be waged against it were practically unknown in Jewish history—except for short and sporadic cases in the Middle Ages, in regard to philosophical polemics around the writings of Maimonides. All of a sudden they became an important issue. Kabbalists were occupied with the issue of correct mystical positions and the dominance of their own tracts. Internal Jewish censorship was activated to prevent the publication of unwarranted positions. Of more importance are certain rabbinic figures known as great persecutors of "heretical" ideas and dangerous persons, mostly crypto-Sabbateans[49]. In this battle

[49] E. Carlebach, *The Pursuit of Heresy.*

they did not spare even major figures of the rabbinic milieu. A vast polemical literature was created in the Sephardi Diaspora to combat the mistaken and dangerous ideas of ex-conversos, who continued to adhere to Catholic views on the Jewish tradition[50]. The terms used in this polemical and confessional battle are directly borrowed from the Catholic repertory.

III.

The sixteenth century witnessed an encompassing passage, taking place in several places of the Jewish Diaspora, from localism and its sanctification (be it in synagogue prayers, family patterns, or community traditions) to managing Jewish life under larger geographical-cultural zones on a supra-local level. It happened in Italy when Jews were forced to move to ghettos in several major cities and abandon smaller communities[51]. Ottoman communities in the European part of the Empire accepted the authority of the Istanbul community, which benefitted from its connections with the Sultanic court[52]. The Ashkenazi Jews in Germany, accustomed to adhere to local community and family traditions for centuries, started to share a position of general heritage common to all speakers of the same native-language, i.e., Yiddish[53]. The Book of religious customs published by Isaac Tirna referred not to a specific Jewish community or family but to the "entire area of Germany, as well as Poland and Bohemia". The shift to trans-localism is even more marked in the Polish case. The recurrent expulsions of Jews from

[50] Y. KAPLAN, *Foi et skepticism dans la diaspora des nouveaux-chrétiens des débuts de l'Europe moderne*, in *La Diaspora des Nouveaux-Chrétiens*, Lisboa - Paris 2004, pp. 21-40; Y. KAPLAN, *The Intelectual Ferment in the Spanish-Portuguese Community of Seventeenth Century Asmterdam*, in H. BEINART (ed.), *Moreshet Sephardad*, vol. 1, pp. 288-314; D.M. SWETSCHINSKI, *Reluctant Cosmopolitans. The Portuguese Jews of Seventeenth-Century Amsterdam*, London - Portland 2000.

[51] R. WEINSTEIN, *The Jewish Ghetto in Relation to Urban Quarters in Italian Cities during the Early Modern Time – Similarity and Differences* (Heb.), in "Zemanim. A Historical Quarterly", 67, Summer 1999, pp. 12-21.

[52] Y. BEN-NAEH, *Jews in the Realm of the Sultans: Ottoman Jewish Society in the Seventeenth Century*, Tübingen 2008.

[53] J.M. DAVIS, *The Reception of the Shulhan 'Arukh and the Formation of Ashkenazic Jewish Identity*, in "AJS Review", 26, 2002, 2, pp. 251-276.

German cities during the late Middle Ages enticed the refugees to move eastward to central and eastern Europe. Polish Jewry witnessed an impressive demographical rise and in the late seventeenth century turned out to be the major Jewish Diaspora and a leading cultural and religious focus. The basis for communal and cultural activity was not the local community but the Polish kingdom as a unified religious and political entity[54]. The community no longer encompassed a restricted number of families and was no longer considered "a sacred institution" (*Kehila Kedoshah* in Hebrew), but contained a large number of Jewish inhabitants. It adopted political patterns of the Christian-Polish city, in respect to treatment of social deviance and criminality or the organization of professional guilds. The codification of Jewish law by R. Joseph Karo allocated a dominant place to Sephardi tradition. As a counter-reaction, Polish rabbis asserted the validity and potency of general Polish-Ashkenazi religious traditions and norms, thus strengthening the distinct identity of the Ashkenazi world as a global entity.

The intensification of supra-local identities of diverse Jewish ethnic collectives (the Hebrew term is *'Edot*) enabled them to survive until the present time. But, dialectically, it enabled the advancement of international and global mechanisms, linking the entire Jewish collective in its response to contemporary history. The parameters of change, mentioned thus far, indicate of "a search for a center", as Elisheva Carlebach felicitously termed it[55]. In a period where politics, wars, economy and trade, as well as cultural and scientific innovations were all managed by larger units—states or empires—the only way to maintain the Jewish culture relevant was to adopt a similar perspective. Since the dispersed Jewish minority lacked any of the material and human resources owned by the majority societies of Islam and Christendom, the strategy undertaken was the creation of a "virtual" or imagined center[56]. Religion was the focus and fundamental arena to give vent to these needs. It led to the creation of the concept of legal unity for the entire Jewish people—the double legal codes of R. Joseph Karo. Theology marked the lines

[54] E. REINER, *"No Jew should learn anything but the Talmud alone": A Dispute over Books and Forbidden Books in 16th Century Ashkenaz* (Heb.), in R. REINER et al. (eds), *Ta Shma. Studies in Judaica in Memory of Israel M. TA-Shma*, Alon Shvut 2011, vol. 2, pp. 705-746.

[55] E. CARLEBACH, *The Pursuit of Heresy*, pp. 1-6.

[56] E. HOBSBAUM - T. RANGER (eds), *The Invention of Tradition*, Cambridge 1995.

between the adherents to such positions and those threatening stability, hence to be persecuted. The international market of book trade and the printing of canonical literature provided a common basis of discussion among the elite, functioning henceforward as an international "republic of scholars". The drive behind these changes was the need for religious reform, occupation with individual consciousness, and making religious experience a significant element in daily life. Centuries would pass until this grand vision could materialize, but it slowly infiltrated to extending parts of the Jewish population.

The early modern Jewish tradition is an interesting case study for global history, as it lacked basic factors of enforcement. It does raise some doubts as to the extent that the big stories of military campaigns, international commerce, and geographical discoveries need to be supplemented by more silent occurrences, such as religious transformations, and their ensuing impact on education, family life, body construction—in short, back to the local perspective.

Renewal and Reform in Sunni Islam

by *Gudrun Krämer*

In the late nineteenth century, Muslim intellectuals such as the noted scholar-cum-activist Jamal al-Din al-Afghani (1838/9-97) referred to the Protestant Reformation, and to Martin Luther more particularly, as a model for the kind of reform needed for Muslims to regain the vigor and unity they had possessed at the time of the prophet Muhammad and the first generations of Muslims, in the seventh century CE, and at the same time fully to enter into modernity. In the twentieth century, outside observers equally called for an Islamic Reformation under the leadership of a Muslim Luther[1]. The call has to be taken with more than the proverbial pinch of salt: what is meant is not the repetition of a process that over the course of several centuries and after much conflict, bloodshed, and war, led from the Reformation to the Enlightenment and thence to liberal modernity. Muslims had to address issues that differed profoundly from the ones faced by Luther and the Protestant and Catholic reformers in the early modern era, and they have to do so now. What Muslim reformers and outside observers alike envision when they speak of an Islamic Reformation today is a critical re-reading of the normative sources of socio-religious thought and practice, one that will free Muslims from the dead load of the past, restore Muslim creativity, revitalize the community, end intra-communal strife, and enable inter-communal coexistence. Peace, openness, and cross-cultural understanding were not the immediate outcomes of the Protestant Reformation. Quite the contrary. They represent the hopes and expectations of the twenty-first century.

[1] For an influential contribution, see D. EICKELMAN, *Inside the Islamic Reformation*, in "Wilson Quarterly", 22, 1998, 1, pp. 80-89. See also A.A. AN-NA'IM, *Toward an Islamic Reformation. Civil Liberties, Human Rights, and International Law*, Syracuse NY 1990; A. FILALI-ANSARY, *Réformer l'islam? Une introduction aux débats contemporains*, Paris 2003; M. BROWERS - C. KURZMAN (eds), *An Islamic Reformation?*, Lanham MD 2004; for al-Afghani as the Muslim Luther, see e.g., A. HOURANI, *Arabic Thought in the Liberal Age, 1798-1939*, London 1962.

There is in fact little evidence that the Protestant Reformation with its wide repercussions on culture, politics, and society in Western and Central Europe had an impact on the Muslim world in its own time[2]. It is also true that the Muslim world did not experience a reformation of its own in either the early modern or the modern period. There still exists a grand tradition of Islamic reform, renewal, and revival that goes well beyond Muslim encounters with Europe in the early modern and the modern era. In Arabic, the relevant endeavors are called *islah*, which in its most literal sense means to make something just, right, and proper (*salih*), or alternatively, renewal (*tajdid*) or revival (*ihya'*). All three suggest the retrieval of a state of soundness and vitality once attained but somehow lost or impaired. By the same token, they suggest a perspective that looks back, to an original state of perfection, or near-perfection, rather than looking forward, towards a better future. Re-form envisaged as revival and restoration can involve subtle and even not so subtle change. The question is whether change and innovation are openly addressed or possibly embraced, or whether, on the contrary, they are passed over in silence or denied. In the Muslim world as well as elsewhere, modified approaches to change and innovation mark a major difference between reform in the pre-modern and the modern age.

For the sake of brevity, my remarks will focus on renewal and reform in the Sunni Arab Middle East, disregarding important developments in Shi'i Islam and the non-Arab Muslim world at large. Even within this circumscribed field, the scope is wide, comprising highly diverse attempts at reforming the individual, community, society, nation, or even humanity as a whole[3]. Theoretically, these attempts could include ascetic and mystical articulations of faith and piety, which—in their different

[2] I am referring here to the religious and cultural spheres rather than the political one, for the political divisions created or fueled by the Reformation also affected relations between Christian and Muslim powers in the wider Mediterranean and the Indian Ocean; for greater detail, see my monograph *Der Vordere Orient und Nordafrika ab 1500* (Neue Fischer Weltgeschichte, 9), Frankfurt a.M. 2016. For a stimulating study of the global situation, see H. SCHILLING, *1517. Weltgeschichte eines Jahres*, München 2017.

[3] I cannot do justice here to the relevant scholarship in Arabic and Western European languages. In a seminal article, Ahmad Dallal has illustrated the diversity of aims, beliefs, and strategies of religious scholars of the eighteenth century who were all described as religious reformers by contemporaries and later observers: *The Origins and Objectives of Islamic Revivalist Thought, 1750-1850*, in "Journal of the American Oriental Society", 113, 1993, 3, pp. 341-359.

ways—equally seek to form the individual and—at least indirectly—to re-form the community. Interestingly, neither is usually categorized as religious reform, a term largely reserved for intentional change of individual religious thought and practice as well as the socio-political order, suggesting a connection between religion on the one hand and politics on the other. Sufism, which is commonly translated as mysticism, but is in fact more diverse, was for many centuries one of the most influential expressions of Muslim piety, culture, and social organization, if not the most important one. The link between Sufism and religious reform is widely acknowledged, especially for the eighteenth, nineteenth, and early twentieth centuries. Yet like mysticism in general, Sufism is usually not subsumed under Islamic reform and will not be treated as such here.

Reform presupposes an object, something that needs to be set right and remade in the light of a model that is either located in the past or in the future. This is also true of Islam. If it is common to speak of a renewal and reform of Islam, it is not Islam as faith and doctrine that reformers seek to reform: according to the Qur'an, Islam is the perfect religion, which cannot be refashioned, updated, or improved. It is Muslims that are in need of correction regarding their beliefs and perhaps even more so, their practices. Like other reformist ventures, Islamic reform is usually framed as a response to, and critique of, processes of social, cultural, and political change that are deemed contrary to, or dangerous to, religion and the community of believers. Again as in other traditions, Muslim reformers usually address concrete phenomena that they consider aberrations if not abominations, ranging from social customs to devotional rites to theological issues. Among the former, the list includes the consumption of alcohol and drugs, as well as various sexual practices; prostitution; black magic; and possibly even dance, music, coffee, and tobacco. Among the theological concerns broadly understood, it comprises the veneration of saints and visits to their tombs if these visits entail belief in the saints' power of intercession; the 'exaggerated' veneration of humans particularly if this involves some degree of idolization or deification; and 'esoteric' beliefs and rituals especially if they include magic and the claim to supernatural powers more generally. In the pre-modern period, these beliefs and practices were commonly described as heresy. In the modern period, they mostly figure as superstition. Reform could also assume a political tinge by addressing iniquity, oppression, and tyranny.

All these phenomena could be covered by the term *fasad*, which suggests the corruption of an original state of soundness and purity. Breaking down corruption into concrete acts, Muslim scholars spoke of blameworthy or illegitimate innovations (*bida'*, sing. *bid'a*), which are objectionable not only on moral grounds but also because the prophet Muhammad and the early generations of Muslims did not know them. Thus, it was not just the consumption of tobacco or the visits to coffeehouses with their potential threat to morality and public order that were categorized as blameworthy innovations but also devotional practices, such as supererogatory prayer or severe asceticism, which could not have been condemned on moral grounds.

Faced with aberrations and illegitimate innovations, Muslim believers are obligated to act. Among the relevant references, none has proved more powerful than the Qur'anic injunction to command right and forbid wrong, or to enjoin good and prohibit evil (*al-amr bil-ma'ruf wa-l-nahy 'ani l-munkar*)[4]. The injunction is phrased in general terms, and it has been interpreted in a variety of ways: one controversy concerns the agents charged with carrying out the command, another with the appropriate modes of implementation. Both are of obvious political relevance, involving as they do the right to resistance against injustice variously defined. Regarding the agents, the question was whether the duty to command right and forbid wrong fell to the individual believer, or to the community as a whole, or to qualified members of the community. Both in religious and perhaps even more in political terms, this made for major differences, with the options ranging from quietism at one end to activism at the other. Regarding the modes of execution, a sequence was constructed that ran from silent disapproval (blaming "in the heart") to verbal admonition (forbidding "with the tongue") to physical intervention (prohibiting "with the hand"). Muslim scholars and activists disagreed as to whether the sequence should begin with 'silent' blame and gentle admonition (preferably to be administered in private and not aired in public) and only in cases of extreme danger to the community culminate in physical action, or whether—on the contrary—it should begin with physical intervention and only be muted

4 The definitive study is M. Cook, *Commanding Right and Forbidding Wrong in Islamic Thought*, Cambridge 2000; see further B. Lewis, *The Political Language of Islam*, Chicago IL - London 1988, and K. Abou El Fadl, *Rebellion and Violence in Islamic Law*, Cambridge 2001.

to silent blame if action jeopardized the integrity of the community and the life of those undertaking it.

Throughout the ages, and particularly in the modern age, reformist thinkers and activists have tended to privilege the responsibility of the individual believer over the collective duty of the community or of select members of the community. The emphasis on individual responsibility, with its concomitant stress on duties rather than on rights, is of obvious interest far beyond the present concern. Regarding the realization of this responsibility, be it individual or collective, the majority has always emphasized the virtue of moderation, at least vis-à-vis fellow Muslims. It is only a minority that has taken the Qur'anic injunction to enjoin good and prohibit evil as an invitation, and indeed a command, to take action even if this resulted in violence and intra-communal strife. Historically, activists have comprised such diverse socio-political groups as the Kharijites of the seventh and eighth centuries CE and the Islamist jihadists of the twentieth and the early twenty-first century. Their Muslim critics have condemned the violence and disruption caused by militant activism as *fitna*, that is a disturbance of the peace and a threat to the integrity of Muslim life and faith. A powerful weapon in the early centuries of Islam, the charge of *fitna* is still employed today in the fight against militant jihadists who propagate an Islamic revolution rather than Islamic reform.

The normative foundation of these controversies is not only scripture (*sola scriptura*), if scripture is solely identified with the Qur'an, or relevation. The third caliph 'Uthman b. 'Affan (r. 644-56) is generally credited with having ordered the collection and redaction of the revelations received by Muhammad in a book comparable to the holy books of the Jews and Christians. Only this collection made it possible for the Qur'an to assume the status of a hallowed artefact it still possesses today[5]. For Muslims, the Qur'anic text is supplemented by the example of the prophet Muhammad and the first generations of Muslims who are invoked as *salaf salih*, the 'pious predecessors', or 'ancestors', who, inspired by the

[5] See S. Wild (ed.), *The Qur'an as Text*, Leiden 1996; D.A. Madigan, *The Qur'an's Self-Image: Writing and Authority in Islam's Scripture*, Princeton NJ 2001; J. Dammen McAuliffe (ed.), *The Cambridge Companion to the Qur'ān*, Cambridge 2006; see also the illustrated contributions by Angelika Neuwirth and Gudrun Krämer in I. Pfluger-Schindlbeck (ed.), *Welten der Muslime*, Berlin 2012, pp. 21-45 and 47-64 respectively.

living presence of the prophet Muhammad, understood and performed Islam in the correct (*salih*) way: they were thus both right and righteous. Neither Muhammad nor the *salaf salih* left any writings to document their teachings in a way comparable to the patristic literature of the Catholic Church. In this sense, they lack a voice of their own. The Qur'an is believed by Muslims to be God's word (*kalam Allah*) and merely transmitted through Muhammad, who had no active part in shaping its form and content. On the contrary, the literary perfection of the Qur'an, one that could not have been achieved by humans, confirmed Muhammad as God's messenger. According to Islamic doctrine, Muhammad worked no miracles: it was the inimitable beauty of the Qur'an (Ar. *i'jaz)* that served as the miracle proof of his prophethood.

The reports (sing. *hadith*, pl. *ahadith*) of the deeds and sayings of Muhammad in his capacity of prophet were later compiled by Muslim men and women who made it their business to collect and transmit them[6]. (In western languages, the transmitters of prophetic traditions are called "traditionists", not to be confused with "traditionalists".) Collectively, in the field of Islamic Studies, the Prophetic Traditions are known as *sunna*, the exemplary practice established by an exemplary person, a concept already familiar in pre-Islamic times. Alongside the exegesis of the Qur'an (Ar. *tafsir*), the study of Hadith and Sunna constitutes one of the main pillars of Islamic scholarship, one that has no parallel in either Christianity or Judaism. Given the status of Muhammad in Islam, it is all the more remarkable that Muslim state authorities did not concern themselves with controlling the Sunna, which was studied and transmitted by 'private' scholars. It is here that the difference between the word of God, which is used in formal prayer and worship and should only be recited in Arabic, and the word of his final messenger comes out most clearly. Unlike the Qur'an, the Sunna is accessible in various collections, several of which assumed canonical status; it is frequently referred to, but not recited in liturgical contexts; and it can be quoted in languages other than Arabic. Over time, the textual authority of the Qur'an and the personal authority of the prophet Muhammad have been variously assessed, with some putting the Qur'an first and the Sunna second, others giving them equal authority as different manifestations

6 See J.A.C. Brown, *Hadith. Muhammad's Legacy in the Medieval and Modern World*, London 2009, as well as *The Canonization of al-Bukhārī and Muslim. The Formation and Function of the Sunnī Ḥadīth Canon*, Leiden - Boston MA 2007.

of revelation, and still others giving priority to the Sunna with its much more numerous and detailed rulings over the Qur'an[7].

But if Muslims had both divine revelation and the role model of the prophet Muhammad to guide them, how could they stray from the path? What went wrong? The standard answer was (and still is) that human weakness, combined with betrayal, and the infiltration of un-Islamic ideas and customs, allowed for corruption to set in, undermining not only the faith and moral fiber of the community but also its material and military power, which had manifested themselves in the Muslim conquests of the seventh and eighth centuries CE. The blame was thus to a certain degree exteriorized. Yet the predominant view of human nature was not entirely pessimistic: Men (and women) might be weak but they were still accountable before God and with the help of divine guidance, they were able to fight corruption and regain the integrity of faith and community possessed by the 'pious ancestors'. Given the requisite will power and determination, their spirit and conduct could be revived. Up until the twentieth century, renewal was frequently envisaged as cyclical, with a 'renewer' (Ar. *mujaddid*) appearing in every century to restore true belief and revive the community. The relevant tradition can be traced back to the twelfth century[8]. In the very different context of Confucianism, scholars have spoken of a "positive anthropology"[9]. The notion fits the Muslim context very well, if one ignores for the moment the element of divine guidance, which has no role in the Confucian tradition.

In studying religious reform and renewal in the Muslim world, the emotional and aesthetic dimensions have perhaps not yet been given due attention. Luther was driven by deep anxiety (the German *Angst*) concerning the conditions of salvation. The conclusion he reached after years of an agonizing search that it was only through divine grace (*sola gratia*) that salvation could be obtained and not through human acts, implied not merely a critique of the indulgences and other malpractices of the Catholic Church and of the individual believers who thought they

[7] A.Y. Musa, *"Ḥadīth" as Scripture. Discussions on the Authority of Prophetic Traditions in Islam*, New York 2008.

[8] E. Landau-Tasseron, *The 'Cyclical Reform': A Study of the Mujaddid Tradition*, in "Studia Islamica", 70, 1989, pp. 79-117.

[9] D.K. Gardner, *Confucianism. A Very Short Introduction*, Oxford 2015.

could buy their way into paradise without demonstrating the proper feelings of faith and repentance. The issue of salvation was of existential importance to himself and his followers. It is difficult to find a similar sense of urgency among Muslims, even though among Muslims, too, the conditions of salvation and the relative weight of human deeds and divine mercy were subject to debate. Sunni theologians held that humans had to strive constantly to follow God's command and that their efforts would be rewarded in the hereafter, or the Other Abode. (While the former entails a temporal dimension, the latter refers to the spatial dimension, illustrating the fact that Muslim notions of paradise and hell are highly complex and not simply temporal[10].) If God was just and merciful, he was also entirely free to distribute reward and punishment. These doctrines left much room for ambiguity and controversy. There were examples of Muslim mystics and ascetics who agonized over their perceived inability fully to give themselves up to God, or to fathom his decree. The majority of Muslims, however, did not experience such anguish, nor did they approve of it. Faced with uncertainty, the majority of scholars, including many Sufis, advocated trust in God (Ar. *tawakkul*) and contentment with his decree (*rida*). At the same time, they called for moderation (*i'tidal*, *wasat*) in all matters, including religion, defining it as the middle ground between neglect and exaggeration (*ifrat wa-tafrit*). Trust, contentment, and the propagation of the middle ground entered into prevalent notions of piety (*taqwa*) that condemned all kinds of 'exaggeration' in religious matters (*ghuluww fi l-din*).

This understanding of piety, based on discipline, balance, and soberness[11], also inspired the majority of Muslim reformers. It called for assiduous work on the body, the heart, and the soul, which had to be 'cultivated' in order to attain the state of calm surrender to God, and God alone. The measures taken to reach this state could be harsh, comprising the classic principles of hunger, silence, sleeplessness, and solitude. But rigorous disciplining of this type was essentially characteristic of asceticism and Sufism, or mysticism more generally, rather

[10] See C. Lange, *Paradise and Hell in Islamic Traditions*, Cambridge 2016, as well as *Locating Hell in Islamic Traditions*, Leiden 2015.

[11] Soberness here means the adherence to Sharia and the abstention from practices considered as esoteric or blameworthy by Sunni Muslim scholars, many Sufis included, from loud *dhikr* (remembrance of God) to music and dance to magic.

than of Muslim reform[12]. The great Muslim mystic-cum-scholar Abu Hamid al-Ghazali (d. 1111) is today the most prominent representative of a path that combined adherence to the Sharia with 'sober' Sufism, at least in the Arab Middle East and the West. It is difficult to know how widely al-Ghazali was read in his own time and over subsequent generations. But ever since his work, notably the massive *Revival of the Religious Sciences* (*Ihya' 'ulum al-din*) was printed in the late nineteenth century, al-Ghazali has served as a reference to Sunni Muslim reformers, including activists of political Islam, such as the Egyptian Muslim Brothers. Referring to an authority in order to enhance one's own legitimacy, however, is one thing. Actually adopting his positions (here: his rigorous scheme of self-disciplining) is another, and the two do not always go together.

Islamic reform thus shared important concerns with reformism in other religious and moral traditions from Confucianism to Christianity, notably the retrieval of original purity and vitality through purification. Still, it unfolded under specific sociopolitical conditions that were quite different from either China or early modern Western and Central Europe. The configuration of religious and political agents and institutions was among the most salient of these differences[13]. From an early date, Islam had known religious specialists and scholars (Ar. sing. *'alim*, pl. *'ulama'*, derived from *'ilm*: religious knowledge) who occasionally fulfilled functions comparable to the Christian clergy and for this reason could be considered as clerics. But they were not ordained priests, and they did not perform or monopolize any sacred rites. More importantly, there never evolved a church as a self-governing body with the authority to regulate religious thought and practice. It is true that in the sixteenth century, the Ottoman state created a religious hierarchy called *'ilmiyye* (again derived from Ar. *'ilm*). But the *'ilmiyye* was not a self-governing body with the authority to decide on religious doctrine and practice. It was a branch of the Ottoman imperial bureaucracy, and it included only those scholars that served the Empire as judges (*kadis*), magistrates, and jurisconsultants (*muftis*). The same applies to similar attempts at "clerical"

[12] See M.H. REID, *Law and Piety in Medieval Islam*, Cambridge 2013.

[13] For greater depth, see my article *Gottes-Recht bricht Menschen-Recht. Theokratische Entwürfe im zeitgenössischen Islam*, in K. TRAMPEDACH - A. PEČAR (eds), *Theokratie und theokratischer Diskurs*, Tübingen 2013, pp. 493-515, and G. KRÄMER, *Der Vordere Orient und Nordafrika ab 1500*.

bureaucratization in early modern Safavid Iran. Several centuries later, in the second half of the nineteenth century, Twelver Shi'i scholars in Iran and the Arab world recognized a 'clerical' hierarchy leading from the local *mullahs* to the most eminent *mujtahid*s, that is to say those religious scholars qualified to practice independent legal reasoning, or *ijtihad*, who were recognized by their peers as 'models of imitation' (Ar. *marja' al-taqlid*) and whom their followers were obliged to follow in legal matters. The step was remarkable because in the case of Twelver Shi'ism it was not the state that established a clerical hierarchy but the highest-ranking religious scholars who acted on their private initiative. Yet it was an informal hierarchy and remains so today. Sunni scholars never organized themselves in comparable fashion. If Muslim reformers therefore called for change, it concerned the character of the religious scholars whom—like their Christian counterparts—they denounced as incompetent, venal, corrupt, and subservient to the rich and powerful. They did not critique the structure and policies of a church for the simple reason that there was no such church. Early modern Muslim state authorities did engage in moral politics, and for this purpose, they also coopted religious scholars. The Ottoman Empire serves as a prime example. They also used what might be called confessional politics to enhance their profile as champions of Sunnism (the Ottoman Empire) and of Shi'ism (the Safavid Empire), respectively. These policies implied measures to impose greater conformity on religious doctrine and practice, restricting the freedom of religious expression and, by the same token, drawing stricter boundaries of what was to be considered orthodox and orthoprax. Next to members of the 'confession' of the political rival—Shi'i Muslims in the Ottoman Empire, Sunnis among the Safavids—, nonconformist and antinomian Sufis were among the prime targets of regulation and reform, both from the state and 'independent' religious scholars. It is perhaps here that the commonality between the European Reformation and confessionalization on the one hand, and confessionalization in the Ottoman and Safavid Empires on the other, is greatest. The latter, however, is still imperfectly understood, making generalization hazardous. We are on safer ground regarding the (contested) link between confessionalization and state-building[14]: in the

[14] For a critique of earlier scholarship on the European Reformation, see H.R. SCHMIDT, *Sozialdisziplinierung? Ein Plädoyer für das Ende des Etatismus in der Konfessionalisierungsforschung*, in "Historische Zeitschrift", 265, 1997, pp. 639-682.

Middle East, the modern state did not grow out of religious reform in general and confessional politics in particular but of political reform aimed at creating centralized states in a world increasingly dominated by European powers. Egypt under the Ottoman governor Muhammad Ali (r. 1805-1848) and the Ottoman Empire in the age of reform, from the Tanzimat (1839-1878) through the Hamidian era (1878-1908) to the Young Turk era (1908-1919), are the principle examples here. Religion was virtually absent from Muhammad Ali's policies of modernization and state-building. Religious symbols, rites, and references were more consciously employed in the Ottoman processes of centralization and modernization. Yet here, too, they served as one element among others and not the primary one. To correct another misperception, state policies of centralization and modernization predated European colonialism in the Middle East and, for that reason, they did not result from colonial intervention. The British occupation of Egypt occurred only in 1882, several decades after the introduction of modernizing reforms in the country by Muhammad Ali and his heirs. The Ottoman Empire was successively penetrated by European capital in the last quarter of the nineteenth century, and it steadily lost territory in Europe and North Africa to Europeans. But it was never formally colonized. The processes of modernization and the articulations of modernity that occurred under these auspices have been variously assessed, as either colonial or local. In the region between Egypt, Syria, and Anatolia, modernization and modernity are best described as 'local'. In the countries subjected to direct colonial rule, that is, North Africa between Morocco and present-day Libya, they are best characterized as 'colonial' (which again does not exclude agency on the part of local actors and intermediaries)[15].

Against the backdrop of modernizing policies of local powers and of European colonial expansion, the dynamics of Islamic reform gradually changed with regards to its aims and contents as much as its social base and modes of action. For many reformers, the defense of Muslim identity, authenticity, and interest in the face of Western hegemony assumed prime importance. None of these motives had figured in either the European Reformation or pre-modern Islamic reform. Resistance to modernization and colonization did not preclude the appropriation

[15] For more detail, see my *Moderne. Arabische Welt*, in F. JAEGER - W. KNÖBL - U. SCHNEIDER (eds), *Handbuch Moderneforschung. Interdisziplinäre und internationale Perspektiven*, Stuttgart 2015, pp. 27-37.

of prevalent ideas of modernity and progress, which were essentially of European origin, although in many cases already filtered through local media. As in other parts of the world, the combination of reason, science, and progress proved attractive to many, Muslim reformers included. Many also argued that Islam provided fertile ground for reason, science, and progress, more fertile ground indeed than Christianity. If European colonialism progressively reduced the appeal of these ideas, it did not obliterate them altogether. In their majority, Muslim reformers continued to defend Islam as a religion of reason and science, while strongly denouncing European colonialism and 'cultural aggression'.

The Sunni (Arab) reform 'movement' of the late nineteenth and early twentieth centuries, of whom the Iranian Jamal al-Din al-Afghani, the Egyptian Muhammad Abduh (1849-1905), and the Syrian Rashid Rida (1865-1935) were the most prominent representatives, had much to do with the perceived weakness of Islam and the Muslim community in the face of European domination and very little with confessionalization tied to state-building. Like their predecessors, Afghani, Abduh, and Rida called for a religious renewal through a re-reading of the Qur'an and a return to the age of the prophet Muhammad and the first generations of Muslims (hence the label 'Salafi' that was later applied to them) so as to retrieve and revive the original purity, power, and unity of the Muslim community[16]. The vision was both religious and political. It aimed at crafting ideas and practices that were both authentic and responsive to modern realities—and it was in this aim that they distinguished themselves most clearly from their reformist predecessors. The 'Salafi' reformers did not shy away from using modern terms to frame their message, and they used new media as well as new forms of association and action to disseminate it beyond their own circles. Still, they remained cautious with regard to the actual articulation of change and innovation. Both were chiefly expressed in the new emphasis on the need

[16] The Salafis that formed in the 1990s have little in common with their predecessors except for the name and their reference to the pious ancestors, and they are not commonly seen as reformers; for the 'historical Salafiyya', see A. ROUSSILLON, *Salafisme, réformisme, nationalisme: Essai de clarification*, in "Hesperis Tamuda", 39, 2001, 2, pp. 15-37, and H. LAUZIÈRE, *The Construction of the Salafiyya: Reconsidering Salafism from the Perspective of Conceptual History*, in "International Journal of Middle East Studies", 42, 2010, pp. 369-389; for the Salafis that emerged from the 1990s, see B. ROUGIER (ed.), *Qu'est-ce que le salafisme?*, Paris 2008, and R. MEIJER (ed.), *Global Salafism. Islam's New Religious Movement*, New York 2009.

to rethink religious and social precepts on the basis of the normative sources at the expense of blind imitation of established opinion, or of human judgement more generally. *Ijtihad*, seeking new legal solutions on the basis of the authoritative sources, or scripture, was thus given priority over *taqlid*, unthinking compliance with established opinions and legal authorities ('tradition', 'convention'). *Taqlid* referred particularly to the eponyms and leading representatives of the various Sunni legal schools (*madhhab*, pl. *madhahib*). Neither of the concepts invoked was new: they were differently assessed and expanded beyond the circles of religious scholars to include the common believer, male as well as female. In a similar vein, new significance was given to established legal concepts, such as the common good (*maslaha 'amma*) and the finality of the Sharia (*maqasid al-shari'a*), privileging the intention and general purpose of Qur'anic injunctions over detailed rulings with the aim of broadening the scope of socio-legal change without abandoning the textual framework of Islamic reform.

The gradual shifts characteristic of Islamic reform in the transition from pre-modern to modern times equally appear in the attention given to theology on the one hand and to active social and political commitment on the other. Theological concerns did play a role in Sunni Muslim reformism up until the eighteenth if not the nineteenth century, but with the important exception of the conditions of belief (*iman*) and unbelief (*kufr*), they seemed to be slowly fading into the background. From the ninth to the twelfth century, many of the most eminent Muslim minds had engaged with the great theological debates over the divine attributes, predestination, theodicy, anthropomorphism, and the createdness of the Qur'an. By the early modern period these debates had by and large subsided. In the eighteenth century, Sunni scholars, reformers as much as their critics and opponents, still discussed the topic of anthropomorphism. By the twentieth century, the focus of Sunni theological reflection had decisively shifted from God to man. The one theological issue that continued to preoccupy religious scholars, Sufis, and ordinary Muslims alike concerned God's mercy or, to use Christian terminology, divine grace and the weight given to faith (*iman*) and deeds (*'amal*), respectively, in judging belief and unbelief as the precondition of salvation. The issue was not resolved.

However, with the exception of antinomian groups, notably specific dervish communities, and individual Sufi masters, all Muslims agreed on the absolute necessity of obeying God's command and fulfilling the obligations set down in Sharia. These obligations included ritual duties, such as prayer, fasting, almsgiving, and the pilgrimage to Mecca and Medina, which in Arabic are known as *'ibadat*, acts of worship. If according to majority opinion, it was faith that ultimately decided the status of the believer, and if faith as an inner condition could only be judged by God, this did not in any way diminish the importance given to the acts of worship that had to be fulfilled. Ideally, the practice of faith should not, as it were, be fragmented and dispersed into discrete acts but translated into pious conduct, corresponding to Max Weber's concept of *Lebensführung*. Interiorization as a religious concept that elevates the believing heart over the obedient body, which worships God in 'exterior' rites and rituals, which is taken as the defining feature of the Protestant Reformation (*sola fide*, *sola gratia*), was not alien to the Sunni Muslim tradition. But it is best known as a Sufi concern and does not constitute a central feature of Islamic reform.

If it has just been said that gradual shifts rather than radical breaks marked the transition of Islamic reform from the pre-modern to the modern era, this also applies to the advocacy of social commitment and political reform, with its stress on legal-cum-moral rather than on theological issues strictly speaking. In previous centuries, many of the men recognized as 'renewers' had equally been active socially and politically. Still, the concern of the moderns with social improvement and communal if not national strengthening marked a significant shift from the program of individual betterment and purification advocated by men like al-Ghazali, who espoused an elitist project that only addressed those men and women with a potential to become what Weber called religious *virtuosi*. Regardless, Islamic reform was not organized until the interwar years of the twentieth century.

What has been called the Salafi 'movement' of the late nineteenth and the early twentieth century was a loose group of thinkers and activists who engaged in intellectual and political work and for this purpose made active use of the newly emerging print media. Among them were pioneers of journalism and what could be called civil society associations that promoted education, moral uplift, and social betterment. Yet the Salafis of the turn of the twentieth century did not create resilient structures, and they did not have a solid base in local society, whether urban or rural.

The first Sunni reform movements deserving of the name, which in one way or another drew on the ideas of the Salafi masters, emerged in present-day Indonesia. In the Arab Middle East, the Egyptian Muslim Brotherhood, founded in 1928, developed into the largest and most influential movement of religious, social, and political reform with a pronounced anti-colonial agenda. Irrespective of their different strategies and practices, the Sunni reform movements of the 1920s and 1930s mobilized a mass following among members of the community that had not been addressed let alone reached by the preceding generation of reformers. With them, the social base of Islamic reform moved decisively from the religious scholars and Sufis of the pre-modern age to 'Islamic' intellectuals, bureaucrats, and activists who in their majority had neither the formal religious training nor the religious credentials of previous generations, lending Islamic reform an entirely new social and educational profile. The Muslim Brothers ultimately had a political project, one that tied moral improvement to collective self-strengthening, be it of the Muslim community, the 'Eastern nation', or the Egyptian nation-state. Over the course of the twentieth and the early twentieth-first century, the principles of religious reform inspired piety movements and Islamist groups of various hues, from quietist Salafi to militant jihadist. Still, the reformers did not realize their two-fold objective of individual reform and collective empowerment, if this entailed freeing Muslims from Western hegemony in the political, economic, and cultural fields. Nor did they initiate a broad and systematic review of the legal and theological legacy of Islam that includes the hermeneutics of scriptural exegesis. It is for this reason that reformist activists and outside observers alike speak of a failure of Islamic reform and the unbroken need for an Islamic Reformation.

To sum up, religious reform has a long history that goes back to the first centuries of Islam. Up until the late nineteenth century, the principle aim of Muslim reformers was to restore the original unity and purity of a community that had split along various lines, by reviving the spirit and exemplary behavior of the early community assembled around the prophet Muhammad. Religious reform implied fighting against ideas and customs that had allegedly crept into Muslim life and diverted it from the straight path, be they illicit practices, such as consuming alcohol and drugs, or illegitimate innovations, such as certain ascetic devotional practices or esoteric beliefs. Religious reform understood as revival and purification, if not restoration, had much in common with pre-modern concepts of reform in other religious and/or moral traditions, from Confucianism to Latin Christianity in its various manifestations. Yet the Protestant Reformation unfolded under highly specific structural and cultural conditions, and some of their defining features, notably the insistence on divine grace as the sole condition of salvation and the concomitant critique of the pope and the church at large, had no parallel in other religious or moral traditions, including Islam. Conversely, the preoccupation of Muslim reformers with legal matters broadly understood, especially in the modern age, was alien to Christian reformers, Protestant as well as Catholic, and even more so to Confucians. Comparing the Protestant Reformation with reform and renewal in Muslim contexts is productive as long as it is used to highlight the specific features of either. To call for a Muslim Reformation, led by a Muslim Luther, is not.

Reform and Revival, Innovation and Enterprise

A Tale of Modern Hinduism

by *Brian K. Pennington*

1. *Introduction*

The history of religions is replete with tales of degeneration and corruption followed by revolt and restoration. The history I refer to here is not the unfolding of events over a succession of years but the manner in which not only historians themselves but also practitioners of religion have framed their stories. Paradigmatic histories of religious traditions often feature great founders and their teachings, a straying from original insights, abuse of power by institutional authorities, and the heroic rescue of a tradition in decline. We could point to histories structured in those ways in all the world's traditions, certainly in the case of Hinduism, as I will discuss below. To no slight extent, however, at least in the case of Hinduism, that narrative bears an unmistakably European imprint. These narratives of rupture and repair are all implicated in rhetorics of authenticity that posit an identifiable tradition moving through history in a linear manner that replicates the European history of Reform and Counter-Reform. These narratives of rupture and repair have, in turn, indelibly marked India's own colonial history, both in the manner that it came to unfold and in the manner in which it has been told. This essay will suggest alternative readings of modern Hindu history that de-essentialize the tradition and de-Europeanize its modern past.

2. *Precolonial reform*

In many respects, what we call Hinduism today could be accurately described as a collection of all the reforming movements its authority has inspired over the course of its long history. I take it as a settled question that the history of religions must treat what we have come to think of as religious traditions as decentered, extended contests to define sources of ultimate authority and the meaning of those sources and must, in addition, resist the World Religions Paradigm that suggests that the labels we employ to identify those traditions such as Hinduism, Buddhism, etc., are historically coherent entities. Hinduism has become emblematic of a tradition without essentials[1], and efforts by many different parties to pull the tradition back towards some fundamental principle from which it had allegedly strayed have been not at the margins but at the very core of South Asian religious life for centuries. Caste, the role of religious authorities, "superstition", image worship, the place of women, and the relative importance of ritual and direct experience have been among the issues that have animated the millennia-long competition to reform or re-reform the tradition. Indeed, the other great religious traditions of South Asia—Jainism, Buddhism, and Sikhism—can themselves be regarded as originally reforming movements within the Hindu world.

Just one example as elaborated by the great South Asian folklorist A.K. Ramanujan will serve to illustrate this point. In the introduction to his classic translations of the poetry of the saints of a twelfth-century group called the Vīraśaivas, Ramanujan describes the emergence of the Vīraśaiva movement as a social upheaval among the poor and low-caste against the ritualized and exploitative religion of the day. Their resentment was directed not just at the high-caste elite, however, but also at contemporary popular practice, which they regarded as meaningless and superstitious ritual that shielded a person from direct experience of the godhead: "Classical belief systems, social customs and superstitions, image worship, the caste system, the Vedic ritual of *yajña* as well as local sacrifices of lambs and goats—all of them are fiercely questioned and ridiculed" in the poetry of the saints[2]. Significantly for our discussion today, the Vīraśaivas regarded their call for a return to experience as a reassertion of the "original inspiration of the ancient traditions"[3]. To use our contemporary language, they and the many groups like them over the course of South Asian religious history thought of themselves not as innovators, but as reformers.

1 B.K. PENNINGTON, *Was Hinduism Invented? Britons, Indians, and the Colonial Construction of Religion*, New York 2005; J.E. LLEWELLYN (ed.), *Defining Hinduism: A Reader*, New York 2005.

2 A.K. RAMANUJAN, *Speaking of Siva*, New York 1973, p. 33.

3 *Ibid.*, p. 30.

3. *Colonial contact and emergent reformism*

It is important to observe, however, that this is exclusively 'our' language, i.e. the language of post-Enlightenment, Europeanized moderns. As in western Christianity, in Hinduism the concept of "reform" has come primarily to signal a specific period and a specific movement and, in a derivative manner, to index a more general, ongoing concern that the tradition return to some true, original, or essential set of teachings. While fluidity and change are characteristic of all cultural institutions, and while some changes in Hindu practice historically would have been directed towards the production of an imagined trans-historical ideal that we could call "reform", in the history of religions, the term "reform" has generally been associated with the configuration of the modern, especially the modern subject. While we could, therefore, describe the kinds of changes the Vīraśaiva's undertook as reforming, that language is our own and not characteristic of these movements' own depictions of themselves. Neither the idea nor the term "reform" is part of Indian discourses about religious change until the nineteenth century, when the word was adopted to describe figures and movements of India's educated elite against orthodox authority and practice[4].

The rupture and rebellion that those titles announce reveal not only a European framework for reading Indian religious reality but also a self-congratulatory assessment of British influence in India as well as a particular way of understanding Protestant Europe's religious history as itself pivoting on a disruption that initiated both modernity and the reformation of western Christianity. Often lauded in the language of heroism, leading religious figures, for example, were sometimes compared to European counterparts. Modernity has been identified with the European Enlightenment's valorization of reason and progress as well as with the self-conscious distinction drawn between the modern and the traditional[5]. That is to say, modernity announces its own advent via a bracketing of the traditional. Scholars have associated it with a number of characteristics that cannot be separated from the idea of reform. Modernity embraced the interiorization of traditional modes

[4] A.P. Sen (ed.), *Social and Religious Reform: The Hindus of British India*, New York 2003, p. 7.

[5] D. Smith, *Hinduism and Modernity*, Oxford 2003, p. 7.

of piety, and mobilizes politics on the basis of religious identity[6]. It highlighted the moral authority of the individual subject and that liberal subject as the basis of civil society and national identity[7]. It congratulated itself on its disenchantment, its supersession of superstition, and its exposure of priestcraft[8]. It created conditions for the appearance of a middle class and its ethic of industry and self-fashioned success[9]. I have argued elsewhere that modernity in India is characterized by diffuse and contested religious authority, politicized religious identities, accelerating global flows across borders, and a milieu of religious innovation[10]. Colonial modernity does not only unfold in colonized space but, as Homi Bhaba, Mary Louise Pratt, and others have taught us, also in the indeterminate zones between colony and metropole, and it disrupts metropolitan meanings and relations as well as those in the colony. Before we pursue the character of reform in Hindu traditions of modernity, at the outset a brief survey of the most significant developments in modern Hinduism might help orient us to consider a question of comparative interest, the serviceability of "reform" as a cross-cultural category.

When the British East India Company assumed the power of taxation in eastern India in 1757, it inaugurated the long and never fully completed process of consolidating its political power in the subcontinent. In service of this end, it recruited a young lawyer, jurist, and orientalist scholar, Sir William Jones, to serve as a junior judge in its Supreme Court of Judicature in Calcutta and to help develop a body of Hindu law by which the company could govern its subjects. An accomplished linguist, Jones embraced the opportunity to study ancient Sanskrit texts,

6 J. FULLER, *Modern Hinduism and the Middle Class: Beyond Revival in the Historiography of Colonial India*, in "Journal of Hindu Studies", 2, 2009, 2, pp. 160-178.

7 P. VAN DER VEER, *The Modern Spirit of Asia: The Spiritual and the Secular in India and China*, Princeton NJ 2014, pp. 98-99.

8 J.B. SCOTT, *Spiritual Despots: Modern Hinduism and the Genealogies of Self-Rule* (South Asia across the Disciplines), Chicago IL 2016; R. YELLE, *The Language of Disenchantment: Protestant Literalism and Colonial Discourse in British India*, New York 2012.

9 B.A. HATCHER, *Idioms of Improvement: Vidyāsāgar and Cultural Encounter in Bengal*, Delhi 1996.

10 B.K. PENNINGTON, *Hinduism in North India*, in B.A. HATCHER (ed.), *Hinduism in the Modern World*, New York 2016, pp. 31-47.

which he did with the assistance of a Brahmin pandit. Within a year of his arrival in India, he had founded the Asiatick Society whose members were for the most part men in East India Company Service who pursued amateur scholarship on the side and made some of the most important discoveries and insights into South Asian history and culture of the age, published through the ground-breaking journal, Asiatick Researches[11]. Jones directed much of his own prodigious scholarship towards the study of the *Dharmaśāstras*, classical and typically sprawling texts that articulated norms for moral and ethical life. They governed everything from marriage to warfare. They are notoriously self-contradictory and decidedly brahminical in their outlook and biases. Under the guidance and interpretation of Jones, however, they were digested so as to provide the foundations for the law that would govern Hindus living under British rule. Yelle calculates that fully 95% of the specific injunctions of the *śāstras*, however, were excised in the process of codifying a law code to govern Hindus[12]. Those laws that corresponded with British ideas of civil law were maintained while those that governed ritual behavior were excised. In short, a code was developed that enfranchised a distinction previously unknown in Hindu thought between civil law and religion[13]. The convergence of law, foreign occupation, and humanistic inquiry represented by the Asiatick Society would prove critical for the emergence of modern Hinduism and incite a series of tensions and contrasts that endure to this day, and demonstrate the impact of European modernity on India: between religious practice and social custom, between the progressive ambitions of a secular democratic republic and the ancient authority of a stratified and gendered social order, between a golden past and a degraded present.

The social and political upheaval created by British rule in Bengal occasioned the rise of a class of English-speaking Indians, often serving in subordinate roles in the East India Company, who were influenced by British manners, customs, and social mores. Their status and material wealth having been established by proximity to the colonial centers of power, the *bhadralok* were often lampooned by their social superiors and inferiors alike for their affectation of English ways, their non-tra-

[11] B.K. Pennington, *Was Hinduism Invented?*, pp. 59-100.

[12] R. Yelle, *Language of Disenchantment*, p. 142.

[13] *Ibid.*, pp. 144-147.

ditional social practices, and their aspiration to appear "modern"[14]. Hatcher refers to them as "bourgeois" to indicate their social location *vis-à-vis* traditional caste hierarchy, their concern for self-fashioning, and their aspiration for material success as a result of emerging economic opportunity[15]. The earliest members of India's modern middle class, these bourgeois individualists were also among modern Hinduism's most important religious innovators, a concept I will develop later in this essay. By means of the voluntary societies that began to spring up all across British India, they fashioned a distinctive set of religious norms that legitimized capitalist accumulation via the domestication of their desires under the governance of the principle of the "godly householder". This modern subject cultivated industry, domesticity, moral leadership, and worldly success, a "worldly asceticism for the bourgeoisie" that produced "a new regime of instructional discipline"[16].

Such were the factors and actors that contributed to the emergence of modern Hindu reform, a movement with two overarching objectives. First, the elimination of Hindu social practices regarded as irrational, backward, or barbaric. These included the practice of widow immolation called *satī*, child marriage, the prohibition against widow remarriage, and the more repressive aspects of caste hierarchy. Secondly, a rejection of irrational, superstitious, or exploitative religious practices and beliefs, principally image worship, excessive ritualism, priestcraft, and polytheism. In the second respect, the oldest and most revered of Hinduism's many sacred texts, the Vedas, were identified as the singular textual authority and reinterpreted to sanction this religious program as a "reform" that would return Hinduism theologically to its allegedly non-idolatrous, monotheistic roots. These concerns—the social, and the ritual, and the theological—drove modern Hindu reform, and the relative weight that any individual or group lent to each of them determined the character of a reform agenda.

[14] S. BANERJEE, *The Parlour and the Streets: Elite and Popular Culture in Nineteenth-century Calcutta*, Calcutta 1989.

[15] B.A. HATCHER, *Bourgeois Hinduism, or, The Faith of the Modern Vedantists: Rare Discourses from Early Colonial Bengal*, New York 2008.

[16] *Ibid.*, p. 70; J.B. SCOTT, *Luther in the Tropics: Karsandas Mulji and the Colonial "Reformation" of Hinduism*, in "Journal of the American Academy of Religion", 83, 2015, 1, pp. 181-209, here p. 196.

Colonial Hindu reform, whether in its social, ritual, or theological guises, was neither cause nor effect of modernization in India; it marked the emergence of the modern itself. That modern, moreover, bore a distinctly Protestant character, as perhaps do all modernities.

The idea of reform functions by means of an idiom of return or correction. Reform implies a tradition gone astray, one that must be directed back into the channels of its original inspiration. It invokes an earlier, pristine practice as exemplar even as it fashions the past to its purposes. For those who use the language of reform to describe themselves or others as reformers, it is a concept that announces an agenda for the future but does so by way of pointing backward. In the words of the historian of Indian reform, Amiya P. Sen, reform represents "a specific reading of the need for change", but their interpretation of their present had implications for the ways these reformers fashioned what came before. "Situating [themselves] in relation with some past", therefore, "became extremely important for both moral and polemical reasons", Sen concludes[17]. The credibility of any program of change stood or fell on the basis of its perceived foundation on the authority of the ancients, but at the same time, particularly in the case of India, it offered the promise of a future reminiscent of a golden past. The force of the concept of reform, therefore, lies less in its descriptive and analytical capacities than in the rhetorical work it accomplishes. For insiders, those who self-identify as reformers, it underscores their commitment to a tradition their enemies might accuse them of abandoning. For those enemies, on the other hand, particularly when accompanied by a snide or ironic tone, it can signal precisely the opposite: a progressive agenda that disdains the past. And for the British outsiders to those discussions, the identification of a Hindu leader as a reformer communicated measured or enthusiastic endorsement, a subtle congratulation for having embraced a European rationality and assumed a Protestant stance vis-à-vis the Hindu tradition. Hence the founder of the reformist organization the Arya Samaj, Dayananda Saraswati, was hailed as the "Luther of India", but so was the journalist Karsandas Mulji[18].

The last several years have seen a renewed scholarly interest in assessing the reform movements of nineteenth-century British India, and I can only

[17] A.P. Sen, *Social and Religious Reform*, pp. 8 and 18.

[18] J.B. Scott, *Luther*.

briefly summarize here the most significant findings of this widespread interest in rethinking the categories of historical analysis that a previous generation of scholars had established. Among the most influential of those earlier scholars was David Kopf, whose 1969 *British Orientalism and the Bengal Renaissance* framed reformism in terms of its debt to British influences[19]. For Kopf, the "discovery" of a Hindu golden age by British Orientalists like Jones provided the intellectual resources with which Indian elites in the center of British power could reimagine a Hinduism that was both modern and Indian at the same time. His was a classic influentialist model by which ideas flowed from the metropole to the grateful colony, but a colony simultaneously intimidated by the imposing task of assimilating elements of European modernity and thereby reinvigorating itself. Kopf wrote in his introduction that the typical member of the elite classes who had ongoing contact with the British through employment or business connections was a "confused but optimistic individual striving to reconcile partially digested alien traits and unsatisfactory indigenous traditions"[20]. This "confusion", Kopf argued, stemmed directly from the disorienting encounter with European modernity and from the wholesale reframing of Indian society and history it seemed to demand. For much of the twentieth century, the historiography of India's modernization entailed the mapping of Europe's own self-understanding onto the Hindu past in service of a European-like future for India. This confused Indian subject was made aware of a previously "unrecognized historical dimension" to his traditions: Orientalists painted a golden age of India, missionaries told of medieval Europe's dark ages, and both inspired Bengali ideas of the perfectibility of all humankind. Modernizing Indians came, in this version of the story, to regard themselves as "products of an exhausted culture and as representatives of one capable of revitalization"[21].

The latest wave of scholarship on Hindu reform has undermined the narrative of the confused or dis-oriented Hindu that informed historiography like Kopf's and pointed to the continuities of nineteenth-century reform with pre-colonial Hinduisms. Two effects are significant for our

[19] D. Kopf, *British Orientalism and the Bengal Renaissance: The Dynamics of Indian Modernization, 1773-1835*, Berkeley CA 1969.

[20] *Ibid.*, p. 8.

[21] *Ibid.*

purposes: first, this reassessment has destabilized our sense of a radical break with past Hindu practice, thereby calling into question the very notion of reform, and second, it has cast doubt on the degree of British influence on modern Hinduism while shedding light on previously unrecognized aspects of Britain's intervention in Indian history.

As Brian A. Hatcher has recently so cogently argued, the very idea of reform wears a Janus face. Its usage in the nineteenth century by British academics and officials to designate some religious movements that originated prior to the arrival of British power served to indicate an undeveloped but indigenous impulse towards the purging of ritual and theological errors such as image worship and polytheism. Observing that "the British seem to have been unable to think about their empire in South Asia outside of a mindset shaped by the fundamental idea of reform", Hatcher notes that British scholars tended to bestow the title of "reformer" exclusively on those Indian religious leaders whose goals appeared fully compatible with the needs and desires of colonial governance: a dedication to social as well as to religious reform and an avoidance of a too-radical program of reform that might spark social unrest. Those values they found only among reformers of their own age, that is, those who had experienced the "stimulating contact with European ideas" that would allow Hinduism to undergo the 'true' reform that Hinduism's medieval reformers could never have achieved[22].

If Hatcher has exposed the rhetorical and political utility of the concept of reform, Robert A. Yelle has levied the still more destabilizing charge that the narrative of European modernity's break with the traditional past is itself, in a quite literal sense, mythical. Yelle's critique takes its point of departure from Max Weber's theory of disenchantment, the idea that the modern world, under the influence of patterns of Christian thought and practice, experienced a "decline of belief in miracles, mystery, and magic" and saw the withdrawal of the gods from the experience and consciousness of human society[23]. The Protestant distinctions between true faith and false religion, meaningful devotion and empty ritual, interior sincerity and vain external display emerged as the tests of

[22] B.A. HATCHER, *Situating the Swaminarayan Tradition in the Historiography of Modern Hindu Reform*, in R. BRADY - Y. TRIVEDI (eds), *Swaminarayan Hinduism: Tradition, Adaptation and Identity*, pp. 6-37, New York 2016, p. 30.

[23] R. YELLE, *Language of Disenchantment*, p. 7.

authentic reform. Applying those European distinctions and declaring the break with the past we invoked earlier, Hindu reformers aimed "to exclude the forms of traditional religion and secure the foundations of modernity as distinct from an irrational, religious past", and the British asserted themselves as the arbiters of that authenticity[24]. In this more radically Weberian analysis, however, the production of a Hindu reformism entailed more than the forcible wresting of elements of social and cultural practice from the authority of religion and the appearance of the secular. It entailed the same self-delusion that a future liberated from history's fetters was achievable: "An originally Christian myth of disenchantment has become the myth of the emergence of the secular out of its religious past, with the breaking of the power of tradition"[25].

The narrative that colonial Hinduism entered onto the path of reform that Europe herself had traced some 300 years previously has thereby reinforced and universalized a particular Protestant self-understanding, fostering "an aura of inevitability of reform by presenting it as a distinct stage of modernization already completed by the West"[26]. This Protestantization of India, celebrated as an emulation of Europe's own decisive break with its medieval past, might now be exposed just as Europe's has. This myth of India's own disenchantment "liberating subjects from oppressive powers" has permitted the production of historically unprecedented but unmistakably Indic asceticisms and subjectivities that defy the received binaries of Europe/India, secular/religious, liberated/enslaved, reformed/traditional[27]. Even in the "most modern of modern Hinduisms" we find markers of the pre-modern that have, in the standard scholarly and reformist narratives, signaled the very same traditional (i.e. irrational and superstitious) Hinduism that the declarations of modern reform have insisted were overcome: myth, extra-textual authority in the person of the guru, other-worldly asceticism[28].

[24] *Ibid.*, p. 11.

[25] *Ibid.*, p. 30.

[26] J.B. Scott, *Luther*, p. 191.

[27] *Ibid.*, pp. 202-203.

[28] T.S. Dobe, *Dayānanda Sarasvatī as Irascible Ṛṣi: The Personal and Performed Authority of a Text*, in "Journal of Hindu Studies", 4, 2011, 1, p. 93.

4. *The question of authority: Reform becomes revival*

The contours of nineteenth-century Hindu reform might come into sharper focus if we consider a movement that succeeded it, often and perhaps unfairly considered a reaction against the progressive agenda of reformers. Inflected differently in different regions of India, the so-called "Hindu Revival" of the later nineteenth century opposed European influences on reforming Hinduism and it became closely associated with the Indian Independence movement and its emphasis on indigenous, South Asian sources of authority. Beginning in the early 1870s and continuing, by one measure, until the first decade of the twentieth century[29] Hindus around India developed new idioms of religious discourse that spoke to the frustrations and resentments of those who had witnessed the denigration of Hindu traditions by Christian missionaries, interventionist bureaucrats, and Hindu reformers that had, in their view, been captivated by European ideas and manners. This determination to find a new voice was occasioned by the clarity with which the Indian elite could now perceive the staunch refusal of the British ever to allow a robust Indian leadership in the empire. The First War of Indian Independence of 1857, known by the British as the Sepoy Mutiny, was the event that opened up the chasm between the two halves of the nineteenth century and sparked the racialization of the empire. A watershed moment in the coalescence of revival as a discourse of resistance to British rule was the 1891 passage of the *Age of Consent* Act, an amendment to the *Indian Penal Code* that set the age of consent for sexual intercourse for girls at 12. This campaign to raise the age from 10 had been set in motion by the case of a young woman named Rakhmabai, who had refused to leave her parents' house to go to live with the husband to whom she had been married at the age of 11[30]. The publicity surrounding the case, including Rakhmabai's own public letters condemning child marriage, prompted an outcry that led eventually to the amendment of the penal code[31]. She wrote:

[29] A.P. SEN, *Hindu Revivalism in Bengal 1872-1905. Some Essays in Interpretation*, New York 1993.

[30] For an account of the controversy, see S.A. WOLPERT, *Tilak and Gokhale: Revolution and Reform in the Making of Modern India*, Berkeley CA 1962, pp. 45-61.

[31] N.A. FALK, *By What Authority?: Hindu Women and the Legitimization of Reform in the Nineteenth Century*, in L.L. PATTON (ed.), *Jewels of Authority: Women and Textual Tradition in Hindu India*, New York 2002, pp. 145 f.

"I am one of those unfortunate Hindu women whose hard lot it is to suffer the unnamable miseries entailed by the custom of early marriage. This wicked practice has destroyed the happiness of my life. It comes between me and the thing which I prize above all others—study and mental cultivation".

Reflecting on her own circumstances and her determination to engage a wider contest, she continued: "I began seriously to consider the former and present condition of our Hindu women, and wished to do something, if in my power, to ameliorate our present sufferings"[32].

The emotional force of Rakhmabai's plea was undeniable, but in the clear light of the late 1880s, however, as the intractability of the empire achieved a state of obviousness, it was hard for many Indian leaders to disentangle social reform from Anglicization or to disassociate religious reform from the crude and distasteful missionary Christianity. The case of Rakhmabai points up the ambiguity of the position in which the revivalists found themselves, and the untenability of the European framework of reform and counter-reform. No educated spokesperson with an eye toward a proud and independent India could defend aberrant social practice, nor were Indians any longer willing to accept the sincerity of Queen Victoria's pledge not to interfere in her subjects' religious practice. The distinction between cultural practice and social custom on the one hand and religion on the other—the post-Enlightenment, European distinction on which the Indian law codes had been built—had proven the wedge that had enabled the dismantling of Hindu institutions. Revivalists like the fiery nationalist Bal Gangadhar Tilak could therefore oppose the Age of Consent bill while also decrying the harm caused by child marriage. As if speaking directly to the ghost of Sir William Jones, and without advocating child marriage itself, Tilak wrote in defense of those who endorsed early marriage and the consummation of that marriage soon after puberty. Referring to the ceremony of *garbhadhān*, the life-cycle rite at which a marriage is consummated and pregnancy presumably initiated, he cited the *Dharmaśāstras*:

"The common rule is for intercourse to take place on that very night when she has the first menstruation after having performed the *homa* (fire) sacrifice. This custom has been practiced for at least 2,500 years since the ancient era of the *sutras*. If you want the *Shastra*, then this is the true way. Take it or leave it, but please do not try to misinterpret the ancient authors. Don't try to oppress them or to oppress our *Dharma*".

[32] Quoted in S. CHANDRA, *Enslaved Daughters: Colonialism, Law and Women's Rights*, New Delhi 1998, pp. 17-18.

Objecting to the British and to reforming Hindus who had selectively highlighted texts and passages acceptable to them but dismissed what they condemned, he continued:

> "You are not told to find new discoveries in *Dharma Shastra,* and you are not asked to bring 'good tidings' [i.e. principles compatible with Christian teachings] out of them. If you don't know how to interpret the *Shastra* correctly, then at least try to remain silent"[33].

Revivalists like Tilak did not oppose social reform. Quite the contrary. They did, however, subordinate it to Indian self-rule, maintaining that reform based on British standards and enforced by British law rather than on Hindu principles at the instigation of Hindu leadership would necessarily undermine Hinduism itself. It is critical to understand that revivalists were also reformers who desired and sought the elimination of social ills. Tilak himself called child marriage an "evil custom"[34]. Revivalists disagreed with reformers not about whether to improve the lives of women and those of low caste nor about the authority of the past. Rather, they disagreed about the pace of change, strategies for implementing it, and the proper authoritative basis for that change. For many revivalists, desirable reforms would have to wait for political self-determination to implement those changes on an authentically Hindu and therefore enduring foundation[35].

The failure of Hindu texts of antiquity to provide a secure and stable model for an indigenous reform prompted an innovation that would have lasting political and religious effects in India. This "brand new construct" was an imagined and romanticized Golden Age of the ancient Aryans, an invocation of an India untainted by the presence of Muslims, whose rule in India the more strident revivalists blamed for the status of women and the social ills such as child marriage and seclusion from which they suffered. An ingenious "new model of authority", it had the capacity to ignite a fervor for social change that could mobilize the masses on the basis of an appeal to an imagined and romanticized past. Ironically this notion of a Vedic past marked by just kings, and a dharmic society in which women were honored rather than exploited, required an embrace of the Orientalist narrative of decline, but it proved

33 Quoted in S.A. Wolpert, *Tilak and Gokhale*, pp. 55-56.

34 N.A. Falk, *By What Authority?*, p. 47.

35 *Ibid.*, p. 146.

a powerful discourse of resistance that enabled a strong assertion of Hindu values over against the West. It drew on the prestige of scripture while escaping classic constraints of scriptural interpretation[36]. The aura of this golden age offered "acceptable grounds for compromise between the goals of nationalists and reformers" while also opening up space for the political participation of women on terms set by the gendered social norms articulated by that age[37]. In the twentieth century, those nativist narratives would turn lethal as that imagined past was distilled into a symbolic arsenal for more poisonous Hindu nationalisms[38].

Dermot Killingley has observed that "Revival is not opposed to reform, it is the idiom in which it speaks"[39]. It is unclear whether the ambiguity of his last two pronouns was intentional, but it underscores what I take to be his larger point, that the periodization of modern Hindu history according to categories derived from Christian history masks the rhetorical and strategic alliance between so-called reform and revival as well as their shared investment in particular uses of the past. In important respects, these common investments indicate how narratives of rupture and repair or degeneration and rescue fall short as a basis for critical analysis of modern Hinduism.

5. *Reform as innovation*

At this juncture I want to take the notion of innovation as a point of departure for a discussion about typologies of religious change, the nature of religious authority, and the relative utility of narratives of rupture and repair derived from post-Enlightenment, Protestant experience. If we look past both the rhetoric of reformers themselves and the categories of reform, orthodoxy, and revival, we might be able to see the early nineteenth century in India in different terms, as something

36 *Ibid.*, p. 151.

37 *Ibid.*, p. 152.

38 P. Bacchetta, *Hindu Nationalist Women: On the Use of the Feminine Symbolic to (Temporarily) Displace Male Authority*, in L.L. Patton (ed.), *Jewels of Authority: Women and Textual Tradition in Hindu India*, New York 2002, pp. 157-176.

39 D. Killingley, *Modernity, Reform, and Revival*, in G. Flood (ed.), *Blackwell Companion to Hinduism*, Malden MA 2005, p. 523.

fully continuous with its own past as well as strategically responsive to an ever-changing present. In the era of reform, the alterations to received practice by an emerging middle class under conditions of foreign occupation from which its members nevertheless benefitted socially and economically might be read as a particularly apt and clever response to an environment they were learning to shape using the technologies and ideas they were uniquely positioned to employ. There are two scholarly habits of mind I would draw our attention to at this moment: we are trained to situate religious change in relation to its past and to reinscribe the terms of analysis derived from the Protestant cultures that produced secularism, the secular study of religion, and even the category religion itself. Both habits of mind, I am arguing, underscore reformism as a critical turn towards a modern Hinduism; both also reinforce our notion of our decisive break with the past and the periodization of religious history that bifurcates traditional and modern forms. These habits—historicizing religion with respect to its past and unself-consciously employing Christian categories—will incline us to see a cohesive and identifiable tradition traveling through time, periodically rescued and recalibrated by heroic actors in the wake of its inevitable decline or corruption.

Hatcher has described Bengal's *bhadralok*, those middle-class leaders who spear-headed much of colonial India's experimentation with religious reform, as bourgeoisie, reminding us that these were India's *nouveaux riches*, of both high and low caste, who had achieved their status via industry or financial savvy[40]. These Brahman and non-Brahman elites participated in a culture of hard work and success. They took advantage of changing socioeconomic conditions and emerging technologies at the same time that they were constantly and competitively devising new modes of transaction and communication. Theirs was a culture of innovation and experimentation, and we should not expect their religious and spiritual inclinations to have stood in sharp contrast.

These emerging elites defined their success not only in monetary terms but also in terms of spiritual attainment and eclectic mastery of multiple sources of authority[41]. Pamphlets and newspapers in the early nineteenth

40 B.A. HATCHER, *Bourgeois Hinduism*, p. 69.

41 B.A. HATCHER, *Eclecticism and Modern Hindu Discourse*, New York 1999, pp. 104-118.

century reveal a vibrant and competitive marketplace for new ideas, new idioms, and new practices. Those we have called India's reformers might, I am suggesting, be just as fruitfully thought of as innovators. Hatcher and Fuller name an impressive number of innovations to their credit: the development of syncretic religious practices, the wide use of vernacular languages rather than Sanskrit, their derivation of forms of ritual suitable to an urbanized environment, their codification of what it means to be Hindu, their appropriation of such British technologies, genres, and social forms as the periodical, voluntary organizations, critical history, and the printing press, and their textualization of a highly oral tradition[42]. Indeed, one of their most successful innovations was the utilization of the British idiom of reform for their own advantage.

The idea of innovation points us first to the historical present and only secondarily to the historical past. As historiographical practice, such a prioritization seems appropriate. For these and perhaps all religious innovators, the historical past is a device for achieving particular ends, not a fixed body of texts and authorities that perpetually orient and guide a tradition. The past always is, in A.K. Ramanujan's words, a "pool of signifiers" whose elements remain available for deployment as they are found relevant or useful in any future historical moment. This pool of polyvalent but authoritative symbols does not exhaust the options for any contemporary religious agent because the symbols, resources, and idioms of the present—authoritative in their own right—remain similarly available as well. The past provides a set of resources to be used selectively to the extent that any particular resource is expedient. Innovation, therefore, stands in relation to the past in a posture of negotiation: give me what I want and need for this project at hand, and in return I will pay you your due respect. Innovation, however, is not always in a position of unchallenged strength, for the past makes its own claims on the present. Its authority must be acknowledged and availed. Successful innovation must strike a balance between submission to received authority and invention of tradition. Hence in the instance of early-nineteenth-century reform, we find regular appeals to the Vedas and Upanishads by those advocating a variety of projects. A cynical reading of those uses would find them 'merely' strategic and selective. A properly historical reading of such religious innovation, however,

[42] B.A. Hatcher, *Bourgeois Hinduism*, p. 9; J. Fuller, *Modern Hinduism*, pp. 168-169.

would regard them in the light of religion's perpetual relationship with its past. Such a reading might, therefore, see the early nineteenth-century middle-class reformers not as radicals initiating a breach in a certain historical trajectory in order to repair a tradition gone astray so much as innovators employing the manifold authoritative resources they have in store. We are reminded here of Sen's own assessment of the function of history by those who produced modern Hinduisms: "The 'past' was undoubtedly a potent means of self-realization. In very few cases however, was the 'present' severely compromised"[43].

6. *Reform as enterprise*

Importantly, these bourgeoisie not only understood spiritual attainment as one marker of success; they also worked in voluntary associations of the like-minded to display and publicize spiritual knowledge and insight. That is to say, they were not only innovators, they were, unsurprisingly, entrepreneurs. Entrepreneurialism is a concept developed in the world of trade, and its use to describe religious activity may strike some ears as odd or defamatory. Reframing reform as entrepreneurialism implies several things I want to make clear. First, it suggests an attempt to build something new but durable. Secondly, it involves a degree of self-interest and self-promotion on the part of the entrepreneur. And thirdly, there is a significant element of risk involved.

To illustrate this I will find it helpful to examine a particular case in which rhetorics of reform and revival have long played a critical role in shaping public opinion and legislative action in India. It is, moreover, an issue that has had a continuous and contested history that ties the Indian present directly to nineteenth-century reformism. The term "devadāsī" refers to various classes of women who are dedicated or ritually married to a deity and are today descended from women who served royal Indian courts as entertainers, dancers, and courtesans in pre-colonial centuries. Their dedication to the deity meant that they were *nityasumaṅgalīs* (ever-auspicious women) who did not marry a human partner. They were among the only Indian women who held property, received an education, and enjoyed a degree of independence from the patriarchal order governed by fathers and husbands. Their social roles

[43] A.P. SEN, *Hindu Revivalism in Bengal 1872-1905*, p. 12.

did not come under the scrutiny of British officials or the first wave of Hindu reformism in the early nineteenth century, during which time the concern for the plight of Hindu women had been focused on child brides and immolated widows. Three factors in the late nineteenth century, however, conspired to subject their lifestyles to the reforming impulse: the influence of Victorian sexual mores on Indian middle and upper classes generally; the adoption of those British values by Indian nationalists as markers of modernity and therefore suitability for self-governance; and the production of pan-Indian, essentialist formulations of Hinduism that disdained some regional practice. As Britain passed into the Victorian era and Queen Victoria herself asserted her direct imperial authority over India in 1877, her colonies came increasingly to legislate more restrictive sexual regimes: as we have seen, child-marriage was criminalized, and in addition, through various means, British men were strongly discouraged from mixing with or marrying Indian women Marriage itself was incentivized to end the practice of long and carefree bachelorhoods once enjoyed by British officials. Secondly, in the effort to demand that higher functions of governance be granted to Indians in line with long-standing British assertions that its benevolent rule was serving to modernize India and make it self-governing, nationalist leaders embraced reforming programs that would demonstrate that Indian leadership had come of age. Finally, however, these leaders were also responsive to the revivalist effort to identify and locate a Hindu past that could authenticate a modern, nationalist program, one, therefore, that predated Hinduism's alleged decline into superstition, idolatry, and priestcraft and its fragmentation into manifold regional practices that did not conform to brahminical or Victorian norms: a golden Hindu past in which women were fully honored as equals while relegated to the domestic sphere as a genuinely Indian but fully equitable social arrangement.

The issue of *devadāsī* reform—that is, the effort to end the practice of the dedication of women and girls to the deity, to rehabilitate *devadāsīs*, and to direct them into lives of conjugal domesticity—was championed by the first female legislator in British India, Dr. Muthulakshmi Reddy. She embraced *devadāsī* reform with passion and determination, drafting a series of bills during her legislative career—only some of which were successful—in order to disrupt the social relations and practices in which *devadāsī* dedication was entangled. In 1929 she introduced an amendment to a Madras Presidency law governing rules at Hindu temples whose purpose was to undermine the *devadāsī* system altogether. Previous governmental efforts, including the outright criminalization of the dedication of girls by the Indian Penal Code, had had little effect, and so Dr. Reddy proposed that the lands to which *devadāsīs* had rights but which technically belonged to the temples to which they were attached be deeded to the women themselves[44]. The aim was to sever *devadāsīs'* ties of dependence on the temple and its high-caste, male leadership. Reddy's proposal suggests her analysis of the root problem: a corrupt priesthood allied to the exploitative institution of the temple.

The wider body of her legislation on reform underscores her engagement in rhetorical practices we have seen develop over the course of a century. In her *Bill to Prevent the Dedication of Women to Hindu Temples in the Presidency of Madras*, Reddy indicated her investment in a narrative of Hinduism's decline:

"Whatever the origin of the practice in ancient days of the dedication of women as Devadāsīs in Hindu temples, it is unfortunately the case that the practice has now degenerated mainly into a method of initiating young women to a life of immorality and prostitution".

The bill goes on to acknowledge the sanction of dedication by the classical legal texts of India, the "shastras", and then to assert, in the face of the very evidence to the contrary she has just cited, that true Hinduism would only endorse monogamy and conjugal sexuality:

"The existence or otherwise of Shastric sanction to the practice of dedication as Devadāsīs is therefore immaterial. The Shastras are against vice and impurity of all kinds, and enlightened public opinion is against tolerating the continuance of a practice which, in the name of service to God, has condemned a certain class of women to a life of either concubinage or prostitution"[45].

The *Madras Hindu Religious Endowments (Amendment) Act*, 1929 underscored the notion that a sanitized image of Hinduism was essential to India's national reputation:

"It is necessary that the sanction of our temple authorities to such a practice of dedication which breeds immorality, promiscuity and irresponsibility in both men and women be done away with in the interest of the individuals and the nation at large and thus the public be disabused of the notion that our religion encourages immorality in either

[44] S.M. Reddy, *My Experience as a Legislator*, Madras 1930, pp. 238-239.

[45] *Ibid.*, p. 244.

man or woman and that the service of these women in any way forms an essential part of the worship in the temples"[46].

When an even stricter version of these earlier proposed statutes, the *Madras Prevention of Dedication Act*, became law in October of 1947, it capped decades of South Indian reforming efforts to regulate sexuality according to the norms of British modernity and to project a essentialized, ethicized, and sanitized Hinduism as the *sine qua non* of India's entry into the company of liberal nation states. It reflected the long process of the stigmatization of *devadāsīs* that that had seen monarchs serving at the pleasure of the British government reconfiguring palace practice and festival processions to exclude *devadāsīs*[47], and the immense popularity of salacious literature by reformed *devadāsīs* such as Moovalur Ramamrithammal. Importantly for the argument I am advancing here today, it also gilded the career of one of modern India's storied founding figures.

The reformer is, by definition, a maverick, one who opposes a s*tatus quo*, a stance that requires the marshaling of support and the construction of networks of resistance. The reformer enters or creates a field of contested ideas and engages that field as a competitive marketplace. Following Bourdieu, we recognize that participation in such a field of competition has an existential character, that its ends can include social status. And we can perhaps agree that there is an instrumental character to religion that could contribute to rising political fortunes and the building of nations. Observing that the "success" of *devadāsī* reform was "a distinctly gendered success that did little for women in these communities but allowed men to reinvent themselves as powerful and legitimate members of the modern, non-Brahmin body politic", Davesh Soneji gives me cause to consider a too-little remarked element of reformism[48]. Soneji was referring most immediately to the fact that Muthuvel Karunanidhi, who served five terms as the Chief Minister of the Indian state of Tamil Nadu over a sixty-year political career, was himself born into a *devadāsī* community. His political success, however, only reflects

[46] *Ibid*., p. 238.

[47] S. KERESENBOOM, *Devadāsīs/Courtesans*, in K.A. JACOBSEN (ed.), *Brill's Encyclopedia of Hinduism*, vol. 5, Leiden 2013, pp. 720-722.

[48] D. SONEJI, *Unfinished Gestures: Devadāsīs, Memory, and Modernity in South India*, Chicago IL 2012, p. 112.

the fact that the politics of *devadāsī* reform, and later, *devadāsī* revival, have traded in ideologies of authenticity and elevated those who employed them into positions of political power and influence. In modern India, rhetorics of reform and revival have provided the ideological and historical resources for the building of powerful religious institutions and elevating the status and reputation of their leaders.

7. *Conclusion*

To return once again to Sen, the framework of reform became something of a trap for those Hindus who sought to implement social and religious changes in line with the demands of the modern. "A progressive outlook upon society", he writes, "when combined with recurring references to the cultural resources of the past produced a powerful dichotomy from which no reformer in British India was really free". Staking a Hindu future on an ancient and imagined past proved an unsustainable proposition, leaving reformers "caught between the dictates of reason and ideology, between intellectually attractive goals and cultural nostalgia", between an imagined past and a contested future[49]. This caught-in-betweenness, I would argue, is precisely the condition that should give us pause about the categories of reform and revival, categories that make reference to a past that is relevant largely as a device for achieving present ends. It could lead us to at least two possible conclusions about Hinduism's association with reform: in the case of Hinduism we can think of reform only in terms of de-Protestantized models for reform, models that problematize the textual claims of reforming movements and the status of the enlightened, moral subject. More radically, we might dispense with this backward-looking framework and recognize that all religious change is at some level "reform", because it is always indexed to received tradition and the authority of the past. In the latter case, we would have to adopt language and models that foreground the needs of the historical present and a vision of the historical future as primary motivating forces. Such models would resist the allure of reformers' own appeals to their past as the rhetoric of insiders to a tradition. It would, perhaps, pursue a history of religion decoupled from the authority of the past.

[49] A.P. SEN, *Social and Religious Reform*, pp. 18-19.

Events of 1517, Accents of 2017

Martyrdom

by *Silvana Seidel Menchi*

1. *Introduction*

The Italian notaries whose task it was to record the questioning of so-called "Lutherans" sometimes found themselves transcribing interrogations conducted under torture. Documents of this kind are relatively rare, but they are all the more significant, in as much as they are necessarily free of apologetical intent[1]. Historians who address these themes today, however, are liable to embarrass their hearers or readers. Martyrdom—understood as the testimony of blood—is a phenomenon that our culture tends to remove, to marginalize, or at any rate to circumnavigate with caution.

The challenge of the present was an important influence in the planning of this conference. It was this challenge that prompted my own choice of subject. If in the past the theme of martyrdom induced historians to extend their studies beyond the interconfessional borders within Europe, or to address the non-European ramifications of Christian culture, today's research tends to transcend all intercultural and interreligious barriers. In this paper, after examining four different interpretations of the testimony of blood in the Reformation period (§ II, III), I attempt to interrogate Jewish and Islamic culture regarding their respective understandings of martyrdom (§ IV, V). Both of these cultural universes are extremely complex, and difficult to achieve consensus about; moreover, current research on Judaism and Islam daily modifies our interpretative paradigms, so my present attempt will necessarily be subject to serious limitations.

I warmly thank Roni Weinstein for his critical reading of this paper. *Translation by Mark Roberts*

[1] S. Seidel Menchi, *Theorie und Wirklichkeit der Verfolgung in norditalienischen evangelischen Kreisen*, in R. H. Guggisberg - B. Moeller - S. Seidel Menchi, *Ketzerverfolgung im 16. und frühen 17. Jahrhundert*, Wiesbaden 1992, pp. 175-192.

2. *Plurality of martyrdom*

With the events that were set in motion in 1517, two different interpretations of the Christian message came into being inside the institution that held the monopoly in the spiritual sphere in Christendom and enjoyed ample powers in the secular sphere. Within a short time, these two interpretations achieved autonomy and consolidated themselves into confessional identities, opposing one another in hostile fashion.

From the biennium 1518/1520 onwards, the term "heresy" forcefully re-entered the politico-religious vocabulary, and those members of the clergy whose duty it was to act as inquisitors grew in stature and importance[2]. In the Iberian peninsula, since 1478—and more drastically since 1492—the tribunals of the Inquisition had assumed the task of ensuring religious conformity in the territory of the *reconquista*, obliging Jews and Muslims to choose between conversion and exile, and repressing occult Judaism[3]. The political authority that this task conferred on the Spanish and Portuguese Inquisition appeared—from the 1520s—to be within the grasp of the clergy who acted as inquisitors in Central Europe, in Bourges and in other centers of France, in Northern Italy[4]. In some of these areas the position of inquisitor had thitherto been little more than an empty title[5]; so the irruption of Luther onto the

[2] For a balanced overview of the state of research early in the present century, see A. Borromeo (ed.), *L'Inquisizione*, Città del Vaticano 2003.

[3] Y. Baer, *A History of the Jews in Christian Spain* [Eng. trans. from Hebrew], 2 vols., Philadelphia PA 1961-1966, vol. 2; H. Kamen, *Inquisition and Society in Spain in the Sixteenth and Seventeenth Centuries*, Bloomington IN 1985. An analysis of the phenomenon from close quarters, M. Bodian, *"Men of the Nation": The Shaping of Converso Identity in Early Modern Europe*, in "Past & Present", 143, 1994, pp. 48-76.

[4] A. Duke, *The "Inquisition" and the Repression of Religious Dissent in the Habsburg Netherlands (1521-1556)*, in A. Borromeo (ed.), *L'Inquisizione*, pp. 419-443; J.A. Reid, *French Evangelical Networks before 1555: Proto-churches?*, in P. Benedict - S. Seidel Menchi - A. Tallon, *La Réforme en France et en Italie. Contacts, comparaisons et contrastes*, Roma 2007, pp. 105-124; A. Del Col, *L'Inquisizione in Italia. Dal XII al XXI secolo*, Milano 2006, pp. 284-341. Regarding the persecution of heresy, it should be noted that in France the duties of the inquisitors were early assumed by the *parlements*, see W. Monter, *France: The Failure of Repression, 1520-1563*, in P. Benedict - S. Seidel Menchi - A. Tallon, *La Réforme en France et en Italie*, pp. 465-479.

[5] The surviving documentation on the activity of the inquisitors in Venice or Modena attest that between 1500 and 1530 such activity was reduced to a very few cases, of

public stage was a shot in the arm for certain faculties of theology, such as those of Cologne and Louvain. Inquisitors became privileged interlocutors with the Roman curia and authoritative political advisors to the emperor, to the princes, to the free cities of the empire, to the governors of the Low Countries[6].

Meanwhile, the proponents of the Reformation drew from the Christian historical memory the terminology of persecution, and adapted it to their own experience. The theme of persecution and the ways of confronting it gave rise to a rich literature that easily crossed linguistic and political borders. Among the authors of these treatises and tracts, letters and exhortations, we find Martin Luther and John Calvin, Philip Melanchthon and William Tyndale, Urbanus Rhegius and Pier Paolo Vergerio, Sebastian Castellio and Lelio Sozzini[7].

The literature of persecution offers three different responses to the problem: martyrdom, flight, and what we may call "the way of Nicodemus". I shall look at each response in turn.

1.

The literature of exhortation to martyrdom begins from the premiss that persecution is the ideal condition for the Christian. Remembering the words of Christ (Matthew 5:11-12; 10:17-23; 24:9; John 15:18-20),

slight importance (Archivio di Stato di Modena, *Inquisizione*, bb. 1, 2; Archivio Storico del Patriarcato di Venezia, *Criminalia Sanctae Inquisitionis*, bb. 1, 2).

6 For a glance at the activity of the Inquisition in the Rhenish region during an actual case, see E. RUMMEL, *The Case Against Johann Reuchlin: Religious and Social Controversy in Sixteenth-Century Germany*, Toronto - Buffalo NY - London 2002, pp. 3-35. Erasmus began to attract the suspicions of the inquisitors from 1519, when his name was systematically coupled with that of Luther (C. AUGUSTIJN, *Erasmus von Rotterdam. Leben, Werk, Wirkung*, München 1986, p. 109).

7 B.S. GREGORY, *Salvation at Stake. Christian Martyrdom in Early Modern Europe*, Cambridge MA - London 1999, *ad voces* Luther, Calvin, Melanchthon, Tyndale, Rhegius. For Pier Paolo Vergerio see A. PROSPERI, *L'eresia del Libro Grande. Storia di Giorgio Siculo e della sua setta*, Milano 2000, pp. 102-130, 211-225; for Sebastian Castellio and Lelio Sozzini: D. CANTIMORI, *Eretici italiani del Cinquecento e altri scritti*, Torino 1992, pp. 162-175; for Castellio: H.R. GUGGISBERG, *Sebastian Castellio 1515-1563: Humanist und Verteidiger der religiösen Toleranz im konfessionellen Zeitalter*, Göttingen 1997.

the pious and godly man cannot subtract himself from persecution, but must accept it as a sign of his election. In persecution suffered in the name of the Gospel, Christ's death becomes our death. Persecution is to be greeted as the prelude to martyrdom, which is the *imitatio Christi* par excellence[8]. The directness with which the theorists of persecution propose to the faithful the prospect of martyrdom is part of the climate of messianic expectation that accompanied the advent of the Reformation. The conviction of living in a new apostolic age, and the sense of the approaching end of time, brought death on the day-to-day horizon of ordinary believers[9].

From the subjective point of view, martyrdom would appear in this climate to be a perfectly rational choice[10]. And from the community point of view, it was the only fruitful strategy for the Reformation movements, or for the Catholic minority in Elizabethan England. The arguments advanced by the apologists for martyrdom are also rational: because of its power as testimony, martyrdom is the weapon by which the faithful achieve victory over the "adorers of idols" or, on the other side, the "heretics". In consequence, the Christian cannot avoid the duty of publicly professing the truth revealed by God, and of denying Babylon, or, on the other side, of challenging the authority of heretical and impious rulers[11].

8 For samples of hortatory writings on persecution and martyrdom, see B.S. GREGORY, *Salvation at Stake*, p. 418, nn. 87, 88, 89. The ability of these pamphlets to cross the linguistic and cultural frontiers of Europe was greater than would appear from this list, as is shown for instance by the case of the pamphlet by Urbanus Rhegius cited in the following note, which was anonymously translated and circulated in Italy (*Libretto consolatorio a li perseguitati per la confessione de la verita Evangelica*, In Milano, M.D.XLV), from the Latin version [Frankfurt, 1543].

9 URBANUS RHEGIUS, *Trostbrieff an alle Christen zu Hildesheym, die umbs Evangeliums willen itzt Schmach und Verfolgung leiden*, Magdeburg, Hans Walther, 1531; CELIO SECONDO CURIONE, *Una familiare e paterna institutione della Christina religione*, s.l. [Basilea, 1549], fols. K4*r*-Lvi*v*. For Luther and his consolatory writings for the time of persecution see R. KOLB, *God's Gift of Martyrdom: The Early Reformation Understanding of Dying for the Faith*, in A. PETTIGREE (ed), *The Reformation. Critical Concepts in Historical Studies*, vol. 1, London - New York 2004, pp. 93-105.

10 B.S. GREGORY, *Salvation at Stake*, pp. 99-111.

11 *Ibid.*, see for instance CELIO SECONDO CURIONE, *Una familiare e paterna institutione della Christina religione*, fol. L5*r*.

These arguments are not restricted to the literature of treatises, but permeate the lived experience of contemporaries. We find them attested in the trial records that have come down to us in Italy, or in Elizabethan England, where they are mainly found in martyrologies[12].

Brilliant as is the communicative force of martyrdom, so—according to this literature—is the effect of recantation dismal. Recantation sees the triumph of Antichrist, it corrodes consciences, it devastates the ranks of the elect. Thus the literature of persecution offers icons—positive and negative—of martyrdom. These icons are emphasized and disseminated by means of print, so as to counter the deplorable effect of public recantation[13].

2.

Beginning in the 1540s, an alternative to the idea of martyrdom makes its appearance. The type of confession of faith that is now held up as a model is that of turning one's back on Antichrist and seeking refuge in those lands that profess the Gospel. To remain in one's country of origin is, for the members of minorities, to risk having to deny Christ. Since the end of the world appears not to be imminent, love of life enters into the vocabulary of dissent, giving rise to a new kind of rhetoric, the rhetoric of exile[14].

Flight, the little martyrdom, is substituted for death as the supreme form of evangelical profession. Its symbolic force consists in proposing to the attention of the community the fact that there exists a supreme value, in the name of which the exile renounces all creature comforts and the company of friends.

[12] S. Seidel Menchi, *Italy*, in B. Scribner - R. Porter - M. Teich (eds), *The Reformation in National Context*, Cambridge 1994, pp. 181-201; for England B.S. Gregory, *Salvation at Stake*, pp. 250-314.

[13] The principle negative icon is that of the Francesco Spiera, *exemplum ad deterrendum* of the bleak despair and dreadful end of those who, like this jurist from Cittadella, deny the known truth; see A. Prosperi, *L'eresia del Libro Grande*, pp. 102-130 and S. Seidel Menchi, *Simbologia della rottura e movimento riformatore in Italia*, in P. Benedict - S. Seidel Menchi - A. Tallon (eds), *La Réforme en France et en Italie*, pp. 438-439.

[14] S. Seidel Menchi, *Simbologia della rottura*, pp. 441-447.

3.

The third option is intellectually the boldest, and consequently the most controversial. It is the option of keeping one's own choice of conscience to oneself. In justification of this tactic there arose a doctrinal edifice that legitimated dissimulation of the known truth and justified simulation, i.e. the active participation in rites, ceremonies, and practices from which the believer had distanced himself in the forum of conscience, *in foro conscientiae*.

The doctrine of the liceity of dissimulation, "Nicodemism", is a Europe-wide phenomenon and it is based on an interiorized concept of the religious life. Living the faith as an experience that exclusively regards the inner person makes it possible to relegate all rites and ceremonies to the sphere of indifferent practices (*adiaphora*) and thus to legitimate one's participation in them[15]. The doctrine of "adiaphora" (1 Corinthians 8-9) had acquired pressing topicality after the publication in 1520 of Luther's treatise *On Christian Liberty*, which relegated a great many religious practices to this category. The "Nicodemite" was a Christian who knew the truth of the Gospel, but who adapted himself to the traditional practices so as not to give scandal to the weaker brethren (1 Corinthians 8). In this specific sense, the term "Nicodemite" was coined by Calvin in his *Excuse à messieurs les nicodemites* (1544).

What these doctrines challenge is a religious practice based on places, times, and ceremonies (including the sacraments), which are seen as carnal manifestations of the faith. The basic conviction is that it is possible to profess the true faith "by night"[16], that is to say in the secret of one's conscience. God searches the hearts and the minds: this was

[15] C. GINZBURG, *Il nicodemismo. Simulazione e dissimulazione relgiosa nell'Europa del '500*, Torino 1970. Despite the disdain that such behaviour aroused in Reformation territory (because of its divisive effect on the persecuted "churches"), we nevertheless find, even in authoritative personages, empathy for those who took refuge in simulation, and compassion for their misery. "Agli infermi che non ardiscono di palesarsi io consiglio che a guisa di Nicodemo, vadano di notte al Signore" [I would advise those of the weak who are reluctant to reveal themselves to go to the Lord by night, like Nicodemus (Jn 3:1-15)], wrote Celio Secondo Curione in the work cited in note 9, fol. L5*r*.

[16] The nocturnal meeting and conversation between Jesus and Nicodemus is narrated in Jn 3:1-2. Later, Nicodemus is identified as he "qui venerat ad Iesum nocte" (Jn 7:50-52; 19, 39).

the basic principle that made it lawful for the Christian to dissemble. Positions reflecting this point of view were taken by Lefèvre d'Etaples, Sebastian Franck, Thomas Wolff, and Bartholomäus Westheimer[17].

3. *A forger at work*

In all parts of Europe and across the denominations there was an exuberant flowering of the literature of martyrdom; in these writings, religious opportunism and dissimulation were perceived as corrosive and deplorable. The literature that legitimated dissimulation, on the other hand, deployed its arguments cautiously and under cover of darkness, recruiting adherents especially in minority communities such as Spirituals and Anabaptists. As regards visibility, therefore, the two opposing options—the testimony of blood and the testimony of conscience—are not comparable. If however we shift our attention from the public area to that of lived experience, this imbalance is corrected in favor of the option for interior faith.

The figures that we have at our disposal are, evidently, somewhat partial. I will limit myself to some data of which we can be certain. In Venice, the number of Reformation sympathizers who were tried by the Holy Office between 1547 and 1586 was 713 (676 Evangelicals and 37 Anabaptists). If we add up the number of those who are mentioned in the trials as supporting the Evangelical cause but who were not themselves put on trial, we arrive at about 2,100[18]. In this same period, 23 sentences of death were issued, of which 20 were carried out (the remaining three having been handed out *in absentia*)[19]. This means that in the relatively turbulent Venetian area, the "Luterani" who actually

[17] C. GINZBURG, *Il nicodemismo*.

[18] A. DEL COL, *L'Inquisizione in Italia*, pp. 492-493 (the above figures do not include the 17 people who in the same period were accused of Millenarian views). According to the inventories, for the entire 16th century the total number of those accused of embracing heresy, heretical propositions, prohibited books and prohibited foods—all crimes that implied adhesion or proximity to the Reformation—amounted to 950 (*ibid.*) At the tribunal of Aquileia and Concordia, the same charges in the sixteenth century amounted to 355: 75 for Reformation ideas, 145 for heretical propositions, 28 for prohibited books, 107 for prohibited foods (*ibid.*)

[19] *Ibid.*, p. 493. In the sixteenth century the tribunal of Aquileia and Concordia issued 10 capital sentences, of which 5 were carried out and the rest pronounced *in absentia*.

suffered martyrdom amounted to no more that 1%[20]. In Bologna, a city that was part of the Papal States, the somewhat incomplete documentation of the Inquisition attests to the presence of between 150 and 200 Protestants: in this case 34 capital sentences were carried out, and 11 or 12 were issued *in abstentia*. In Bologna, obviously, the collaboration between the Inquisition and the secular arm was closer than in Venice[21]. Even in these more perilous conditions, however, the proportion of those bearing witness with their blood did not exceed 20-25%. The others, for the most part, had chosen to profess their faith in the privacy of their own consciences. Of the three options open to dissidents, the first made the greatest impression on the public stage; but it was the third that was most practiced.

The succession of the three options listed above makes manifest a basic tendency that was already well defined in the Europe of confessional conflict: the tendency to distance oneself from the testimony of blood, to spiritualize the notion of martyrdom, to interpret it as bearing witness by living. This concept—for which there is no lack of precedents in medieval theology and iconography—finds particularly vivid expression in a text whose argument I should now like briefly to summarize.

It is a treatise entitled *The two kinds of martyrdom (De duplici martyrio)*, described in 1530 as a recently discovered writing by Saint Cyprian, bishop of Carthage[22]. This saint, a master of rhetoric, had written extensively on the theme of the martyrdom of blood and had himself been martyred in 258, during the persecution of Valerian. In the treatise

20 A. Del Col, *L'Inquisizione in Italia*, p. 495. For the procedure of the tribunals see: T.F. Mayer, *The Roman Inquisition. A Papal Bureaucracy and Its Laws in the Age of Galileo*, Philadelphia PA 2013.

21 G. Dall'Olio, *Bologna*, in A. Prosperi, with V. Lavenia and J. Tedeschi (eds), *Dizionario storico dell'Inquisizione*, Pisa 2010, vol. 1, pp. 211-213.

22 [Divi Caecilii Cypriani] *Liber vnus De duplici martyrio ad Fortunatum, quem in vetustissima bibliotheca repertum adiecimus: Vtinam liceat et caetera huius viri salutifera scripta pervestigare.* We find this title in *Diui Caecilii Cypriani episcopi carthaginensis et martyris Opera iam quartum accuratiori vigilantia a mendis repurgata, per Des. Erasmum Roterod. Accessit liber eiusdem apprime pius ad Fortunatum De duplici martyrio, antehac nunquam excusus*, Basileae, ex Officina Frobeniana Anno M.D.XXX (Colophon: Basileae, in Officina Frobeniana per Hieronymum Frobenium, Ioannem Heruagium et Nicolaum Episcopium, Anno M. D. XXX. mense Ianuario), fol. b3*v*. The treatise occupies the final 20 pages of text (fol. X8*v*-Z4*r* corresponding to pp. 508-527).

On the two kinds of martyrdom, the author widened and diversified his discourse. If the "martyr", etymologically, is "he who bears witness", the title of martyr belongs to all who bear witness to God, those who bear it by dying and those who bear it by living[23].

Although the author makes obeisance to the salvific cross, his hidden agenda is to ascribe to unbloody martyrdom as high a position as, or even a higher position than, bloody martyrdom on the scale of Christian perfection. Unbloody martyrdom, he observes, has an ampler extension than the other kind, because it has no need of torturers to shine in the eyes of God. The fury of persecution passes away, "but the struggles and the martyrdoms by which pious men give glory to God continue undiminished"[24]. Moreover, the author argues, it is the testimony of life that gives value to the testimony of blood, and not the other way round, because the martyrdom that has not been preceded by a virtuous life has no value[25]. Theologically speaking, this is an error: the blood of the martyr washes away all sins.

[23] *De duplici martyrio*, fol. Z2*r* (p. 523),"[Paulus] scribens ad Hebraeos orsus ab Abel vsque ad Gedeonem ingentem sanctorum catalogum recenset, in quo plures sunt qui non defuncti sunt morte violenta, imo pauci sunt qui sic mortui sunt. Et tamen de omnibus pronunciat: *Et hi testimonio fidei probati inventi sunt*, perspicue declarans etiam vita bona peragi martyrium fidei. Ecclesiae quidem usus discernit illos cognominibus, martyres appellans eos qui violenta morte decesserunt, confessores qui constanter in cruciatibus ac minis mortis professi sunt nomen domini Iesu, parati mortem oppetere vel potius martyrii supremam coronam ambientes. Apud Deum tamen quicunque carnem suam crucifixerunt cum vitiis et concupiscentiis, quicunque Christo vere commortui sunt eique in baptismo consepulti sunt – vt iam non sibi vivant neque mundo cui semel mortui sunt, sed ei qui pro ipsis est mortuus – martyres sunt nec martyrum corona fraudabuntur".

[24] *De duplici martyrio*, fol. Y4*r-v* (pp. 515-516), "Neque enim semper saeuiunt Nerones, Diocletiani, Decii ac Maximini; nunquam tamen cessat diabolus exercere Christi militiam professos. Et fortassis erunt posthac donante Christo tempora quibus nullae tyrannorum persequutiones affligent ecclesiam; nunquam tamen defutura sunt certamina, nunquam martyria quibus homines pii glorificent Deum."

[25] *De duplici martyrio*, fol. Y5*v* (p. 518), "Haec quum ad hunc habeant modum ... conemur assiduis exhortationibus excitare fidelium animos, ut tota etiam vita martyrium, hoc est testimonium, reddat Deo. Quod adeo negligendum non est, ut nisi ea praecesserit, martyrium quod sanguine perhibetur non sit martyrium. Frustra enim cervicem praebueris carnifici, nisi prius occideris *membra quae sunt super terram*, hoc est affectus qui militant adversus spiritum – odium, invidiam, avariciam, superbiam, libidinem – quibus quicunque servit Deum quodammodo abnegavit, et Christum ore profitens vita Satanam Deum confitetur".

Christians who deny Christ under torture deserve more indulgence, according to this treatise, than those who practice vice: the former give way to the promptings of nature, too strong to be overcome by human willpower, yet continue to honor Christ in their consciences; the latter consign themselves voluntarily to the power of Satan. Apostasy is committed not only by those who burn incense before idols, but by all those who serve in the ranks of evil and obey its commandments[26].

In the concluding peroration, finally, the experience of the martyr dissolves into the Christian's daily struggle. A financial disaster, a family bereavement, the loss of a loved one, a cruel illness: each of these experiences confers on the Christian the crown of martyrdom. Every Christian, of whatsoever rank or degree, has their cross to bear; if they bear it with patience, they give glory to God by their witness. Thus the glory of martyrdom turns out to be the crowning of an interior disposition rather than a bodily experience. Hidden martyrdom—martyrdom as the testimony of conscience—is more severe than professing one's faith by the shedding of one's blood[27].

In an age that saw opposed and irreconcilable choices of conscience in parliament, on the street, in courts of law, in princes' palaces, and on battlefields, the treatise on twofold martyrdom communicates the message that fidelity to one's own faith does not necessarily demand the shedding of one's own blood. It transfers martyrdom from the level of the physical event to the level of interior experience. It is a forgery, well attuned to topical themes and well argued[28]. Some scholars still consider it genuine today. It made little impact in a Europe inundated with martyrologies. It is however a prophetic text, one that anticipated the perplexity of Western culture faced with the experience of martyrdom.

[26] *De duplici martyrio*, fol. *Zr* (p. 521), "Merito fidelium aures abominantur apostatae vocabulum; verum hoc non ibi tantum execrandum est, quum incenso thusculo ... renunciatur professioni nominis Christi, sed ubicunque contemptis Christi legibus obtemperatur Satanae. Nec enim refert quid sonet lingua, quae si sonet Christum, quum animus sit deditus criminibus, non est professio sed hypocrisis".

[27] *De duplici martyrio*, fols *Z3v-Z4r* (pp. 526-527).

[28] The forger is Erasmus of Rotterdam. See S. SEIDEL MENCHI, *Introduction* to *De duplici martyrio*, in DESIDERII ERASMI ROTERODAMI *Opera omnia recognita et adnotatione critica instructa notisque illustrata*, series VII, vol. 1, Leiden (forthcoming).

4. *Analogies or divergences?*

However much Christian martyrdom of the early centuries was influenced by the Hebrew Bible—in particular, 2 Maccabees 7 and Daniel 3[29]—the actual experience had a very different impact in the two cultures, the Jewish and the Christian.

The waves of violence that from the eleventh century periodically afflicted the Jewish communities in Europe made the state of persecution an historical constant for the Jews, and incised martyrdom onto the horizon of their awareness with an urgency that has no parallel among the Christian population. In response to these recurrent attacks, a part of rabbinical culture devised theories that extended the range of options open to the individual faithful (whose experience was incorporated into the definition of martyrdom), so that he or she might not be bound to a forced choice. In particular, the persecutions that accompanied the First Crusade (1096) inspired two significant extensions of the concept of martyrdom.

- The rabbinical doctrine offered a positive response to the question of whether a Jew who is obliged to choose between conversion and death might permissibly commit suicide, and whether his suicide might be regarded as "sanctification of the Name" [Kidush HaShem], that is to say as active martyrdom.
- A similar response was given to the question of whether the persecuted believer might licitly kill his own children and other family members in order to prevent their baptism and conversion to Christianity[30].

Although these options have given rise to a lively debate, and no unequivocal solution has been found[31], it is nevertheless clear that the more persecution threatened daily living[32], the more cautious and flexible

[29] J.W. van Henten, in collaboration with B.A.G.M. Dehandschutter - H.J.W. van de Klaauw (eds), *Die Entstehung der jüdischen Martyrologie*, Leiden 1989, p. 7.

[30] H. Soloveitchik, *Halakhah, Hermeneutik, and Martyrdom in Medieval Ashkenaz*, in "The Jewish Quarterly Review", 94, 2004, pp. 77-108, part 1, and pp. 278-299, part 2, in particular p. 79; S. Goldin, *The Ways of Jewish Martyrdom*, Turnhout 2008, pp. 95-96; A. Gross, *Struggling with Tradition. Reservations about Active Martyrdom in the Middle Ages*, Leiden - Boston MA 2004.

[31] A. Gross, *Struggling with Tradition*, p. 84.

[32] K.A. Fudeman, *These Things I Will Remember: The Troyes Martyrdom and Collective Memory*, in "Prooftexts", 29, 2009, pp. 1-30.

became the doctrine that regulated behavior in critical situations. Thus, rabbinic literature does not encourage the aspiration to martyrdom but, on the contrary, tends to limit the cases in which the Jewish believer is obliged to choose death rather than to transgress a commandment of the law. Roughly from the third century and onward, such extreme cases are reduced to three: "If a Gentile tells an Israelite to transgress one or all of the commandments of the Torah—excepting idol worship, incestuous relations, and the spilling of innocent blood—he should transgress the commandments and not be killed"[33]. The same tradition authorizes recourse to cunning, and even to dissimulation, in order to avoid the choice between conversion and death (sixteenth- and seventeenth-century Spain)[34]. The first duty of the faithful Jew is to defend his own life until the point where he is placed in a desperate position regarding the observance of his own faith. The lively presence of the testimony of blood in Jewish historiography reflects, indeed, the importance that this form of witness has had in molding the collective memory of Israel[35]; yet Jewish culture has shown itself more attentive to the lacerations imposed on the believer by the prospect of martyrdom, than has been the case with Christianity.

An extension of the concept of martyrdom to include not only the testimony of blood but also the testimony of life, such as—as we have seen—is found in Christian culture in the period of the Reformation, is not unknown in Islamic culture. In the lexicon of Islam the martyr was, originally, the one who "renders testimony"—with his life, and not necessarily with his death. Western historiography on the Muslim martyr devotes particular attention to positions such as that of Jalal al-Din al-Suyuti (d. 1505) who enlarged the definition of martyrdom so far as to recognize as martyrs all those who aspired to martyrdom. Among those who "die in the path of Allah" [*jihad*], Suyuti lists—possibly relying on an earlier tradition—seven categories: those who die of a stomach complaint, or by drowning, or of the plague, or in a structural collapse, or in a fire, or of pleurisy, and the women who die

[33] S. Goldin, *The Ways of Jewish Martyrdom*, p. 69; but see also *ibid.*, pp. 341-342.

[34] M. Bodian, *In the Cross-Currents of the Reformation: Crypto-Jewish Martyrs of the Inquisition 1570-1670*, in "Past & Present," 176, 2002, pp. 66-104.

[35] It has been observed that "Jewish martyrology anticipated Jewish historiography by many centuries", and the Jewish religion has been called "eine Religion des Martyriums", see J.W. van Henten, *Die Entstehung der Jüdischen Martyrologie*, pp. 1-2.

in childbed—all these deserve the title of martyr[36]. Going even further, this line of thought confers the title of martyr on those who say certain prayers, or who carry out specific ceremonies, or who sincerely ask God for the gift of martyrdom and who then die, even in bed[37].

The concept of martyrdom proper to Sufism recalls even more directly the evolution of the Christian concept. Sufism created the figure of the living martyr. This is the ascetic or mystic whose life of prayer, fasting and solitude is considered tantamount to martyrdom[38]. By an analogous conceptual operation, late-antique and medieval Christian theology recognized monks and nuns as the heirs of the martyrs and accorded them—now that the age of persecution was finished—the same pre-eminence that the church of the earliest centuries had accorded to those who testified with their blood[39].

In Shi'ite Islam, the martyr par excellence is the victim of co-religionists with a different view of the faith. For the Shi'ites, too, to persevere in one's faith for an entire lifetime has the same value as falling on the field of battle: constancy in the faith confers on the believer the title of martyr, just like those who fought alongside the Prophet[40]. Moreover, the choice of simulation or dissimulation is legitimated by legal and theological arguments in this minority community[41].

[36] D. COOK, *Martyrdom in Islam*, Cambridge 2007, pp. 33-34.

[37] *Ibid.*, pp. 34-36, 167; M. HATINA, *Martyrdom in Modern Islam. Piety, Power, and Politics*, Cambridge 2014, pp. 53-54.

[38] D. COOK, *Martyrdom in Islam*, pp. 63-64; M. HATINA, *Martyrdom in Modern Islam*, p. 50.

[39] One medieval iconographic testimony directly assimilates the scholar (Saint Augustine) and the ascetic (Saint William of Malval) to the martyrs: just as the martyrs exhibit before the heavenly throne the instruments of their martyrdom or the mutilations they suffered (Saint Agatha with her severed breasts), so Saint Augustine shows the codices that contain his Rule—the fruit of his labours as writer and thinker in the service of the Church—and Saint Willliam shows the herbs that attest to his ascetic life, and in particular to the rigours of his diet (M. SEIDEL, *The Frescoes by Ambrogio Lorenzetti in Sant'Agostino in Siena*, in M. SEIDEL, *Italian Art of the Middle Ages and the Renaissance*, vol. 1, Venice 2005, pp. 360-367).

[40] M. HATINA, *Martyrdom in Modern Islam*, p. 51.

[41] M. BASSIOUNI, *Menschenrechte zwischen Universalität und islamischer Legitimität*, Berlin 2014, p. 141; see also T. BAUER, *Die Kultur der Ambiguität. Eine andere Geschichte des Islams*, Berlin 2011.

To assimilate these Islamic utterances to the Christian discourse on "bearing witness" as the habitus of everyday life is, however, an operation that demands caution. In the Muslim concept of martyrdom, the figure that is historically, symbolically, and emotionally predominant is that of the warrior who, on the field of battle, fights to the death, in the front line, and who continues the struggle against desperate odds, in order to ensure the victory of God. The warlike concept of martyrdom is congenital to the birth and growth of the Islamic empire, driven forward as it was by serried ranks of religiously and politically motivated combatants, determined to advance or to resist to the last man, in order to achieve the aim of religious and political dominion[42]. Islamic tradition celebrates as glorious victories certain battles the followers of the Prophet won against armies that were three times more numerous than they. Despite the "*de facto* waning of the ethos of jihad and martyrdom in the battlefield" in the centuries of the modern age, the ideal of bearing testimony by dying in battle reappears periodically in dissident communities or in marginal Muslim groups[43].

Authoritative legal opinions in the early centuries of Islamic culture even legitimated the choice of solitary combat, in which the believer on his own attacks an overwhelming enemy force: if he is devoted to God and is sincere in his "intention" to cause harm to the infidel, his action is lawful (Mohammad ibn al-Hasan al Shaybani, d. 805; Abu Hamid al-Ghazali, d. 1111)[44]. The "Islamic humanism" that we have learned about from Shahab Ahmed opens up the perspective to the future, but does not protect us from the trials of the present[45].

[42] D. Cook, *Martyrdom in Islam*, pp. 12-44; M. Hatina, *Martyrdom in Modern Islam*, pp. 36-39, 43.

[43] D. Cook, *Martyrdom in Islam*, p. 41-42; M. Hatina, *Martyrdom in Modern Islam*, p. 53.

[44] *Ibid.*, pp. 36, 40, 47, 65.

[45] S. Ahmed, *What is Islam? The Importance of Being Islamic*, Princeton NJ - Oxford 2016.

5. *Conscience*

We have seen that transferring martyrdom from the level of physical experience to the level of interior experience calls into play the principle of conscience. To what extent can this link be found in the three monotheistic religions?

The importance that the appeal to conscience assumes in the thought and action of Luther is a postulate that has no need of demonstration. Because of Luther, "the critical role of conscience in Protestantism had been established once and for all"[46].

Rather less well known is the appeal to conscience in the vocabulary of Catholic culture. This is an area that historians need to explore more thoroughly. To do so they need to examine the sources produced by Catholic institutions invested with judicial authority, especially the transcriptions of interrogations, and the texts of moral controversy. I will mention three examples.

- The appeal to conscience occurs in the interrogations by episcopal *vicarii* of Catholics who apply to the church courts in situations of personal or family conflict, especially in cases of matrimonial uncertainty. The episcopal officials who were responsible for solving these disputes took it upon themselves to *perscrutare* the souls of the faithful, to "peer into" their hearts. Their preferred interlocutors were women: the *vicarii* took pains to ensure that these women, who were often young or extremely young, were able to express themselves freely, separating them from their families so as to subtract them from paternal or maternal pressure. The young women were exhorted to reflect deeply and to take responsibility for their words; continual appeals were made to their "conscience" (sixteenth-century Venice)[47].
- Another area of the concept of "conscience" that is worthy of exploration is the literature of casuistry. After centuries in which the early-modern casuists were the subject of vigorous polemical attacks (Pascal's *Lettres Provinciales*, 1657), this literature is now emerging as a fruitful field of research. A forthcoming book by Stefania Tutino,

[46] M. VAN CREFELD, *Conscience. A Biography*, London 2015, pp. 67-69.

[47] C. CRISTELLON, *L'ufficio del giudice. Mediazione, inquisizione e confessione nei processi matrimoniali veneziani (1420-1532)*, in "Rivista Storica Italiana", 115, 2003, pp. 851-898.

and a collection of essays edited by Carlo Ginzburg, promise to open up a new field of studies in this area[48].

- Lastly, the most authoritative documentation on the subject of conscience is found in the archives of the Holy Office of the Inquisition. Their opening in 1998 aroused enormous interest in the scholarly world[49] and has given rise to a veritable avalanche of publications[50]. The most important series of documents, the protocols of the tribunal (*Decreta Sancti Officii*), remains however unpublished. On the basis of my own transcription of the first fascicle of protocols (1548-1558), I can however report that the term "conscience" occurs in them twelve times.

The most significant of these occurrences is from the mouth of the pope himself. On April 29, 1557, Paul IV informed his prelates about a brief he intended to promulgate. On that day the tribunal of the Holy Office—presided over as usual by the pope—comprised nine cardinals, three archbishops, the Master of the Sacred Palace (the pope's personal theological advisor), and four theologians and canonists who acted as consultants. The papal brief concerned the use of torture during interrogations "in trials for heresy", both for the accused and for witnesses. The procedure could lead—as the direct result of voting by members of the tribunal—to "the mutilation of a member [of the body] or the shedding of blood" of the accused, or of a witness, "even unto natural death *inclusive*"[51]. Evidently some members of the tribunal were troubled in conscience, fearful of incurring a state of irregularity from any shedding of blood consequent upon their decision. The pope therefore, "wishing to safeguard the security and tranquility of their mind and conscience",

[48] S. TUTINO, *Uncertainty in Post-Reformation Catholicism: A History of Probabilism* (forthcoming); C. GINZBURG (ed.), *Norms and Exceptions. A Comparative Approach to Casuistry*, forthcoming.

[49] *L'apertura degli archivi del Sant'Uffizio romano* (Atti dei convegni Lincei, 142), Roma 1998.

[50] For an overall balance of research on the Inquisition, see M. VALENTE, *Nuove ricerche e interpretazioni sul Sant'Uffizio a più di dieci anni dall'apertura dell'archivio*, in "Rivista di storia della Chiesa in Italia", 66, 2012, pp. 569-592.

[51] Città del Vaticano, Archivio della Congregazione per la Dottrina della Fede, *Decreta Sancti Officii*, I, Die Iovis 29 Aprilis 1557.

authorized the members of the tribunal to take decisions that would result in the use of torture, and to pass sentences that would have as a consequence "mutilation and shedding of blood even unto natural death *inclusive*", all this without incurring any irregularity; and the pope even absolved them of any irregularity they might have contracted earlier[52].

Conscience is a force that can speak a different language in the pope and in the cardinals assembled at the Holy Office, becoming a potential factor of divergence and obliging the pope to resort to the principle of authority so as to ward off a potential schism. In other words: even the pope bows before the argument of conscience. My conclusion is that "conscience", despite its considerable fluctuations of meaning, and varied intensity of presence, is an authority recognized by the different cultures in the Christian world, independently of confessional boundaries.

What can we say about the role of conscience in the other two monotheistic religions?

The history of the twentieth century has conferred an extraordinary tension on the term "conscience" in Jewish culture, a tension that is expressed in a flourishing literature of study and analysis. In this literature, however, the term "conscience" occurs especially in the expression "freedom of conscience", or else we find it in connection with the debate on human rights[53]. In other words, studies of conscience coming from Israel, or focusing on Jewish communities, refer basically to the history of the last two centuries. An authoritative Israeli histo-

[52] Città del Vaticano, Archivio della Congregazione per la Dottrina della Fede, *Decreta Sancti Officii*, I, Die Iovis 29 Aprilis 1557: "Nos securitati et tranquillitati eorum mentis et conscientiae occurrere volentes ... votum et sententiam eorum non solum quoad questionem et torturam ipsis reis pro delictis, quibus pro tempore inquisiti accusati seu denuntiati fuerint, sed etiam ad condignam poenam et mulctam etiam usque ad mutilationem seu sanguinis effusionem usque ad mortem naturalem inclusive, absque alicuius censure vel irregularitatis incursu, dicere et eisdem Congregationibus interesse et immiscere possint, licentiam et facultatem concedimus, ac quoad preterita si aliquam forsan irregularitatem incurrissent cum omnibus predictis dispensamus".

[53] M. WYSCHOGROD, *Judaism and Conscience*, in A. FINKEL - L. FRIZZELL (eds), *Standing Before God: Studies on Prayer in Scripture and in Tradition with Essays in Honor of John M. Oesterreicher*, New York 1981, pp. 313-328; M.R. KONWITZ (ed.), *Judaism and Human Rights*, 2nd ed. New Brunswick NJ - London 2001, see in particular *Freedom of conscience*, pp. 157-212.

rian has even asserted that prior to the twentieth century the Hebrew language did not possess a term that translated the Latin concept of *conscientia*. "Modern Jews took the idea of conscience from Christianity, or rather the Christian peoples among whom they lived after leaving the ghetto during the nineteenth century"[54]. This judgment finds however a correction in the description that Roni Weinstein has given of the genesis of Jewish modernity. In his reconstruction, the practice of confessing sins, heavily emphasized in post-Tridentine Catholicism, had a profound innovative effect on Jewish theology and on the Kabbalah, in the forms that these assumed in Safed especially in the seventeenth century. Assiduous vigilance over sin, and the training of the faithful in the examination of conscience, entered into Jewish culture and lastingly molded the experience of the individual believer[55]. As a consequence, the dialogue between Judaism and Christianity on the concept of conscience dates back at least to the seventeenth century.

In historical and juridical studies dealing with Islam, on the other hand, the term "conscience" does not occur at all, so far as I know. A concept that can have a certain affinity with that of conscience is "intent" or "intention". "Intent" is indeed considered "a fundamental concept of the whole of Islamic religious law", "a component of nearly every relevant action, from purification and prayer, to sales and divorce, to fornication and murder". When we read that "in Islamic law, intentions are a constitutive element of human action, the internal component of the actions prescribed, proscribed, and evaluated by Muslim legal scholars"—and that "intent is subjective, invisible, silent, 'internal'"—we are apt, as scholars of Western formation, to suppose that here is an Islamic equivalent to the dimension of conscience[56].

In the Sunni doctrine analyzed by Paul Powers, in particular, "intent"—generally conveyed in Arabic by the word *niyya*—is the interior completion necessary for full observance of the precepts and commandments

[54] M. van Creveld, *Conscience*, p. 22.

[55] R. Weinstein, *Kabbalah and Jewish Modernity*, Liverpool 2016, especially chap. 6, pp. 123-141; see also J. Garb, *The Psychological Turn in Sixteenth Century Kabbalah*, in G. Cecere - M. Loubet - S. Pagani (eds), *Le mystiques juives, chrétiennes et musulmanes dans l'Egypte médiévale (VIIe-XVIe siècles). Interculturalité et contexte historique*, Cairo 2013, pp. 109-124.

[56] P.R. Powers, *Intent in Islamic Law. Motive and Meaning in Medieval Sunni Fiqh*, Leiden - Boston MA 2015, quotation at pp. 1, 3.

of worship as regulated by Islamic law. The exterior performance of the ritual action commanded (prayer, fasting, pilgrimage, etc.) is not enough; it must be completed by the interior intention to fulfill that specific commandment. Through the *niyya* or intention, the one who acts mentally defines his or her action as an act of ritual worship, in accordance with the legal taxonomy of prescribed actions. So "intent" is the (necessary) interior completion of the exterior action required by law. The "intent" guarantees that Muslim believers have fully performed their religious duty. Martyrdom, understood as immolation on the field of battle, also requires the right "intention"[57].

I see no correspondence between intention as thus defined and the concept of conscience, because the latter does not have a fixed prescriptive or proscriptive dimension, does not have a complementary or integrative function, and does not harmonize the exterior/physical level and the interior/mental level of a prescribed ritual. Conscience is a dimension of interior exploration, that does not harmonize but divides, and that does not always obey the (religious) commandments. Conscience can separate an individual from his faith community and isolate him (Luther).

However, one impressive synthesis of Islamic culture—impressive for its boldness and profundity—indentifies the concept of Self as the central pillar of historical Islam. Shahab Ahmed writes:

"Our conceptualization of Islam should be such that when we think of Islam, we should concomitantly think of the meaningful exploration of the self with its associated components of self-awareness, of personhood, of identity, of the individual, of the collective, of the personality, of self-action".

Ahmed is well aware that this position of his goes against truths that are unequivocally shared by the culture with which he identifies himself.

"Our received habits of conceptualizing Islam as discourses of prescription rather than as discourses of exploration have considerably obstructed us from recognizing the place of discourses of the Self as central to and constitutive of human and historical Islam"[58].

According to this perspective, the concept of conscience in the world of Islam depends on the exercise of self-exploration.

[57] *Ibid.*, pp. 61-82.

[58] S. AHMED, *What is Islam?*, pp. 341-342.

6. *Conclusion*

The question at the beginning of this paper was whether martyrdom can be regarded as an experience that unites or divides the three monotheistic religions considered here. The challenge of the present impels us to the conclusion that this experience is a factor of division between Judaeo-Christian and Islamic culture; but an ear more attentive to the plurality of voices, especially more recent voices, manages to identify—through an analysis of this concept—a basic area of dialogue.

Faith v. Identity

The Protestant Factor in Contemporary European Freedom of Religion or Belief

by *Marco Ventura*

1. *Introduction*

The universal human right to freedom of religion or belief as enshrined in article 18 of the UN *Universal Declaration of Human Rights* is challenged from outside as well as inside the West. References to the Protestant element lie at the heart of the challenge. The individual, choice-based and faith-centered definition of freedom of religion or belief is contested in the name of an alternative understanding of religion, rather conveying a collective, tradition-based, and precepts-centered notion of religious freedom. Although the faith-based, predominantly individualistic notion of religious freedom is more immediately associated to the Protestant legacy, the collective, identity-based notion is equally relevant to Protestants, especially in certain areas and for certain churches. This text aims to locate and analyze the Protestant factor in contemporary European freedom of religion or belief by first drawing the picture of contemporary freedom of religion or belief, and secondly focusing on the role and implications of the Protestant factor.

Driving this analysis is the assumption that three factors are seminal for the understanding of developments in the area of freedom of religion or belief. The first factor is the sense of history upon which each nation, society, and community builds its internal process of identity-making; the second belongs to trajectories of religion in the global, regional, national, or local context; the third factor belongs to the interaction of law and religion and its politics, in particular of human rights and religion. No comprehensive and profound understanding of the dynamic picture of contemporary religious freedom is possible without taking into proper account these three factors.

With the expression "contemporary European religious freedom or belief" I designate both the descriptive side of the multifaceted experience of religious freedom in today's Europe, and the normative side prescribing how conflicts pertaining to what individuals and groups define as their religious freedom should be regulated and adjudicated. From a European perspective, since the demolition of the Berlin Wall and the attack on the Twin Towers, both sides have undergone significant change as a result of a threefold process. First comes the process leading from a theistic, strongly Christian understanding of religious freedom to the inclusion of non-Christian believers and communities and even of atheistic and non-theistic beliefs in what European law and public policies term today as freedom of religion or belief (hence the acronym FoRB). Second is the emerging Atlantic conversation bridging together European countries' governments, European institutions, and the US and Canada in the forging of the concept and description of freedom of religion or belief as well as in the international strategies supposedly leading to the protection and promotion of freedom of religion or belief worldwide. Essential to this component of the threefold process is the dialogue between European states and European institutions on the definition of a common standard of protection of freedom of religion or belief, within Europe and abroad. The third component is the emergence of new religious freedom-related claims, with immigrant groups and alienated traditional Christians resorting to this right in order to preserve their practice against the enlarging scope of threatening rights and policy principles, in particular non-discrimination and equality rights, gender equality, LGBTQI rights, freedom of expression and association, defense rights through due process and fair trial, children's rights, and animal rights.

This attempt to locate the multifaceted Protestant factor in contemporary European freedom of religion or belief will entail looking at how contemporary actors refer to the Reformation as a crucial foundational stone in the historical emergence of religious freedom, and describe the impact of the Protestant legacy on current geo-politics of religious freedom. I will argue that the main Protestant challenge to the contemporary concept and operation of religious freedom lies in the tension between faith and identity, and more particularly between a faith-based religious freedom and an identity-based religious freedom. This challenge is doubly Protestant: first because it is related to Protestant theology, history, and recent developments, although its genealogy is much richer; secondly because Protestants are very active in promoting both versions of religious freedom. Hence, my conclusion is that the tension between a faith-based religious freedom and an identity-based religious freedom in turn poses a vital challenge to contemporary Protestants.

2. *Contemporary European freedom of religion or belief*

Contemporary European freedom of religion or belief is deeply rooted in the emergence and progressive definition of religious freedom in the West. At the dawn of the twentieth century, two Italian scholars significantly contributed to the modern Western understanding of religious freedom while themselves reflecting wider developments in the Anglo-Saxon, German, and French world.

Francesco Ruffini, a Turin-based professor of church and state law and legal history, whose scholarship was impregnated with English "ecclesiastical law", American separation of church and state, as well as with German *Kirchenrecht* and *Staatskirchenrecht* (through his intellectual and personal association with Emil Friedberg), published in 1901 his seminal history of the idea of religious freedom, and endeavored in the following years to bridge both the history and the "idea" of freedom with the legal protection of the right thereof. In so doing, Ruffini built upon the European and North American conversation of his time and paid special attention to Protestant development in the Netherlands, Switzerland, and the Nordic countries[1].

In 1917 Santi Romano, a Sicilian professor of constitutional law at the University of Pisa, also drawing upon a solid knowledge of church and state law, published his book on the plurality of legal systems, challenging the assumption that state law would be the only possible and legitimate legal system, and recognizing church laws—not only Roman

[1] See F. Ruffini, *Religious liberty*, New York - London 1912 and F. Ruffini, *Corso di diritto ecclesiastico italiano: la libertà religiosa come diritto pubblico subiettivo*, Torino 1924. Ruffini's understanding of Protestant laws was based on the work of Emil Friedberg and in particular on his *Lehrbuch des katholischen und evangelischen Kirchenrechts*, Leipzig 1879. Ruffini translated and published Friedberg's work in Italian.

Catholic canon law, but also the law of "schismatic" churches—as equally plausible legal systems[2].

As the two Italian scholars suggested, based on their sense of the evolving Western legal doctrine and anticipating the seminal contribution to the understanding of the interaction of law and religion by Harold Berman[3], himself an Episcopalian, the historical process leading to the right to religious freedom, and the theory and reality of church autonomy, concurrence of legal systems, and legal pluralism went hand in hand.

After World War II, when the UN *Universal Declaration of Human Rights* was adopted in 1948 and the process of European integration was begun, the time was ripe for religious freedom, together with the other human rights, to be enshrined not only in new national constitutions, such as in France and in Italy, but also in the *European Convention for the Protection of Human Rights and Fundamental Freedoms* of 1950. Article 9 of the *European Convention* was set to protect "freedom to change his religion or belief and freedom, either alone or in community with others and in public or private, to manifest his religion or belief, in worship, teaching, practice and observance". This formulation of religious freedom was based on the assumption that religion could be legitimately changed, thus that religion was ultimately a matter of choice, primarily of individual choice ("everyone has the right"). In so doing, the *European Convention* incorporated the Western elaboration to which Francesco Ruffini had given voice. On the other hand, the doctrine of Santi Romano on the existing plurality of legal systems, and the necessity for a developing civil society to integrate such plurality, was not incorporated. References to "manifestation in community and in public", and to "observance of religion or belief", did not imply that the legal order of the state had to leave room for competing nor-

[2] See also S. Romano, *L'ordinamento giuridico: studi sul concetto, le fonti e i caratteri del diritto*, Pisa 1917 (eng. transl. *The Legal Order*, transl. by M. Croce, Abingdon 2017). In this work Santi Romano affirms Roman Catholic canon law as a legal system, and opens the door for recognizing other ecclesiastical legal systems when he writes: "there are institutions that affirm themselves by assuming an antithetical position to the others, which in their turn can deem the former to be unlawful, as is the case with entities pursuing goals in conflict with state law, or schismatic churches in the eyes of the church they left", p. 19. Also see S. Romano, *Lezioni di diritto ecclesiastico*, Pisa 1921.

[3] I refer in particular to H. Berman, *The interaction of law and religion*, Nashville TN 1974.

mative religious systems. Nevertheless, such references paved the way for attempts to lead the interpretation of freedom of religion precisely in the direction of "institutional" religious freedom, possibly allowing for the existence of religious legal systems parallel to the legal system of the State.

The threefold process forging contemporary European religious freedom is rooted in the post-war interactions between the religious element and the European integration process. Yet, it goes much beyond those foundations.

The move from theistic-only freedom of religion to freedom of religion or belief, this latter encompassing theistic as well as atheistic and non-theistic beliefs, entails the very re-definition of the scope of freedom of religion[4]. The Cold War divide between communist atheists and capitalist, free-market-oriented believers, like those evangelicals who engineered Wall Mart as documented in the account by Bethany Moreton[5], is replaced by the shifting boundary between theistic believers and the unaffiliated. Whereas the percentage of global atheists is decreasing according to the Pew Research Center, the unaffiliated are fast growing in the West, including in the US. They are predicted to become the majority group in the Netherlands (49%) and France (44%) by 2050[6]. The "nones" are not necessarily atheists though: more often, they partake in the quest for new forms of spirituality[7]. If traditional believers, which in Europe means followers of Abrahamic religions, are no longer the exclusive beneficiaries of freedom of religion, competition

[4] For the inclusion of atheistic and non-theistic beliefs in the definition of religious freedom, see the case European Court of Human Rights, Kokkinakis v. Greece, 1993, at paragraph 31 where the Court stated: "As enshrined in Article 9, freedom of thought, conscience and religion is one of the foundations of a 'democratic society' within the meaning of the Convention. It is, in its religious dimension, one of the most vital elements that go to make up the identity of believers and their conception of life, but it is also a precious asset for atheists, agnostics, sceptics and the unconcerned".

[5] See B. MORETON, *To Serve God and Wal-Mart: The Making of Christian Free Enterprise*, Cambridge MA 2009.

[6] The Pew Research Center data on the future of world religions can be accessed at http://www.globalreligiousfutures.org [accessed March 1, 2017].

[7] On the emergence of spirituality in the context of law and religion, see F.M. GEDICKS, *God of Our Fathers. Gods for Ourselves: Fundamentalism and Post-Modern Belief*, in "William & Mary Bill of Rights Journal", 18, 2010, 4, pp. 901-914.

is triggered amongst an increasingly complex array of actors—including secular societies and associations of humanists—with differing views on the substance of religion- or belief-based claims as well as on the institutional infrastructure under which those claims should be adjudicated. Article 17,3 of the *Treaty on the Functioning of the European Union*, as adopted in Lisbon in 2007, mandates the European Union to recognize the "identity" and "specific contribution" of "churches and religious associations or communities" and of "philosophical and non-confessional organizations" alike, and to engage in "an open, transparent and regular dialogue" with the same communities and organizations. The inclusion of "churches, religious associations or communities" and "philosophical and non-confessional organizations" in the same provision mandating for a dialogue between them and the European Union bodies has been saluted by the latter as an acknowledgment of equality between the two categories, although churches do not seem ready to sit at the same table with atheistic organizations and the like[8].

The second process through which contemporary European freedom of religion has developed pertains to the emerging European standard, the connected competition between individual States and supranational entities, and the struggle against global violations of religious freedom[9]. Two contradictory elements coexist in the European convergence on freedom of religion[10]. On the one hand, the European supervision and

[8] I have discussed inclusion of "churches, religious associations or communities" and "philosophical and non-confessional organizations" in the same provision mandating for a dialogue between them and the European Union bodies in the context on the debate on the religious competence of the European Union in M. Ventura, *L'articolo 17 TFUE come fondamento del diritto e della politica ecclesiastica dell'Unione europea*, in "Quaderni di diritto e politica ecclesiastica", 22, 2014, 2, pp. 293-304.

[9] I understand this process based on the outcome of the Religio West project and the Religare project. The Religio West project led by Olivier Roy at EUI worked on transatlantic developments. See in this context M. Ventura, *Dynamic Law and Religion in Europe. Acknowledging Change. Choosing Change*, European University Institute Working Paper, Religio West Project, 2013. The Religare project has worked on new demands of freedom of religion or belief. See M.C. Foblets - K. Alidadi - J.S. Nielsen - Z. Yanasmayan (eds), *Belief, Law and Politics. What Future for a Secular Europe?*, Farnham 2014.

[10] I have discussed this contradiction in M. Ventura, *Balancing Convergence and Divergence. The Challenge for European Law and Religion*, in M. Lugato (ed.), *La libertà religiosa secondo il diritto internazionale e il conflitto globale dei valori / International Religious Freedom and the Global Clash of Values*, Torino 2015, pp. 89-102.

the consequent limitation of national sovereignty are opposed in the name of both the protection of cultural identity and the benefit of subsidiarity-based governance. In this case, religion is understood as an ingredient of culture, tradition, and identity, out of the individual's reach, as well as a key social factor the control of which is vital to the relevant community and should not be relinquished to higher powers. In the last two decades, populist movements have capitalized on the rejection of the "plot" between European technocrats and alien religions threatening the national purity and unanimity, as documented by Pantelis Kalaitzidis for Greek orthodox nationalists, Tim Peace for the British National Party, Duncan McDonnell for the Italian Lega Nord, and Susi Meret for the Danish People's Party[11]. On the other hand, the European involvement in the global struggle for the promotion and protection of religious freedom—something the same populist actors advocate, often in the interest of fighting anti-Christian persecutions—depends on the very existence of such thing as a European doctrine and standard in full compliance with international human rights law. The process leading to the adoption of the *EU Guidelines on the Promotion and Protection of Freedom of Religion or Belief* in 2013[12] and their subsequent implementation bears constant witness to the tension between the two elements. The strategic alliance between the EU and the US on the agenda of defending and promoting religious freedom worldwide makes the tension between transatlantic, Western convergence and the national, cultural case for divergence even greater. Anxieties across Europe about the global persecution of Christians push political leaders to call for action. European action requires a consistent European framework in support of religious freedom for all everywhere, this being the only sustainable rationale for an international initiative. Diplomats try to keep the foreign policy initiative as disconnected as possible from any domestic loss of sovereignty on religious affairs. However, reality does not always conform to the project of increasing interference abroad with little interference at home.

The third process is the emergence of new demands of religious freedom. On the one hand, immigrant groups resort to religious freedom

[11] See N. Marzouki - D. McDonnell - O. Roy, *Saving the People: How Populists Hijack Religion*, London 2016.

[12] See Council of the European Union, *EU Guidelines on the Protection and Promotion of Freedom of Religion or Belief*, June 24, 2013.

in order to frame claims of a new kind in the European landscape. In issues pertaining to the family and marital or paternal authority (e.g. polygamy, repudiation, and kafala), dress code, relations between men and women, food, and many others, believers claim they should be entitled to act according to their religious precepts. Although individual agency is crucial, as we know from field research on practices amongst European Muslims[13], demand not to be interfered with by the government in the compliance with religious precepts is framed in terms of cultural identity and collective tradition. To the increasing demand from recently established communities corresponds the growing alienation of those groups of believers who see themselves as the successors of majority faith communities and thus as custodians of local tradition and identity: these groups are alienated not only because of their increasing social shrinking, but because of the State's endorsement of new rights, especially in the area of LGBTQI and of reproductive rights. Religious freedom is thus framed from both constituencies—new and old religious groups—as a right preserving a threatened collective identity and personal conscience from other fundamental rights or principles. Ultimately, as we will see in the next paragraph, this leads to the very neutrality and impartiality of the State, and the superiority of the law of the land, vis-à-vis religious normativity, being questioned.

3. *The Protestant factor and the present challenge*

Traces of the inextricable knot holding together the history of Reformation and the history of religious freedom can be found in each component of the threefold processes shaping contemporary European religious freedom.

The transition from religious freedom to freedom of religion or belief, and the dynamic growth of new forms of belief and religiosity in need of protection, can be associated with Protestant ideas of individual and collective creativity in the interpretation of the Scripture, in personal and social ethics, and in the ordering of the community. The decline of traditional religiosity in Europe and the emergence of beliefs can be

[13] This can be observed through Eva Brems's research on face veil wearers in Europe witnessing new individual trajectories amongst Muslim communities in Europe; see E. Brems (ed.), *The Experiences of Face Veil Wearers in Europe*, Cambridge 2014.

associated to Brad Gregory's "unintended reformation"[14], the evolution of Protestant society into a secularized society, especially in the Anglo-Saxon and Nordic landscape. Pointing at the Nordic experiment, Ara Norenzayan sees the Protestant legacy in what he defines as "cooperation without God" and the replacement through civil government of the lost power of the eye of God as the guarantor of moral and social order[15].

As for the supranational, European component, since the very early post-World-War-II documents on religious freedom of churches in Great Britain and the Council of Churches, European developments in this area have been the effect of the Protestant thrust for ecumenical dialogue, the human rights activism of Nordic Lutherans, and cooperation of North American and European Protestants[16].

Regarding new claims related to religious freedom, the Protestant element can be located at the two extremes of the spectrum. Conservative Christians struggling with same-sex marriages and resorting to religious freedom in order to strengthen their claims to conscientious objection often belong to Protestant Evangelical Churches or to other Protestant churches. At the same time Protestants, ranging from Methodists to Lutherans in the Nordic countries and to the churches of the Anglican Communion, are also a vital component of the Christian support for liberal legislation on issues of family, filiation, sexual orientation, gender equality, and end of life. Such a scheme is blatant in the US of the culture wars, but can be identified in Europe as well.

If Protestants feature prominently in the emergence of "religion or belief", in the transatlantic initiative and in the new demand of religious freedom, the challenge to Protestants deriving from contemporary concept and operation of European freedom of religion or belief is also threefold.

[14] See L. CHRISTOFFERSEN, *Church Autonomy in Nordic Law*, in L. CHRISTOFFERSEN - K.Å MODÉER - S. ANDERSEN (eds), *Law and Religion in the 21st Century – Nordic Perspectives*, Copenhagen 2010, pp. 563-592. On the connection between Protestant theology and secularization, see B.S. GREGORY, *The Unintended Reformation*, Cambridge MA 2012.

[15] I quote A. NORENZAYAN, *Big Gods. How Religion Transformed Cooperation and Conflict*, Princeton NJ 2013, in particular the last chapter.

[16] On the process leading to the EU's policy on religion, and the Protestant element, see the work of B. MASSIGNON, *Des dieux et des fonctionnaires. Religions et laïcités face au défi de la construction européenne*, Rennes 2007.

First, contemporary religious freedom challenges the Protestant doctrines of separation of church and state and establishment of churches. Both have strong historical roots in the trajectories of Protestants. Both are in the process of being redefined. Since the *Religious Freedom Restoration Act* of 1993 and more vigorously in the last decade, the US Supreme Court has attenuated separation of church and state in the case of public display of religious symbols like the Ten Commandments in the Summum case of 2009[17] and sectarian Christian public prayer at a city council, like in the Town of Greece case of 2014[18], while allowing for broad exceptions from the general law when free exercise was at risk, as authors like Marc DeGirolami see fit[19], to the unprecedented extent of granting the Pentecostal owners of a retail company exemption from the Obamacare contraception mandate, thus construing a company as a quasi church[20]. In the meantime, Protestant establishment has been softened in nearly all the old national-church countries (Finland, Sweden, Norway, Iceland, Scotland and England) to the exception of Denmark. Even more important, establishment is now advocated by scholars such as Lisbet Christoffersen. Establishment is seen as a crucial feature of the Nordic social model, one that is even more precious today, when society and the governments have to deal with an increasingly multi-religious society with its challenging parallel religious laws. Christoffersen is adamant, however, that no establishment related provision should impinge upon individual or collective freedom of religion[21].

Secondly, conservative Protestants have joined forces with Catholics and the Orthodox, with Mormons as well, for the conceptualization and

[17] US Supreme Court, Pleasant Grove City v. Summum, decided on February 25, 2009.

[18] US Supreme Court, Town of Greece v. Galloway, decided on May 5, 2014.

[19] See M.O. DeGirolami, *The Tragedy of Religious Freedom*, Cambridge MA - London 2013.

[20] US Supreme Court, Burwell v. Hobby Lobby, decided on June 30, 2014.

[21] See L. Christoffersen, *Church Autonomy in Nordic Law*, in L. Christoffersen - K.Å. Modeér - S. Andersen (eds), *Law and Religion in the 21st Century – Nordic Perspectives*, Copenhagen 2010, pp. 563-592. This was the case in Christoffersen's paper at the at the 2016 Oxford symposium of the International Consortium for Law and Religion Studies (program of the symposium at http://www.iclars.org/event.php?event=13 [accessed March 1, 2017]).

advocacy of institutional rights of churches. Jean-Pierre Schouppe has offered the most comprehensive illustration of this doctrine, based on the case law of the European Court of Human Rights[22].

In cases in which individuals claiming their rights were infringed attacked churches on employment or freedom of expression and associations, the doctrine of church autonomy was mobilized in order to establish the priority of church rights over individual rights[23]. In the Siebenhaar case, the German courts and the European Court of Human Rights in 2011 accepted that a Catholic worker in a kindergarten of the Protestant Church of Baden was dismissed because of her conversion to the Universal Church (the Protestant Church of Germany, EKD intervened in the procedure before the European judges in support of the German government against the individual claimant)[24]. The doctrine has been most successfully applied before the US Supreme Court in the case of a Lutheran Church in Michigan, a member congregation of the Lutheran Church-Missouri Synod, the second largest Lutheran denomination in America, when a teacher's unlawful dismissal for health reasons was deemed legitimate on grounds of her being a minister of the church (judges applied the so called "ministerial exception")[25]. The decision was later referred to before the European Court of Human Rights in the case of a Roman Catholic married priest unsuccessfully claiming his entitlement to keep the position as professor of Catholic

[22] On institutional freedom of religion, see J.-P. SCHOUPPE, *La dimension institutionnelle de la liberté de religion dans la jurisprudence de la Cour européenne des droits de l'homme*, Paris 2015.

[23] Religious autonomy can be defined as the "competence of religious communities to decide upon and administer their own affairs without governmental interference", as well as the "right of self-determination for religious groups"; W.C. DURHAM Jr., *Religion and the World Constitutions*, in W.C. DURHAM Jr. - S. FERRARI - C. CIANITTO - D.D. THAYER (eds), *Law, Religion, Constitution*, Farnham 2013, pp. 3-36, at p. 6.

[24] European Court of Human Rights, Siebenhaar v. Gemany, decided on February 3, 2011.

[25] See US Supreme Court, Hosanna-Tabor Evangelical Lutheran Church and School v. Equal Employment Opportunity Commission, decided on January 11, 2012. I have discussed the case in M. VENTURA, *L'eccezione ministeriale in Hosanna-Tabor. Dall'ingerenza visibile all'ingerenza invisibile*, in P. ANNICCHINO (ed.), *La Corte Roberts e la tutela della libertà religiosa negli Stati Uniti d'America*, Fiesole 2017, pp. 66-73. Also see the special issue of the "Oxford Journal of Law and Religion", 4, 2015, 2.

Religion in a state school in Spain despite the disagreement of church authorities, thus showing the inter-denominational potential of the autonomy doctrine[26].

Thirdly, Protestant churches are crucial in the discussion on religious laws. Again, the Protestant element can play in different, sometimes opposing ways. The Protestant legacy can be one of state legal monopoly, and subordination of church laws, this leading to cultural, political, and even constitutional resistance to parallel legal systems, sharia law in particular. In contrast, Archbishop of Canterbury Rowan Williams has produced the most structured advocacy of the need for the law of the land not to be the legal monopolist, and for religious laws to interplay, and even compete with the law of the land for the allegiance of community members[27]. In his effort to draw a set of "Christian laws" from the various canon laws and church orders, Norman Doe has paved the way for the unprecedented exercise of building a corpus of interdenominational Christian rules[28]. Such effort stems from the unsuccessful but highly significant attempt at producing a covenant for the churches of the Anglican Communion: it is thus deeply tied to contemporary developments of European Christians, in connection with non-European churches.

Protestants are challenged on their doctrines on legal pluralism, the viability of autonomous legal orders, the neutral and impartial character of the state in post-establishment countries, and the limits to state regulation, while being themselves in charge of reshaping their own

[26] See European Court of Human Rights, Grand Chamber, Fernandez Martinez v. Spain, decided on June 12, 2014.

[27] For Williams's speech on religious laws, see R. WILLIAMS, *Civil and Religious Law in England: A Religious Perspective*, in "Ecclesiastical Law Journal", 10, 2008, pp. 262-282. I have discussed the issue of human rights within religious laws in M. VENTURA, *Human rights within religions*, in S. FERRARI (ed.), *Routledge Handbook of Law and Religion*, Abingdon 2015, pp. 161-178. Also see from a Protestant perspective L. CHRISTOFFERSEN, *Religion as a Factor in Multi-Layered European Union Legislation*, in R. MEHDI - H. PETERSEN - E.R. SAND - G.R. WOODMAN (eds), *Law and Religion in Multicultural Societies*, Copenhagen 2008, pp. 111-130, and L. CHRISTOFFERSEN, *Shari'a: Is Shari'a law, religion or a combination? European Legal Discourses on Shari'a*, in J.S. NIELSEN et al. (eds), *Shari'a as Discourse*, Farnham 2010, pp. 57-76.

[28] For the project on Christian laws, see N. DOE, *Christian Law. Contemporary Principles*, Cambridge 2013.

internal legal orders. Accordingly, their threefold challenge includes 1) theology, in particular the interpretation of Scripture, and political theology understood as the secularization of theological concepts; 2) ethics; and 3) church authority and laws.

The threefold challenge—on separation and establishment, church autonomy and religious laws—pertains to European majority or minority Protestants in their connection to the emerging internal competition from "ethnic" Pentecostal churches. In the global world, the challenge cannot be isolated from North American developments, with US Protestants reduced to little more than 50%, and largely Evangelicals[29], as well as Protestant trajectories in the rest of the world, in particular non-mainstream Protestants suffering persecution, as it is the case in Russia, and mainstream Protestants under the formatting pressure by the government in China and Vietnam.

At the heart of the threefold challenge to contemporary Protestants lies the fundamental question of the alternative between individual faith-based religious freedom and religious freedom based on the assumption that membership of a faith community is a given, handed over from the family and parents, not to be departed from regardless of personal feelings, a matter of allegiance to one's own people, collective tradition and identity[30]. As opposed to faith-based religion, identity-based religion sees opting out through conversion as repugnant, something to which it is suitable to react with social hostility and law-sanctioned punishment.

[29] The Pew Research Center data on the US religious landscape can be accessed at http://www.pewforum.org/religious-landscape-study/ [accessed March 1, 2017].

[30] The clash between faith-based religion and identity-based religion is presented by Silvio Ferrari in the following terms: "if the accent is on individual conscience and freedom of choice, the public sphere will be open to those religions which are ready to recognise individual freedom in their internal organisation and which therefore do not insist too much on membership by birth (as opposed to membership by choice), which do not sanction the apostate too heavily, and which do not resort to extreme forms of proselytising. If, instead, the emphasis is on the identitarian and cultural value of religion, traditional religions will be appointed as gatekeepers of the public sphere and access to it will be granted only to those minority religions that have a doctrine and an organisation which is not too far from that of the dominant religion in a country", S. FERRARI, *Law and Religion in a Secular World: A European Perspective*, in "Ecclesiastical Law Journal", 14, 2012, 3, pp. 355-370. Also see M. VENTURA, *The Changing Civil Religion of Secular Europe*, in "The George Washington International Law Review", 41, 2010, 4, pp. 947-961.

With immigrant communities largely advocating their right to obey God-given, non-negotiable precepts as essential to the preservation of their religious and cultural identity, traditional majority and minority communities in Europe are also pushed by analogy to prioritize the collective over the individual, and identity over faith. This is how I interpret the Eweida case, involving a British Airways' employee who claimed she was entitled to wear a cross by analogy with Muslim and Sikh employees entitled to wear the veil and the turban[31].

The Protestant legacy is so rich and diversified that Protestants might side with faith, or with identity, or just reject the opposition between faith and identity, depending on the circumstances, or based on their membership of mainstream Protestant or Baptist and Pentecostal groups. The Protestant diversity on the clash of faith and identity featured spectacularly during the controversy over the display of the crucifix in state schools in Switzerland, Germany (Bavaria), and Italy. Although Italian Protestants, Waldensians in particular, opposed the display of the crucifix in Italian state schools, European Protestants largely preferred to stand for religion against the alleged anti-religious threat inherent in the anti-crucifix movement, thus joining in the pro-crucifix international front led by the Italian government and supported by the Holy See and the governments of Orthodox countries. An Evangelical Protestant law firm based in the US masterminded the litigation in Strasbourg through its European office[32]. Reformed Calvinist John Witte Jr. drafted a praise of the 2011 ruling of the European Court in favor of the Italian government[33]. Judges accepted the argument that "the presence of crucifixes in State-school classrooms, being the result of Italy's historical development, a fact which gave it not only a religious connotation but also an identity-linked one, now corresponded to a tradition". They also accepted the argument that "beyond its religious

[31] See European Court of Human Rights, Eweida and Ors v. The United Kingdom, decided on January 15, 2013.

[32] See P. Annicchino, *Winning the Battle by Losing the War. The Lautsi Case and the Holy Alliance between American Conservative Evangelicals, the Russian Orthodox Church and the Vatican to Reshape European Identity*, in "Religion and Human Rights: an International Journal", 6, 2011, pp. 213-219.

[33] See European Court of Human Rights, Grand Chamber, Lautsi v. Italy, March 18, 2011, at paragraphs 67 and 68. I have discussed the case in M. Ventura, *Creduli e credenti. Il declino di Stato e Chiesa come questione di fede*, Torino 2014.

meaning, the crucifix symbolized the principles and values which formed the foundation of democracy and western civilization"[34].

4. *Conclusions*

The individual, faith-based, and pro-choice religion upon which Episcopalian Eleanor Roosevelt built the religious freedom of the *Universal Declaration* of 1948, the immediate antecedent of article 9 of the *European Convention* of 1950, is often identified as the only, exclusive dimension of the Protestant legacy, regardless of the collective, cultural and national character of mainstream Anglicanism, Lutheranism, Calvinism and even Methodism. In particular, Protestant culture is associated with the deeply internalized conviction that God is able to judge not only the external conduct, but also the internal will and thoughts[35].

Critics of culture-blind Western neo-colonialism identify such association: 1) as a factor making religious freedom incompatible with any universalistic project, since the Protestant character relativizes this right in its scope and goal (this position has been presented by Prakash Shah at the 2016 Oxford symposium of the International Consortium for Law and Religion Studies[36]; 2) as a factor making religious freedom, consciously or not, deliberately or not, a missionary tool, a vehicle of conversion and neo-imperialism, in religion and beyond; this position has been indirectly taken by Indian courts, such as the Supreme Court on same-sex sexual intercourse, and most recently by the High Court of Gujarat in its decision against the operation in the State of a US software company commercializing Pokemon Go like augmented reality technologies[37]; 3) as a vector of social secularization, possibly

[34] See J. WITTE, *Lift High the Cross? An American Perspective on Lautsi v Italy*, in "Ecclesiastical Law Journal", 46, 2011, 3, pp. 341-343.

[35] This is what psychologists Adam Cohen and Paul Rozin affirm they observed in some experiments: ee A.B. COHEN - P. ROZIN, *Religion and the Morality of Mentality*, in "Journal of Personality and Social Psychology", 81, 2001, pp. 697-710.

[36] Program of the symposium at http://www.iclars.org/event.php?event=13 [accessed March 1, 2017].

[37] On same-sex sexual intercourse, see Supreme Court of India, Suresh Kumar Koushal and ors. v. Naz Foundation and ors., decided on December 11, 2013. On augmented

conducive to a secularist project of the kind Saba Mahmood blames for the failure of the state in North Africa and the Middle East. She forcefully demonstrates how seemingly benign concepts such as religious freedom "have been historically intertwined in a colonial agenda and also served to privilege specific forms of religiosity, in particular individualized, Protestant Christianity, at the expense of Coptic and Eastern Orthodox Christianity"[38].

This position is commonly held in the name of non-Western concepts of human rights, for instance "Asian values", or straightforwardly against the Western export of allegedly inefficient and divisive schemes in the colonies. If Talal Asad is critical of the falsely neutral secular state, in fact a Christian state for him[39], authors like Jakob De Roover and Prakash Shah openly challenge the Protestant forging of concepts of religion in non-Western countries, India in particular, and the related imposition of religious freedom[40].

Such criticism confirms Larry Siedentop's account of Western Christian history as the "invention of the individual", deeply linked to the construction of the distinction between the space of ethics and the space

reality technology, see High Court of Gujarat, case of Nantic Inc., decided September 7, 2016.

38 See S. MAHMOOD, *Religious Difference in a Secular Age. A Minority Report*, Princeton NJ 2016. Mahmood's contention needs to be understood in the context of critical research on politics of religious freedom, and in particular of the joint research project of the same name (see the blog *The immanent frame* at http://blogs.ssrc.org/tif/the-politics-of-religious-freedom/). See in particular W.F. SULLIVAN - E. SHAKMAN HURD - S. MAHMOOD - P.G. DANCHIN (eds), *Politics of Religious Freedom*, Chicago IL 2015. In this context, the idea of the impossibility of religious freedom has been advanced: see W. SULLIVAN, *The Impossibility of Religious Freedom*, Princeton NJ 2005.

39 See T. ASAD, *Formations of the Secular: Christianity, Islam, Modernity*, Stanford CA 2003.

40 See J. DE ROOVER, *Europe, India, and the Limits of Secularism*, Oxford 2016. On the Protestant forging of religion in India, and consequences on ideas of the Secular State and religious freedom, see P. SHAH, *The Difference that Religion Makes: Transplanting Legal Ideas from the West to Japan and India*, in "Asian Journal of Comparative Law", 10, 2015, 1, pp. 81-97. Also see, specifically on castes, M. FÁREK - D. JALKI - S. PATHAN - P. SHAH (eds), *Western Foundations of the Caste System*, London 2017. For a more systematic and detailed account of the Protestant impact on the religion of India, see G.A. ODDIE, *Imagined Hinduism. British Protestant Missionary Constructions of Hinduism. 1793-1900*, New Delhi 2006.

of legal regulation, the rejection of theocracy and the emergence of the secular state[41].

The many Protestant variations and genealogies make the Protestant factor intrinsically plural. For one thing, the individual, choice-based, sincere, and personal faith upon which religious freedom has been established as a foundational right after the World War II in Europe and the West is as central to the struggle with religious conflict, as it is contested in the name of family-given, collective, cultural, and national religion, in Europe and beyond. Although Protestant theology and practice would predominantly side with choice-based religious freedom, significant fractions of the Protestant world might feel more at ease with culture-based religious freedom. An internal competition is taking place within Protestant churches on the opposition between choice and allegiance to tradition and culture, between faith and identity. While the global conversation affects such "competition within", it also depends upon it, thus making the Protestant experience definitely crucial.

[41] L. SIEDENTOP, *Inventing the Individual. The Origins of Western Liberalism*, London 2014.

Reform, Reformation, Confessionalization

The Latin Christian Experience

by *Heinz Schilling*

I.

The topic of the 58th Study Week of the Istituto Storico Italo-Germanico in Trento "The Protestant Reformation in a Context of Global History" is a comparative, not a normative one. Within our scholarly community that might go without saying.

To the general public however, at least in Germany, the normative understanding of Luther and the Reformation is still present, if not prevailing. With regard to the integration of Muslims into western society or the end of Islamist fundamentalism, it is often said that "Islam needs a Luther or a Reformation"—a sentiment that is occasionally applied to other world religions too.

To celebrate the Reformation within Latin or Western European Christianity as a landmark in world history and as a decisive engine of modernity became a central element in Protestant identity during the nineteenth century. The tone was set by the head of German Idealism, the Berlin philosopher Georg Wilhelm Friedrich Hegel. Hegel identified Luther and the Reformation as the breaking through of *Innerlichkeit und Individualität* (inwardness and individuality), which in his eyes were constitutive for the modern world—in contrast to the Middle Ages, when people could not act according to their inwardness and individuality, but were subordinated to forces outside of their personalities[1]. This

The reflections in this article are based on my extensive writings during the last decades on Luther, the Reformation, and the confessional cultures in Early Modern Europe. To avoid excessively detailed notes, the following references are mostly to these earlier publications, each with ample annotation.

[1] "Mit der Reformation beginnt … das Reich des Geistes, wo Gott als Geist wirklich erkannt wird … Die Zeit von da bis zu uns (hatte) … dieses Prinzip in die Welt hin

assessment was substantiated by Max Weber and Georg Jellinek to a monopoly of Protestantism in the rise of capitalism and democracy. Even at the end of the 1920s and with Nazi barbarism at hand, there was no doubt to Adolf von Harnack, professor of theology and the most influential agent in cultural and educational policy during the Weimar period, that "modernity ... was initiated by the hammer-blows to the doors of the castle church in Wittenberg"[2].

In the meantime, the mandarins of the German academic world have gone and with them their big picture of a Europe-based world history as well. The memorial culture that will shape the fifth centenary of the Reformation is quite different. It is characterized by a democratic and pluralistic atmosphere, instead of a monarchist authoritarian one; by endeavor for ecumenical understanding instead of hostility and zeal for confessional dissociation; by global perspective instead of euro-centrism. This fundamental change in the perspective of evaluation gives us the chance for a new understanding of Luther and the Reformation as well as of their impact on world history, specifically on the rise of modernity.

In concluding our conference and its sophisticated discussions, I make some suggestions for a historically adequate answer to the question of whether or not Luther's Reformation should or could be a model for similar changes within other world religions with subsequent "modernizing" impacts on their respective world civilizations.

einzubilden, aber so, daß dies noch die Form der Freiheit und Allgemeinheit gewinnen mußte" ["With the Reformation the realm of the spirit was established, where God is really recognized as spirit ... The time from then to us tried to incorporate this principle into the world, but in such a way that it still had to acquire the form of freedom and commonality"], H. SCHILLING, *Die Reformation – ein revolutionärer Umbruch oder Hauptetappe eines langfristigen reformierten Wandels?* in W. SPEITKAMP (ed.), *Konflikt und Reform*, Göttingen 1995, pp. 26-43, n. 3.

[2] "The modern age began along with Luther's Reformation on 31 October 1517; it was inaugurated by the blows of the hammer on the door of the castle chruch at Wittenberg", quoted by H. SCHILLING, *Martin Luther: Rebel in an Age of Upheaval*, Oxford 2017, p. 524, with n. 1, p. 577.

II.

1. *October 31, 1517: A landmark in world history?*

In a European-comparative and global perspective, the publication of the ninety-five theses was not at all the only event in 1517 that generated fundamental change[3]. Apart from Luther's protest against the papal indulgence system, several other events were crucial for the shape of the early modern and modern era. Most important and of long-lasting "significance in world affairs" was the surrender of the last Sultan of the Mamluks, Tuman Bay, outside Cairo in February 1517 to the Ottoman Sultan Selim I. The capture of Cairo became a landmark in world history because it opened the Arabian Peninsula to the Turks and enabled the sultan to transfer the caliphate, the highest spiritual dignity in the Muslim world, for centuries to Istanbul. This tradition ended only ninety years ago, after World War I, when Ataturk founded the Turkish Republic after the last sultan had to go into exile. For a short time the caliphate lived on as a spiritual honor without political impact, but it was abolished definitely on March 3, 1924 in accordance with Ataturk's policy of secularization.

The significance of the surrender at Cairo in February 1517 in world history becomes striking by a counterfactual evaluation: almost simultaneously with the capture of Cairo by the Turks a Portuguese fleet, commanded by the Viceroy of the Portuguese Entrado da India Lope Soarez de Albergaria, attacked the harbor town of Dschidda (Jidda) on the Arabian peninsula, close to Mecca. The aim was to safeguard shipping to India and the spice islands of Indonesia by establishing a Portuguese stronghold on the Red Sea. The operation failed—but the significance of a possible success on world affairs is striking: not the Muslim Ottomans, but Catholic Portugal dominant on the Arabian Peninsula! That would have given a totally different direction to world history—with consequences up to the present situation in Syria, where Muslim extremists try to revive an Arabian-based—and anti-Turkish—caliphate exactly in a region, where it was usurped by the Ottomans 500 years previously.

[3] The folowing is discussed in more detail in H. SCHILLING, *1517 – Weltgeschichte eines Jahres*, München 2017.

Perhaps even more important than this key event in politics was the encounter with alien civilizations (in Yucatan with the first contact of Christians with the Mayan civilization, or in the far east by a Portuguese mission to the Imperial court of China). This encounter became fundamental for the emergence of a new world view and self-understanding of Europeans, at least for the educated and the intellectuals.

2. *Reform and Reformation in Latin Christianity*

To identify the Christian capacity for religious and societal change with Luther or the Protestant Reformations alone is misleading. The Protestant Reformation was part of an overarching process of fundamental religious, cultural, and social change. It was an apogee in the long "temps des réformes" in the sense of Pierre Chaunu and Jean Delumeau, embracing the centuries between roughly 1450 and 1650[4]. Luther was at the same time both a product and a powerful engine of that change, which impacted not only on church and religion, but on society as a whole.

It is well known that Luther's plea for reform, which ended in a breach with Rome, was part of an ongoing dispute about spiritual and institutional reforms within Latin Christianity. Parallel to Luther's Protestant model, other concepts of reform were developed in different parts of Europe. Because of the Protestant self-interpretation of 1517 as a radical universal change in world history, all these efforts were discredited because they generated only modifications within the given system, whereas only Luther and his followers were held to have established a new ecclesiological and spiritual basis.

This polarization set the tone for centuries for the respective interpretations of the Reformation and the Counter-Reformation. But this is no longer adequate for a trans-confessional evaluation of the events of the early sixteenth century and their impact on European and world history. Luther and the Protestant Reformations, on the one hand, and the reforms of the Roman church, on the other hand, were sprouts of the same roots. This can be verified by many examples. Two of them are most striking, as they are traditionally linked exclusively to

[4] H. SCHILLING, *Reformation – Umbruch oder Gipfelpunkt eines Temps des Réformes?*, in H. SCHILLING, *Ausgewählte Abhandlungen*, Berlin 2002, pp. 11-31, here pp. 26 ff.

Protestantism—by the demand for the translation of the Bible into the vernacular and the use of the vernacular in Sunday services and by scholarly research on the Bible.

From the beginning, Protestant identity was based on high esteem for the Bible. Luther's widely admired knowledge of Scripture and his academic position as "bible professor" at the young University of Wittenberg were the foundations of his prestige and for the legitimacy of his theology. Soon it became part of Protestant identity that the new and professional way of reading and interpreting the Bible began with Luther. The same is true with regard to the translation of the Bible into the vernacular. Both claims do not match the reality of 1517. Before Luther, the high esteem of vernacular translation was already part of the demands for ecclesiastical reforms. This is documented by the *Libellus ad Leonem* written by Paolo Giustiniani and Vincenzo Quirini, high-ranking members of the Camaldolese order, to Pope Leo at the moment of his succession to the *cathedra Petri* in 1513. These two reform theologians recommended to the new pope that the Bible be translated and read in the vernacular during services. This would be the only way to make the Christian religion understandable not only to the congregation, but also to many priests, who often read the Latin without having understood the meaning[5].

In 1517 the most up-to-date professional project in biblical studies was based not in Wittenberg, but in the Spanish city of Alcalá in Castile[6]. Because of the famous *leyenda negra*—the very successful anti-Spanish propaganda of the Protestant Dutch and English competitors—late medieval and early modern Spain is regarded as a backward country with no vision of reform and modernity. Reality was quite different: Spain, mainly Castile, during the decades around 1500 experienced the strongest reform efforts in Latin Christendom. The leading figure here was the Archbishop of Toledo Francisco Jimenez de Cisneros, an influential councilor at the Castilian Court, who for several months in 1517 was regent for the young Archduke Charles, the future emperor. Born in 1436, Cisneros became an adherent of mystical spirituality and of the religious reforms expressed in the teaching of Catherine of Siena, Girolamo Savonarola, and especially of Erasmus of Rotterdam.

[5] H. Schilling, *Martin Luther*, p. 272.

[6] H. Schilling, *1517 – Weltgeschichte eines Jahres*, pp. 232 ff.

He promoted the printing industry to increase the spread of reform books; in 1499 he established a new university at Alcalá—the soon-to-be famous *Complutense*, after Complutum, the former Roman name of the city. Alcalá immediately became the intellectual and spiritual center for humanistic and philological studies in Christian religion and theology, very similar to the Saxon University of Wittenberg, which was founded three years later.

Cisneros' reform project reached its apogee in the spring of 1517, when the editorial work on a new edition of the Bible, begun fifteen years previously, came to fruition. A group of high-ranking scholars had finished the manuscript of the Old Testament, the New Testament having been printed already in 1514. This Complutensian Polyglot Bible was an impressive document of the Spanish impetus for reform—the first complete Bible in polyglot versions. The Old Testament was arranged with each page in three columns—Hebrew on the outer part, Latin in the middle and Greek on the inner part of the page, and in annotated form at the bottom of the page were Aramaic texts and their translation into Latin. The impact of the Complutensian Polyglot Bible was very limited, not so much due to the fact that—because of diplomatic and academic quarrels, especially with Erasmus—the manuscript only went into print in the 1520s, but in consequence of the completely new framework that the reform discussions had meanwhile reached by virtue of Luther's intervention in late October 1517. As time went on, an antagonism between Luther's program and that of Rome's Tridentine Reform came into being, which soon affected the most central points of Christian belief: the Lord's Supper, the meaning of grace, the priesthood, the position of Christ's mother Mary, and last but not least also the use of the Bible[7].

This polarization set the tone for centuries for the respective interpretations of the theology, spirituality, and the general cultural impulses of the Reformation on the one hand, and of the Counter-Reformation on the other. But this is no longer adequate for a trans-confessional evaluation of the events of the early sixteenth century and of their

[7] For more details, see the chapter "Antagonismen und kommunizierende Röhren im nachreformatorischen Verhältnis der Konfessionen", in H. SCHILLING, *Luther und die Reformation 1517-2017*, in U. SWARAT - T. SÖDING (eds), *Heillos gespalten? Segensreich erneuert? 500 Jahre Reformation in der Vielfalt der ökumenischen Perspektiven*, Freiburg i.Br. 2016, pp. 17-30, here pp. 23-26.

impact on European and world history. As is shown by the Biblicism of Cisneros, or by Emperor Charles' Christ-centered piety as displayed on his deathbed[8], and by many other examples, the Reformation and the reforms of the Roman church had the same roots. In this perspective it seems inadequate to impute to October 31, 1517 the quality of a radical universal change, let alone of a paradigm shift in the sense used by Thomas S. Kuhn.

3. *Specific profile of Luther's type of reform: Redirection of religion towards the world*

The specific profile of Luther's theology was a redirection of existential religion towards the world. In addition to the scholarly treatment of the Holy Scriptures, the secularizing capacity is a second essential for the exemplary meaning of Luther and the Reformation for modernizing developments in other world religions.

Luther's teaching on justification, which formed the theological core of his rebellion against the papal church, reached out beyond the narrowly religious sphere to have momentous impact on mentalities and behavior. The transition from medieval good-works-based piety to evangelical grace-based devotion founded on the "by faith alone" principle set a course towards the modern vocational ethics that determined the Christians' correct action in the world. Previously monasteries, abbeys, religious foundations, and other consecrated locations had provided the principal setting for faith and for the activities that sprang from faith. Now the Christian individual and Christendom as a whole were to live out their faith and prove themselves in their faith in their everyday experiences in the world. By this, "holiness" (previously reserved to the priestly life and especially to the life of the monk) was brought into the world. In serving the community (*ecclesia*), the family (*oeconomia*), and the state (*politia*), holiness provided a new dynamic that the special status of the clerical calling (*vocatio*) had previously held back from the world.

With Luther's eschatological theology uniting faith and world and identifying the world as the place where salvation unfolded, that which was

8 Described in detail by H. SCHILLING, *Martin Luther*, pp. 616 ff.

of the world became part of salvation. Marriage, sexuality, work, and politics were all re-evaluated and given a new legitimacy. A dynamic that had been absent when medieval performance-based devotion had held sway was now present in both private and public life. To believe without acting in the world was now just as sinful and far from God acting in the world without believing. Luther unleashed a dynamic that contributed fundamentally to the secular reshaping of early modern Europe and, in the longer term, to the emergence of the modern. On this basis religion would help shape the modern world for centuries, culturally, socially, and politically. In consequence of the Reformation "it was a hand-to-hand conflict between the Christian and the world"—thus at the height of German anti-Christian barbarism, the definition of the relationship between the Christian religion and secular world by Dietrich Bonhoeffer, the prominent adversary to Nazi ideology and martyr on the basis of Lutheran theology[9].

Neither scholarly treatment of the Holy Scriptures and the idea of explaining them to the people in the vernacular, nor the redirection of religion toward the world and the devotion of the Christian to shape society, politics, and culture was a singular profile of the Protestant Reformation. On a different theological and institutional basis, Roman Catholicism also contributed to the rise of a modern unified, rationally functioning, and disciplined society by implementing general rules and norms for marriage and family life, for education and training, for obedience and duty, for moral standards and behavior, for the role of men and women in the home and in public, etc. On this basis, a modern Christianity that "paved the way for the modern bourgeois spirit in Europe" came into being also in Catholic regions of Europe, although Catholic leaders in Rome liked to display a marked anti-modernism from time to time.

The widespread network of the Jesuits especially made a decisive contribution to the dissemination of modern styles of thinking and behavior, among the princes and nobility as well as among the emerging early modern educated middle class elites. Particularly significant was the impetus given to middle-class society, into which the Jesuits introduced "sufficient new ideas to worry the upholders of tradition in the catholic

[9] D. BONHOEFFER, *The Cost of Discipleship*, New York 1995, p. 48.

camp—new ideas on the level of the family and of society, as well as on the manner in which religion is lived in everyday life"[10].

Both Protestantism and Tridentine Catholicism became agents of early modern secularization. But it was a religious interference in matters of the world, by which the world became secularized in a peculiar way—not by separation from religion, but by a new "worldliness" (*Welthaftigkeit*) of religion, which had to realize its energy primarily not in the sacral, but in the secular sphere.

4. *Competition between different concepts of reforms and antagonism and fundamental hostility of confessional systems*

The specific outcome of the reform process, which was started by Luther on October 31, 1517, was the deep structural differentiation of Europe's culture and civilization, which opened wide channels of dynamism and fundamental change and became the roots of modernity. This too was part of a long process that began in the Middle Ages. But only Luther was ready to push this process of differentiation into the very center of Western European civilization—to the church and Christian religion. Erasmus in contrast still advocated the unity of the *populus Christianus* and the integrity of the church as the common house of all *gentes*, all European peoples, which "eadem omneis habet domus"[11]. With regard to pluralism and freedom not the humanist Erasmus, but the theologian Luther was the agent of modernity!

But—and this seems crucial for our comparison with other world religions, which did not experience comparable ecclesiastical, religious, and spiritual reforms—the path into modernity was neither the intention of Luther nor the direct result of his theology. Religious differentiation as

[10] L. Chatellier, *L'Europe des dévots*, Paris 1987, p. 127 and p. 151; L. Chatellier, *Le catholicisme en France, le 16e et 17e siècles*, 2 vols, Paris 1995; L. Chatellier, *The Religion of the Poor. Rural Missions in Europe and the Formation of Modern Catholicism, 1500-1800*, Cambridge 1997; H. Schilling, *Calvinist and Catholic Cities – Urban Architecture and Rituals in Confessional Europe*, in "European Review", 3, 2004, pp. 293-312. On the social and cultural impact of confessionalization in general, see W. Reinhard - H. Schilling (eds), *Die Katholische Konfessionalisierung*, Gütersloh 1995.

[11] Erasmus of Rotterdam, *Querela Pacis*, in *Ausgewählte Schriften*, ed. by W. Welzig, vol. 5, Darmstadt 1968, pp. 59-451, here p. 394.

the precondition for modern pluralism was introduced into European civilization not by theology or ideology let alone as a Reformation program, but by the simple fact, that Luther and his co-Reformers in Zurich and Geneva in contrast to their medieval predecessors survived and became able to organize in alliance with the princes and urban magistrates separate Protestant churches on the basis of early modern territorial states or cities.

Europe's path to modernity was not (so much) opened by Luther's theology or the Reformation as a religious, societal, and political event or movement, but by the internal formation of European societies and states along confessional lines and the competition of these confessional systems. This was not at all a harmonious and peaceful process.

On the contrary, as both sides considered their interpretation of the Bible as the only and absolute truth, a kind of confessional fundamentalism came into being and the Reformation period ended in a clash of churches, cultures, identities, and states. For more than a century, Europe suffered within and between societies from religious wars with contemptuous hate, inhuman hostility, violence, assassinations, and murderous terrorism quite similar to our present experience—with only one difference: the instruments and communication were still archaic, based on craftsmanship techniques.

III.

Of course, the Christian or "Western" experience with Reformations—the Protestant Reformations as well as the Tridentine Catholic one—has to be outlined in more detail. This cannot be done at this moment. Instead, I will summarize my arguments in seven theses:

First, the idea that non-Christian world religion needed a Luther to keep up with western civilization is too simple and does not capture the complex European experience in developing from pre-modern to modern civilization. In opening the historical perspective beyond the traditional national and European boundaries, it becomes evident that there is no reason to privilege the Protestant Reformation as 'the' key impulse for fundamental, modernizing change in "world affairs"—thus the subtitle of the "Archiv für Reformationsgeschichte/Archive for Reformation History", the leading Protestant journal in the field.

Second, apart from the Reformation, several other events and developments of the first decades of the sixteenth century, even of the year 1517 itself, had a similar deep and long lasting impact on "world affairs". Even more important, simultaneously with the declaration of Luther's theology and the subsequent process of Reformations broad streams of new world-knowledge (*neues Weltwissen*) flowed into Europe with new and deep intellectual, scientific, and scholarly stimulation.

Thus, the early modern time of dynamism and change and Europe's departure to modernity was the result of a kind of syndrome with three leading forces in its center—the recollection of ancient culture by Humanism and Renaissance; the new knowledge of a wider world; and—of cause course—the Reformations of Christianity, provoked by Martin Luther.

Third, also within the European context itself, the Lutheran Reformation has to be contextualized. It was not a singular event, but a specific variation within a long tradition of reform in Latin Christianity. And it was accompanied by a second early modern reform—the Tridentine Reform, as the response of Rome to Wittenberg's challenge (in the sense of Arnold Toynbee's theory of evolution of civilizations). Both—the Protestant Reformations as well as the Tridentine Reform—ended in the formation of new, early modern church organizations with a deep impact on the culture and politics of the respective societies, as well as on the behavior, mentality, and everyday life of their members. These confessional churches differed substantially from their medieval predecessors—the Protestant churches as well as the Roman Catholic one. Not the Reformation, but both confessional churches represented a "modern Christianity" (Louis Châtellier) and consequently were agents of secularization, though at a different speed and to a different degree.

Fourth, in Europe the path to modernity was not paved by the Reformation itself. On the contrary, it was Luther's failure in his aim to reform the church as a whole that opened the way for fundamental change. Luther was not an advocate of plurality, but stuck to the traditional idea of unity, based on absolute and exclusive religious truth. Yet it was just this sticking to traditional unity and absolute religious truth that in reality fostered cultural differentiation and plurality: As Luther—in contrast to Erasmus—valued dogmatic truth higher than Christian unity and peace, religion as the ideological heart of European civilization broke up into two different interpretations—in the long run even into a plurality of truths. Since both sides insisted that their respective religious truth was the only and absolute one, the breaking down of the Christian unity (and the differentiation of religious truth) did not mean freedom and plurality, let alone enlightenment. Europe had to pass a long period of deep religious, political, and military conflict before the murderous clash of confessional fundamentalism was fenced in by a rational settlement. Only then was the door opened towards the modern, secular world characterized by freedom, tolerance, and pluralism—a century and a half after Luther's Reformation!

Fifth, the overcoming of confessional fundamentalism became possible by the authority of secular Roman law, which had resisted the religious and ideological antagonism of the confessional churches. But—and this is important in our comparative perspective—the fencing in of religious fundamentalism was not accomplished in confrontation with but in concordance with religion. Thus the nowadays widespread idea that Islam and other non-Christian societies would modernize quickly, if they would get rid of their excessively high esteem of religion, cannot be confirmed by the European historical experience.

The end of confessional fundamentalism within western Christianity by the middle of the seventeenth century was not achieved by eliminating religion out of public life, but by a change within the religious ideas of the confessions themselves: The change from confessional orthodoxy to Pietism, from dogma to "devotion of the heart" (*Herzensfrömmigkeit*), reactivated the peace tradition of Christian theology, which had been blocked but not eliminated by confessional fundamentalism. The symbolic representation of the Christian peace tradition became important for religious as well as political peace in Europe—the *Madonna della Pace* as well as the *Dove of Noah*—in 1648 the symbol for the reclaimed peace between God and mankind, and today in a secularized version the emblem of the international political movement for a general peace on earth.

Sixth, important too with regard to the present problem of relations between Christians and non-Christians, especially Muslims, in Europe and the World in general: the European settlement, that ended the murderous hostility of the Reformation-born Christian confessions, was and is not based on harmonizing or neglecting religious differences, but on the will to oblige the respective believers (and civil society as a whole) to endure them.

Seventh, taking the Christian experience during the half millennium after the Reformation into account, it is evident, that the slogan "Islam needs a Luther or a Reformation" does not hit the historical reality. It is much too simple to serve as a pragmatic instruction for the present and the future.

Contributors

Pierre-Antoine Fabre, Professor, School for Advanced Studies in the Social Sciences, Paris

Thomas Kaufmann, Professor, Georg-August-University, Göttingen

Gudrun Krämer, Professor, Free University, Berlin

Silvana Seidel Menchi, Professor emeritus, University of Pisa

Brian K. Pennington, Professor, Elon Univeristy, North Carolina

Paolo Prodi, Professor emeritus, University of Bologna †

Wolfgang Reinhard, Professor emeritus, Albert-Ludwigs-University, Freiburg

Heinz Schilling, Professor emeritus, Humboldt-University, Berlin

Martin Tamcke, Professor, Georg-August-University, Göttingen

Marco Ventura, Professor, University of Siena and FBK-Center for Religious Studies, Trento

Roni Weinstein, Hebrew University, Jerusalem

Finito di stampare nel mese di novembre 2017
dalla Litoseibo, Bologna - www.litoseibo.it